T0196559

THE HOLIEST LIE EVER

Glorified by Myths, Mysticism, Symbolism,
Rituals and Traditions.

ALEXANDER SMITH

Order this book online at www.trafford.com
or email orders@trafford.com

Most Trafford titles are also available at major online book retailers.

Printed in the United States of America.

ISBN: 978-1-4669-4582-1 (sc)
ISBN: 978-1-4669-4581-4 (hc)
ISBN: 978-1-4669-4583-8 (e)

Library of Congress Control Number: 2012914150

Trafford rev. 08/02/2012

 www.trafford.com

North America & international
toll-free: 1 888 232 4444 (USA & Canada)
phone: 250 383 6864 ✦ fax: 812 355 4082

Myths, Mysticism, and Deception Present in Faith

CONTENTS

Even if you are a minority of one, the truth is the truth.

—Mahatma Gandhi

Preface

I was born in Cullinan, Gauteng, in South Africa and am the youngest of four children. I was raised in a staunch and strictly religious family. The Christian religious sect that I was born into was all I knew while I was growing up, and I therefore entered into various positions within the church structure, even practicing as a minister at one point. I spent most of my life until my late twenties serving the church that I believed in and grew up in.

Through my studies, I had the privilege to travel the world, and little did I know that soon, my world would change. I happened to be in Egypt during one of my travels, and being a Christian at the time, I was interested in tracing the paths and history of Christianity. Keep in mind that I was a very staunch Christian at the time that I was in Egypt. I stumbled upon many contradictions and myths that related directly to Judaism and Christianity.

The more I looked and the deeper I got into all of these shocking aspects, the more troubled and disturbed I started to feel. I was shocked and angry at first, so I decided that I wanted to prove that Christianity is the true religion of God. My mind had been conditioned since I can remember; it was therefore extremely difficult for me to accept and understand these facts that I had uncovered. At first, I was offended and shocked; this turned into anger and outrage until I started to accept and understand the truth. It was not too late to live and strive for the actual truth, even though I had been misled for so many years. I have experienced my fair share of trials and tribulations in my own life; I have never and will never intend to make out as if I have had it easy because I have found the truth. The truth makes sense of many life experiences concerning the positive and negative; it allows you to accept and move on, striving toward the future.

To my astonishment, I discovered that many religions share the same origins; and others adopt, alter, and modify the content of other religions either to benefit their own religion or to discredit others. When I started understanding the truth, I was excited and anxious to discuss it with anyone and everyone that came into contact with me, but I soon realized that people did not want me to tell them about these facts because they felt threatened and uncomfortable; they felt that I was challenging their religion in a negative light. Soon people started labeling me as the Antichrist; at first, it used to upset me immensely because that simply was not true. I have always and will always believe and know that God exists; he just is not what you believe him to be.

Do you know, for the first time, that I was able to actually see what was happening around me? I was no longer blinded by faith or manipulated by religion. I started to see how many of the world's religions and churches were misleading people, how

1

they were manipulating their members and followers by using these myths and lies to deceive people. It was hard to believe that I had never noticed this before.

I eventually found a like-minded partner in my life that was searching for the truth, Liza-Mari. We got together under the strangest of circumstances and started putting parts of my research into the form it is today. This book has been made possible from our passion and drive to get the truth out to the masses.

The main purpose of this book is to open the eyes of everyone who has been deceived over the years by their religion, their religious leaders, and their churches. Everyone deserves to be given the opportunity to know the truth and to live their lives in the best positive and free way. Everyone has a task that they need to fulfill in their lives; everyone is unique, and everyone can be the best, positive, loving, and good people that they can be. Religion is the largest stumbling block to spiritual growth, and people need to be made aware of this.

May you, the reader, become enlightened with the knowledge and truth within these pages. Let us take those blindfolds off . . . for yourself and the greater good of society.

Author Alexander Smith is an inventor who has a profound passion for researching world religions and for discovering and understanding all the aspects in the true meaning of spirituality.

INTRODUCTION

Society today is composed of a series of institutions, from political, legal, to religious institutions. Further institutions exist, that of social class, family values, familial values, and occupational specialization. It is obvious, the profound influence these traditionalized structures have in shaping our understandings and perspectives. Yet of all the social institutions, we are born into, directed by, and conditioned upon, the religious system exists as one of the most unquestioned forms of faith there is. How it is conducted and how it truly affects society are ignored by the great majority of the population. There is nothing more unacceptable than a crisis of consciousness. Our minds are finding increased difficulty of accepting old norms, the old patterns, and ancient traditions. One of the main reasons for this crisis in consciousness is because of what is going on around us in our environment. Mankind has nurtured the misery, conflict, destructive brutality, and aggression; and from that, it has formed a society based along those lines.

It is no measure of health to be well adjusted to a profoundly sick society.

—J. Krishnamurti

You are not born with bigotry, greed, corruption, and hatred. You pick that up within a society. Society cannot be rectified by existing religious notions concerning the conduct of human affairs. People need to be freed from old superstitions. We have been raised to serve the established institutions. We are such an abominable sick society that suffers from corrupt behavior; this artificial reality must be eliminated to rebuild foundations for a spiritual and sustainable new world that strives toward world unification. We should ultimately be working toward a common good for all human beings without anyone being subservient to anyone else.

This would mean that we need to allow our minds to be open to new information at all times, even if it threatens our current belief system and our identities. Sadly, society has failed to recognize this, and the established institutions continue to paralyze growth by preserving outdated religious and social structures. Religion has been built upon lies, corruption, fraud, and deception. Simultaneously, however, the population suffers from fear of change. For this conditioning assumes a static identity and challenging one's belief system usually results in insult and apprehension. Mankind's perception of being wrong is erroneously associated with failure. In fact, to be proven wrong should be celebrated because it is elevating someone to a new level of understanding, furthering their awareness.

There is no such thing as a clever human being because it is merely a matter of time before their ideas are updated, changed, or eradicated. This tendency to blindly hold on to a belief system, sheltering it from new transforming information is nothing less than a form of intellectual materialism. The religious institution perpetuates this materialism not only by its self-preserving structures but also through the countless number of people who have been conditioned into blindly and thoughtlessly upholding these structures, therefore becoming self-appointed guardians of the status quo.

People are like sheep that no longer require a sheepdog to control them because they control each other by ostracizing those who step out of the norms. This tendency to resist change and uphold existing institutions for the sake of identity, comfort, profit, and power is completely unsustainable by any means. To continue supporting these institutions' norms will irrevocably entail further imbalance, fragmentation, distortion, and, eventually, destruction on an unprecedented scale. It is time to come back to the truth and not allow ourselves to be led by the nose by church fathers that concoct clever ways to maintain mysticism and blind faith.

Religious authority has been a product used over decades of time where control and obedience has been the reality. This authority is no longer relevant to society. You need to get rid of the aberrant behavior that your religion fosters and manifests among the masses.

Islam, Christianity, Judaism, Hinduism, and all the others exist as barriers to spiritual, personal, and social growth. For each group perpetuates a closed-world view. This limited understanding that they acknowledge is simply not possible in an emergent spiritual universe. Still, religion has succeeded in shutting down the awareness of this emergence by instilling the psychological distortion of faith upon its followers. These institutions reject logic, original truths, and new information in favor of traditionalized outdated beliefs.

The traditional concept of God is really a method of accounting for the nature of things. Unfortunately, the true concept of God has been lost and has never truly been understood. People have invented their own stories out of lack of understanding, and they have made God in their own image. God is portrayed as a man who becomes angry if people do not behave appropriately according to the norms of these institutions; he creates floods and earthquakes, and people say it is an act of God. People have adopted a grotesque perception of whom and what God is.

Ideologies that separate humanity such as religion need earnest reflection in the communities with regard to its value, purpose, social, and spiritual relevancy. The most relevant change must first take place within yourself, awake from your slumber, and open your eyes to the truth that is staring straight at you. Cast off the web of lies that you have clung to for dear life. There is nothing to be afraid of. The real revolution is the revolution in consciousness, and each one of us first has to eliminate the divisionary materialistic noise we have been conditioned to think is true while discovering, amplifying, and aligning with the goodness coming from our true spirituality and oneness.

Once we understand that the integrity of our personal existences is completely dependent on the integrity of everything else in our world, we have truly understood the meaning of unconditional love. How can you love God but hate his creation at the same time? Love is extensionality and seeing everything as you, and you as everything can have no conditionalities, for in fact, we are all everything at once. There is only one race, and that is the human race.

Hatred does not cease by hatred, but only by love; this is the eternal rule.

—Buddha

There are numerous sections where I talk frankly in this book; please keep in mind that I do so not out of harshness, not out of cruelty, not for the passion of my purpose, but because I want you to understand what I am saying. Your prejudices, your fears, your religious authorities new and old are all barriers to understanding. I cannot make myself clearer than this. I do not expect you to agree with me; I do not want you to follow me; I want you to understand what I am saying and to explore, inquire, and search for the truth.

Facts are usually very uncomfortable for most people because it tends to shock and anger some of you. Facts challenge age-old beliefs and the very basis of religious systems that you may have based your whole life on. People still persist with ancient ignorance, myths, and beliefs. Many cling to unproven centuries-old myths, which is religion.

I have painted a broad picture of the contents of this book in this introduction. What I am trying to do in all these pages is to encourage bringing about a transformation of the mind, not accepting things on face value and for the way that they are. Instead truly understand it, emerge yourself with it, examine it, give your heart and mind with everything that you have within yourself that you have to find the truth. In these pages, I bring many aspects and truth to your attention. At the end of the day, it depends on you and not on somebody else because to understand the truth is to transform what is.

Chapter 1

Religion: Origin and History

In this chapter, we will discuss religion in general, where religion originated and the history behind it. To understand the concept of religion, we need to discuss it briefly. Religion is a system of religious beliefs or a body of people accepting a system of religious belief.

The history of religion refers to the written record of human religious experiences and ideas. This period of religious history begins with the invention of writing about five thousand years ago (3000 BC) in the Near East. The prehistory of religion relates to a study of religious beliefs that existed before the advent of written records. The Pyramid Texts from ancient Egypt are one of the oldest-known religious texts in the world dating from 2400 to 2300 BC. Writing played a major role in sustaining organized religion by standardizing religious ideas regardless of time or location.

The word religion" as it is used today does not have an obvious precolonial translation into non-European languages. Daniel Dubuisson writes that "what the West and the history of religions in its wake have objectified under the name 'religion' is . . . something quite unique, which could be appropriate only to itself and its own history." The history of other cultures' interaction with the religious category is therefore their interaction with an idea that first developed in Europe under the influence of Christianity.

Religion can be seen as evolving with human culture, from primitive polytheism to an eventual monotheism. To have an understanding of religions and their origin is important because religion has been a major force in many human cultures. Religion has often shaped civilizations' laws and moral codes, social structure, art, and music. Religion has also been the source of numerous brutal wars throughout human history.

Origin: To see where the origins of religion started, it will take us back to the earliest of times when human beings started investigating their surroundings in order to understand why and how their systems and life cycles in their surroundings worked. From this came the need and desire to find out some sort of truth or at least a logical answer. From the human beings' primitive understanding, they formed their own deductions and conclusions. The conclusions are not necessarily correct, but it served as the most logical answer to their questions. This is where religion, belief, habits, and traditions followed.

The earliest evidence of religious ideas dates back several hundred thousand years to the Middle and Lower Paleolithic periods. Archaeologists noted intentional burials of early *Homo sapiens* from as early as three hundred thousand years ago as evidence of religious ideas. Other evidence of religious ideas includes symbolic artifacts from Middle Stone Age sites in Africa. However, the interpretation of early Paleolithic artifacts, with regard to how they relate to religious ideas, remains controversial. Archeological evidence from more recent periods is less controversial. A number of artifacts from the Upper Paleolithic (50,000-13,000) are generally interpreted by scientists as representing religious ideas. Examples of Upper Paleolithic remains associated with religious beliefs include the figurines of deities, elaborate ritual burials, and cave paintings.

In the nineteenth century, various theories were proposed regarding the origin of religion, which replaced the earlier claims of Christianity. Early theorists Edward Burnett Tylor and Herbert Spencer proposed the concept of animism, while archaeologist John Lubbock used the term "fetishism." Meanwhile, religious scholar Max Müller theorized that religion began in hedonism, and folklorist Wilhelm Mannhardt suggested that religion began in "naturalism," by which he meant the mythological explanation of natural events. All of these theories have since been widely criticized; there is no broad consensus regarding the origin of religion.

However, religion is how human beings relate to that which they regard as holy, sacred, spiritual, or divine. Religion is commonly regarded as consisting of a person's relation to God or to gods or spirits. Worship is probably the most basic element of religion; but moral conduct, right belief, and participation in religious institutions are generally also important elements of the religious life as practiced by believers and worshippers and as commanded by religious leaders, traditions, ancestors, and their scriptures.

Conviction plays a prominent role; without conviction, there cannot be any belief. Therefore, people are constantly searching for their own truth and their own answers to the conundrum of spiritual existence.

<u>Religion at the Neolithic Revolution</u>: Through most of human evolution, humans lived in small nomadic tribes and practiced a hunter-gatherer lifestyle. The emergence of complex and organized religions can be traced to the period when humans started to abandon their nomadic hunter-gatherer lifestyles in order to begin farming during the Neolithic period. The transition from foraging tribes to states and empires resulted in more specialized and developed forms of religion that were reflections of the new social and political environments required to manage a civilized society. While small tribes possessed supernatural beliefs, these beliefs were adapted into the smaller populations.

The religions of the Neolithic peoples provide evidence of some of the earliest-known forms of organized religions. The Neolithic settlement of

Catalhoyuk, in what is now Turkey, was home to about eight thousand people and remains the largest-known settlement from the Neolithic period. James Mellaart, who excavated the site, believed that Catalhoyuk was the spiritual center of central Anatolia. A striking feature of Catalhoyuk is its female figurines. Mellaart, the original excavator, argued that these well-formed, carefully made figurines—carved and molded from marble, blue and brown limestone, schist, calcite, basalt, alabaster, and clay—represented a female deity of the great goddess type. Although a male deity existed as well, "statues of a female deity far outnumber those of the male deity, who moreover, does not appear to be represented at all after Level VI." To date, eighteen levels have been identified. These figurines were found primarily in areas that Mellaart believed to be shrines. One of the sites where a possible shrine existed had a figurine of a goddess seated on a throne flanked by two female lions that was found in a grain bin, which, as suggested by Mellaart, might have been a way of protecting the food supply or ensuring their harvest.

Axial Age: The period from 900 BC to 200 BC has been described by historians as the Axial Age. According to Jaspers, this is the era of history when "the spiritual foundations of humanity were laid simultaneously and independently . . . And these are the foundations upon which humanity still subsists today." Intellectual historian Peter Watson has summarized this period as the foundation of many of humanity's most influential philosophical traditions, including monotheism in Persia and Canaan, Platonism in Greece, Buddhism and Hinduism in India, and Confucianism and Taoism in China. These ideas would form the foundations of religious institutions in time, for example, as platonic philosophy formed part of the foundations of Christianity.

Value of Religion:

Organized religion emerged as a means of providing social and economic stability to large populations through the following ways:

- Organized religion served to justify the role of the central authority, which in turn possessed the right to collect taxes in return for providing social and security services to the people of the state. The empires of ancient Egypt and Mesopotamia were theocracies, with chiefs, kings, and emperors playing dual roles of spiritual leaders and political leaders. Most state societies and chiefdoms around the world have these similar political structures where political authority is justified by divine sanctions.

- Organized religion emerged as a means of maintaining peace between unrelated individuals. Tribes consisted of a small number of related individuals. However, states and nations were composed of thousands and millions of unrelated individuals that needed to cooperate in order for the civilization to function and develop. Jared Diamond argues that organized religion served to provide a bond between unrelated individuals who would otherwise be more prone to enmity. He argues that the leading cause of death among hunter-gatherer societies was murder.

Let us have a look at the earliest of times until the middle AD 1500s, when people believed that the earth was flat and rested upon four pillars. This was considered the unequivocal truth, so much so that if anyone said anything to the contrary, they would be blasphemous and considered to be profane, tried in the royal courts, burned alive, and condemned to an eternal hell. However, it was soon discovered that this was not so—that the earth is indeed round.

<u>Middle Ages:</u> Newer present-day world religions established themselves throughout Eurasia during the Middle Ages by Christianization of the Western world, Buddhist missions to East Asia, the decline of Buddhism in the Indian subcontinent, and the spread of Islam throughout the Middle East, Central Asia, North Africa, and parts of Europe and India.

During the Middle Ages, there were numerous religious conflicts; here we list a few:

- Shamans were in conflict with Buddhists, Taoists, Muslims, and Christians during the Mongol invasions.
- Muslims were in conflict with Hindus and Sikhs during Muslim conquest in the Indian subcontinent.
- Muslims were in conflict with Zoroastrians during the Islamic conquest of Persia.
- Christians were in conflict with Muslims during the Byzantine-Arab Wars, Crusades, Reconquista, and Ottoman wars in Europe.
- Christians were in conflict with Jews during the Crusades, Reconquista, and Inquisition.

Many medieval religious movements emphasized mysticism, such as the Cathars and related movements in the West, the Jews in Spain, the Bhakti movement in India, and Sufism in Islam. Monotheism was the defining form of Christian Christology and in Islamic Tawhid. Hindu monotheist notions of Brahman likewise reached their classical form with the teaching of Adi Shankara.

<u>Modern Period:</u> European colonization during the fifteenth to nineteenth centuries resulted in the forceful spread of Christianity to sub-Saharan Africa, the Americas, Australia, and the Philippines. The invention of the printing press in the fifteenth century played a significant role in the rapid spread of the Protestant Reformation under leaders such as Martin Luther and John Calvin. Wars of religion followed, such as the Thirty Years' War, which devastated central Europe from 1618 to 1648. Both Protestant and Catholic churches competed ruthlessly to Christianize the world.

The eighteenth century saw the beginning of secularization in Europe, gaining momentum after the French Revolution. By the late twentieth century, religion had declined to only a weak force in most of Europe.

In the twentieth century, the regimes of Communist Eastern Europe and Communist China were extremely antireligious. A great variety of new religious movements started to get momentum in the twentieth century, many proposing a combination of different forms of belief or practice of elements that formed the new established religions. The following of such new movements is relatively low, usually only consisting of 2 percent or less worldwide in the 2000s. Followers of the popular classical world religions account for more than 75 percent of the world's population, while followers of indigenous tribal religions have fallen to 4 percent globally. As of 2005, is has been estimated that 14 percent of the world's population are nonreligious.

Blasphemy: In Christianity, blasphemy has points in common with heresy but is differentiated from it in that heresy consists of holding a belief contrary to the current orthodox belief. Therefore, it is not blasphemous to deny the existence of God or to question the established tenets of the Christian faith unless this is done in a mocking and derisive spirit. In the Christian religion, blasphemy has been regarded as a sin by moral theologians; Saint Thomas Aquinas described it as a sin against faith. For the Muslim, it is blasphemy to speak with disdain not only of God but also of Muhammad. Blasphemy is irreverence toward a deity or deities and, by extension, the use of profanity.

In many societies, blasphemy in some form or another has been an offense punishable by law. The Mosaic Law decreed death by stoning as the penalty for the blasphemer. Under the Byzantine emperor Justinian I (reigned 527-565), the death penalty was decreed for blasphemy. In the United States, many states have legislation aimed at the offense. In Scotland until the eighteenth century, it was punishable by death; and in England, it is both a statutory and a common-law offense. It was recognized as a common-law offense in the seventeenth century; the underlying idea apparently was that an attack on religion is an attack on the state. This proves that authority morphed into truth. Can you see the extent of control, corruption, and influence that religion has had on many civilizations? Their religion is believed to justify their authority.

The Natural Elements: Then there is the universe that has always captured the imagination of mankind. The strange sparkling specs against the black cloth draped over the earth when the sun rests for the day and the brilliant stripes formed in the night sky by shooting stars. The human race and their ignorance of the universe in ancient times developed many varied and unique explanations for what they witnessed. From these explanations, myths were formed and established; these stories, fables, and myths were in turn told and retold over generations, some of which have survived and are still believed until today. For example, when you wish upon a falling star, your wish is believed to come to fulfillment; however, do not share it with anyone as it will not come true.

Humanity witnessed the magnitude of power that the various elements held and therefore attributed each element or a combination of elements to various gods, goddesses, and deities. Offerings and sacrifices (sometimes animal or human, depending on the severity of devastation and need) were made to appease the gods and prevent their wrath from devastating their society, and in turn, gifts would be bestowed upon them from these gods in the forms of plentiful harvests, protection, and the general well-being of their peoples. The portrayal of the elements as gods with human qualities made humankind capable of relating to them in a divine and spiritual way.

Religious practices and theories concerning rituals and ceremonies were reserved for chosen disciples or holy men to undertake the responsibility of the successful completion of practices. The chosen follower that dealt directly with the gods was usually the oldest of that civilization or the wisest who had to possess certain attributes for them to carry out their divine position and spiritual path for them and their people. The teachings and communication from these divinely elected followers were perceived to be the will of the gods.

From this came the dawning of religious structures in its earliest forms with different ranks of authority and jurisdiction. These structures were initially formed to dominate and govern their people. New gods were forged that had added human qualities. These new gods assigned orders and values to the ordained individuals in secret to convey to their followers. The people became God-fearing and accepted what they were told by the gods. From this came blind belief, conviction, and unwavering faith in religion.

When there was drought, it was due to nonbelievers or people living in sin. A sacrificial ceremony had to be performed, and the people were reprimanded in order to preserve certain values which would guarantee blessings if they were obedient to these religious values. Group prayers were formed, and the people with divine power bestowed upon them by the gods had to articulate with the gods and oversee the ceremony. Bizarre sounds and convulsions are executed by the ordained religious official to demonstrate to the followers what an arduous task it is to communicate with the gods. Drumbeats and chanting are accompanied by attendants to create a mystical and receptive atmosphere among the believers.

These practices established certain values as religious laws that had to be customary as part of the daily lives of the followers who were part of the religious assembly. These religious laws became governance laws, and those that did not abide by them were chastised, ostracized, punished, or killed. Rigid laws were passed, and the elders of the religious groups had more power and control over the obedient members than ever before. The elders ensured that the elected members who conversed with the gods were under their influence, and they received titles or names in order to be recognized by society as the ordained one, such as priest or priestess.

This office over the years has grown into one of the most powerful professions. Holiness is also associated to this title. Therefore, a religious leader is considered to be a person with integrity. Advice and support is sort from such a holy ranking official because they are believed to possess immense wisdom. Followers did not always comprehend what these religious leaders taught then, but they would not venture against anything that the religious leaders had conveyed to them. When an inquiry was made about an unreasonable or unjust statement made by the religious leader, the holy official's statement would be taken in higher regard, and his word would be explicitly accepted. The general accepted reasoning was that it was "the will of the gods," irrespective of how illogical or irrational their ideologies may have seemed. The most popular answer to any illogical action was that the gods do not think like humankind. From here the phrase originated into "The wisdom of the gods is foolish by man and so the wisdom of man is foolish by the gods." Up until today, this is unequivocally one of the most enduring arguments that the church uses. Who would dare undermine the authority of a god?

Immense power and freedom was granted by the gods to the holy religious leaders that were in turn accepted by their peoples; with this indoctrination in place, higher ranking officials supervised lower ranking officials to oversee that the religious group spoke with the same voice. The high-ranking religious leaders had more responsibility than the lower ranks, and their benefits were also substantially greater. Even government heads solicited advice from these high-ranking religious leaders. This rudimentary structure formed the foundations for the first church that was established; these institutions yielded immense spiritual governance over their followers also referred to as their "flock." Well-cultivated values were established, and the word "holy" was incorporated into these values. Even the lower ranking holy officials were now considered to be holy. To be holy is considered to be divine, exalted, or worthy of complete devotion as one perfect in goodness and righteousness.

This was how the first rudimentary idea of a church structure was physically and mentally formed in the minds of society, which led to spiritual governance for the peoples. Well worked out and refined values were brought in place, and the word "holy" was associated before it that included all their workings and scriptures that were produced by the church.

Since the earliest of times, there were individuals that exploited the emotions of people, working on people's fears and overpowering them with threat, force, guilt, and fear which granted church complete authority over society. This is the most successful recipe for psychological manipulation.

Let us have a look at how religion forged its path through the years to rise to the fine art practiced today and known as the church or the Christian religion. Two thousand years ago, the church was not as established as today. There are three variants of religion that we will discuss: the old Egyptian religion of Amen-Ra, the old Greek religion, and finally the Christian religion which originally came from the Kumran religion.

You will be required to be attentive when we venture into these religions especially if you belong to the Christian religion, even though you may snicker at their beliefs, myths, and false gods. Try not to pass judgment, and instead view the bigger picture for what it is worth, as there are many similarities between the various religions that we will discuss further in the book. The full explanations of the similarities will be provided in chapter 11 under the heading "The Jesus Story and His Predecessors."

In this chapter, we have only discussed religion in general, its origins, and the history thereof. Religious structures will be discussed in the following chapter.

The religious beliefs in gods were previously in existence long before the old Oriental religions originated. There is substantial proof that the first peoples such as the old cave people had gods and practiced their own form of tradition or religion during the time when fire was discovered and tamed.

Humankind has since its existence showed frailty and obedience toward the elements, for the elements were considered to be superior, particularly the unseen elements. It was concluded that it was unequivocally the act of gods. Everything that could not be mastered was a god of some kind.

One ought to query if the modern and enlightened religions of today are genuinely as enlightened as they proclaim. Even with modern technology, mankind persists to blindly follow that which they have no true knowledge of. Most individuals believe that if they have read their Bible or Holy Book and performed some form of study concerning certain religious aspects that they are qualified to speak or preach haphazardly about what they have no true knowledge of.

These preachers or holy officials utter various mythological events with confounded conviction as if it were the truth.

A rhetorical question: If a refined educated individual conveys a certain aspect and is not the truth even if the individual does not know that it is untrue, should this untruth become the truth purely because the speaker did not know that it is actually untrue? Any reasonable person would reckon that it would remain false no matter how spiritually it was intended. A falsification cannot be made holy.

From the earliest of times, humankind has been fascinated with the universe, the big unknown, which was at that time totally out of reach for mankind. Mythical stories came into existence, and this became known as the "house of the gods." The gods controlled the elements on earth from their heavenly throne. That seemed logical at the time to refer to the heavens as the "heavens of the gods."

Later it was realized that all these elements and their gods worked in harmony; therefore, it was considered that there was a supreme god over the lower order gods. The birth of the Almighty God came to be. The heavens and all on earth belonged to him and the heavens became God's heaven.

This god was so almighty that man was not worthy enough to speak directly to him, so it came to be that a mediator or savior was required to communicate between God and humanity. There were more than sixteen known saviors before the story of Jesus. More about these saviors will be discussed in chapter 11.

Superincumbent religious structures formed around astrotheology, today known as theology. Theology is the discipline of religious thought that is restricted in its narrower sense because of origination and format, to Christianity, but in its broader sense, because of its themes, to other religions. The themes of theology are God, man, the world, salvation, and eschatology (or the study of last times). Theology became influential and heavily relied upon by many traditions and religions as long as it was trusted to be true to time and true to the seasons. Theology seemed to be entirely unchangeable and was compared to the elements and seasons because they would approach and pass like clockwork and maintain a logical order and harmony. Theology, as believed by the ancients, was thought to have existed before time, and that it will always be there even long after humanity no longer existed and so another concept came to be. The god's unchangeable heaven, or in other words, the eternal god was unchangeable. This God as he was, he is, and shall remain forever more. He is the Alpha and the Omega, the beginning and the end. Perhaps the information that has been provided thus far might seem to be thumb sucked and difficult to believe or accept its validity; however, please bear with me.

There is no need to be convincing; this is factual history for anyone who seeks it. This book has not been compiled to instill fear or apprehension; the purpose of this book is to offer the naked truth, no sugar coating or half-truths.

All this knowledge and wisdom took place long before you and I even existed. Why should you not be allowed to know the truth? The truth is available for everyone.

Why do we follow a severally distorted version out of fear; are we afraid to question or inquire? Does the scripture not teach you to investigate all and keep only the good, i.e., advantages, positive, desirable, and needed information? That is exactly what truth is; it is wholesome and untainted because the truth sets us free from the ties that we are bound with, be it bonds made by religion, tradition, or myth.

When we have the facts, we do not have blind faith; we no longer need to wonder about our faith because we know the facts; we know for certain. With facts, you do not need convincing, you do not need to hope, and you do not have to simply blindly accept without question.

Believing in something is beneficial to spiritual growth as our spiritual well-being is connected to all facets of our lives. However, our faith should be based on proven facts and the admission of ultimate truth.

God does undeniably and undoubtedly exist. However, God is not what the religious institutions make you believe God is. Know God not from prayer, wishful thinking, or from the beliefs in the traditional doctrines of a religion. How can you be part of your faith without question? We all have hidden deep within ourselves an inquiring and inquisitive nature. If your faith is true, there should be millions of righteous saved souls in the heavens. Think about the possible magnitude of righteous souls that were there before you and me. I reckon it must be an inconceivable quantity. Do they all rest forever in the lap of father Abraham, or do they all rule as kings or priests? The state of human death has always been shrouded by mystery and superstition, and its precise definition remains contentious due to the differences in culture, religion, and legal systems.

Religion in general has made human beings stupid and totally illogical. Do you also mumble, stamp your feet, and clap your hands so that the Holy Spirit can come over you? Do you also fall down and foam at the mouth? How mockingly do you want to make your God out to be?

Are you perhaps one of those who want to be an old Job, or do you want to be a David or a Moses or an Elijah? Do you not perhaps think that God would want you to be the best that you can possibly be? What would God do with an oversupply of Jobs, Davids, and Elijahs in heaven or on earth? Therefore, he made each of us into our own unique image and person to be the best that we can be.

Do not lose your faith in God just because you have seen the myths and lies for what they are. But there is a more unique way, and that is the naked truth without all the lies, myths, rituals, habits, and symbolism.

Read all these chapters to get the full picture. Go over to the next chapter, "God: The Concepts by Man."

Chapter 2

God: The Concepts by Man

Christianity is a major religion, stemming from the so-called life, teachings, and death of Jesus of Nazareth (referred to as the Christ or the Anointed One of God) in the first century AD. It has become the largest of the world's religions. Geographically, the most widely diffused of all faiths, it has a following of some 2 billion believers. Its largest groups are the Roman Catholic Church, the Eastern Orthodox churches, and the Protestant churches; in addition to these churches, there are several independent churches of Eastern Christianity as well as numerous sects throughout the world.

The Identity of Christianity

At the very least, Christianity is the faith tradition that focuses predominantly on the figure of "Jesus Christ." In this context, faith refers both to the believers' act of trust and to the content of their faith. That tradition, viewed as a system of belief and behavior, leads people to see Christianity as one of the world's religions, alongside Hinduism, Buddhism, Islam, and others.

As a tradition, Christianity is more than a system of religious beliefs. It also has generated a particular culture, set of ideas, and ways of life, practices, rituals, symbolism, and artifacts that have been passed down from generation to generation through the twenty centuries since Jesus first became the object of this faith. Christianity is both a living tradition of faith and the culture that the faith leaves behind. The main agent of Christianity is the church and the community of people who make up the body of believers and worshippers. Christianity may incorporate, along with such believers, their doctrines, customs, and historical episodes.

To say that Christianity "focuses" on Jesus is to say that whatever else it comprehends is secondary; Christianity brings these mythical realities together in reference to a distorted ancient historic figure. Few Christians would be content to keep the figure of an ancient Jesus as a merely historical reference. Although their faith tradition is historical, with examples, such as they believe that encounters and communication with the divine occurs among ordinary humans through the ages, the vast majority of Christians focus their faith in Jesus as someone who is also a present reality. There are many inclusions and references in their tradition, and therefore they speak of "God" and "human nature" or of "church" and "the world," but they would not want to be nor would they be called Christian if they did not bring their attentions first and last to "Jesus Christ."

While there is something simple about this focus on Jesus as the central figure, there is also something very complicated. That complexity is obvious when one tries to envision the more than twenty-two thousand separate churches, sects, and denominations that make up the Christian faith tradition today. To project these separate bodies against the background of their development in the nations of the world gives you an idea of the variety present in, what is supposed to be, one religion.

Due to the complexity fostered in Christianity, it is natural that through the ages, both those in the tradition and those surrounding it have made attempts at simplification. Two ways to do this have been to concentrate on the "essence" of the faith, and thus on the ideas that are integral to it or to be concerned with the "identity" of the tradition and on the boundaries of its historical experience, even though many ideas and views vary quite dramatically. Simplification will never truly be acquired due to heated and contentious issues among the different sects and denominations.

Scholars in the modern world have tended to locate the focus of this faith tradition in the context of monotheistic religions. Christianity addresses the historical figure of Jesus against the background of, and while seeking to remain faithful to, the experience of one God. It has consistently rejected polytheism, which allows for many gods, and atheism, which makes Jesus a purely and ordinarily human figure without divine or transcendent reference.

To monotheism as an element of the faith tradition of Christianity, one may add that, with rare exceptions, Christianity refers to a supposed plan of salvation or redemption. That is to say, the believers in the church picture themselves as in a plight from which they need rescue. What do Christians need to be saved from? They believe that they have been distanced from their source in God and therefore need to be saved. Christianity is based on a particular experience or scheme directed to the act of saving—that is, of bringing or "buying back," which is part of what redemption means, these creatures of God to their source in God. The agent of that redemption is Jesus Christ. The Christian religious institution plays on your feelings; they put you on a continuous roller-coaster ride of emotions, from guilt to redemption and back again to guilt. They do this to maintain an artificial sense of control over their members and followers.

By the late twentieth century, Christianity had become the most widely disseminated faith on Earth. Virtually no nation has remained unaffected by the brutal, forceful, and ruthless activities of Christian missionaries; although in many countries, Christians are only a small fraction of the total population. Most of the countries of Asia and of Africa have Christian minorities, some of which, as in India and even in China, number several million members. The concentration of Christians, however, remains in the popular domain of Western culture.

The Essence of God

On the basis of Christian religious experiences, the myths and mystics of Christianity throughout the ages have agreed in the belief that one can make no definite assertions concerning God, because God is beyond all concepts and images to humanity as his wisdom is incomprehensible or foolish to man. Even though the Christian Bible states that nothing will be hidden from God's children. Inasmuch as human beings are gifted with reason and logic, however, the religious experience of the eternal and the transcendental demands historical clarification for the many inquiring minds emerging from today's modern age because people are no longer comfortable to conform to old norms, old traditions, and old ways.

Therefore, in Christian theology, two tendencies stand in constant tension with each other. On the one hand, there is the tendency to arrange and organize the idea of God as far as possible. On the other, there is the tendency to eliminate the accumulated collection of current conceptions of God and to return to the understanding of the utter transcendence of God, as they perceive this to be the only way to understand God.

Theologians, by and large, have had to acknowledge the limits of human reason and language to address the "nature" of God, who is beyond normal human experience but who is unequivocally intertwined with it. When it concerns the divine human contact, it became necessary and possible for them to make some affirmations about the experience, the disclosure, and the character of God.

The word or the name God is generally familiar to every person, irrespective of culture or creed. This concept is considered holy with everyone whether you are a Christian, Hindu, Muslim, or any other religious follower. It does not matter if you do not belong to a religion; there is still however a higher power that is in essence a God to you.

If you ask anyone the following question, you will receive a broad diversity of answers. Some answers are ambiguous while others are more straightforward. "Who is God, or what is God?" Many of you will now have a frown, a grin, or a raised brow. How could I ask you such a question? you might ask. Yes, I'm asking because if you think about it earnestly, this is not an aspect that is usually discussed; this topic is prevalently avoided. It is widely accepted that each of us have some sort of knowledge of who or what God is, an inborn knowledge of some sort that everyone is allegedly supposed to possess.

Here are a few examples of the answers I have received from numerous people. Astonishingly, most answers were brief and obtuse.

- He is our Heavenly Father.
- He is the strength within us.
- He is our creator.
- He is the wise one over all things.
- He is the creator of all things.
- God is God.
- He is the almighty.

The list continues indefinitely; however, these are the most common responses. There are so many books that are written about God. Most people would tell you that it does not matter how you serve God. There is only one God, and we all serve him. Would you tend to agree with such a statement? Let us have a look. There are so many who pray to a god high above the sun, moon, and stars. Then there are those that believe that God is among us. Then there are others who take the middle way that believe God is in the heavens, but that his spirit is with us at all times. Then there are still others who would say that God is within each of us or at least his spirit. At the end of the day, there are so many concepts regarding God that it would be logical to say that he cannot possibly be all of these at once because it does not describe one God.

What does the Bible say to help clear up this matter? Even in the Bible, there are various viewpoints. In the Bible, it says that God does not have the outward form of man, and that God is spirit. However, it also says that God is the strength and wisdom in our midst. How do you understand God or this concept? It is ironic that most people think of God as a manly figure because he is our father and we speak of God as "him" or "he." No one has spoken of God as a "thing" or an "it." If God does not have the form of man and he is the unseen higher power, as no person can proclaim that they have undoubtedly seen God, why do we give God human qualities and characteristics? Perhaps, we do this to be able to relate to God in a human way.

Some of us see God as one mighty power while others think God to be three parts in one, i.e., the Father, the Son, and the Holy Spirit. If either of this is true, then why did God say that he will send his Son to the world? He would then have stated that he himself would arrive. Why then does his Son proclaim that he is going to his Father to prepare a place for the chosen people?

When we talk about unity, then it would mean that we need to be one of thought and one of spirit. A marriage embodies unity between husband and wife, is it not? Even though they are still two separate human beings, each with their own character traits, personalities, and desires, they have become one and united to strive toward their ambitions and aspirations together. The couple work at their unity "which is their marriage" and conquer many obstacles and challenges as one force.

When people say that God comprises of three entities in Christianity as the Holy Spirit, Jesus Christ, and the Father, we speak of unity. This idea and theory goes as far back as two thousand years; let me enlighten you with some history.

In Egypt, when the Jews lived in exile, they were introduced and influenced by the Egyptian religion of Isis, the Virgin Mother. Isis proclaimed that she was the strength and wisdom in the midst of mankind. Isis was the eternal mother who gave birth to Horus, who was also the son of Osiris, the eternal god of the underworld.

Isis declared that she is what she is; Isis was known as "Is."

Today, we see a remarkable resemblance to what God has declared that he is the strength and wisdom in the midst of mankind, the eternal Father.

The Father declares that he is what he is: the Father is known as "Is."

After the death of Isis, a new religion was brought forth that was not reflective of the life span of a human being but instead to exist for an eternity.

The religion of the mediator Amen-Ra representing the sun, the Son of God and the Son of Righteousness was recognized and accepted by the Egyptian people. The tradition of a son that gave his life to humankind and that offered eternal life to the world originally meant that as long as the sun shined, there would be eternal life on earth.

The sun god Ra had substantial influence on the foundation and forming of Christianity. We have briefly mentioned this aspect which will be discussed further and more depth in chapter 10.

The son of God—the Son of Righteousness: Amen-Ra; and the son of God—the Son of Righteousness: Jesus Christ.

When the Jews took flight from Egypt and Canaan fell to ruin, today known as Palestine, they were introduced to yet another mediator known as "the comforter" god "El," the planet Saturn.

The god El—the comforter and the Holy Spirit—the comforter seem synonymous.

Should you write these similarities off as mere coincidence? This will be discussed more depth in chapter 10.

What do you believe the word "God" means to mankind? Why this word in particular; is there a reason for this?

> Gospel: The message or teachings of a religious teacher.

> Obedience: The act or instance of obeying the belief structure.

> Duty: A moral obligation or the force of moral obligation.

Work these views out on your own merits. It does not matter how you look at it because it comes back to what I have revealed to you so far. You will not learn these facts and views on a school or church bench because the truth is being withheld from you purposefully. There are very few religious leaders that have this knowledge available to them.

Within the Christian religion, they endless search for explanations to questions that suit their belief system; they sift through old translations and find certain terms such as the supposed name of God.

The name Jehovah or Jeh actually means "we." Now there are religious groups that no longer talk about God but instead of Jehovah. Let us be serious for a minute. If Jehovah was truly the name of God, which child would call their father on their first name, i.e., John or Graeme? How could anyone fathom to call their biological father on his first name, let alone God our Father on his? Nowadays, the church groups have become so laid back and arrogant to refer to God as Dad or Daddy.

There is an ingenious word play performed to an exact refined art to attract people to the church groups. For example, are any of the following statements familiar? "If you do not stop doing this or that, then God will punish you!" and in the same breath you are told "Give your life to Jesus, and he will forgive you."

This is further proof that people make God out to be a stern, strict, and rigid god that does not forgive easily; but they tend to place Jesus, his Son, above him by making Jesus look like the good guy because it is perceived that God is the strict and unforgiving one. It tends to resemble the "good cop, bad cop" team in the films. When we refer to the Holy Spirit, this holy figure has been watered down and generalized as if the Holy Spirit does not qualify for any godlike status.

Everything revolves around Jesus, the Son of God, who is the Salvation and the Savior. What is decisively new in the Christians' Bible of the New Testament is that faith in God lies in the fact that this faith is predominantly about a particular person, teaching, and work of Jesus; it has become difficult to discern between theology (doctrines of God) and Christology (doctrines of Christ).

Nevertheless, in the Christian understanding of Jesus as being one with the Father, there is a constant possibility that faith in God will be absorbed in a "monochristism"; in other words, the figure of the Son in the life of faith will overshadow the figure of the Father and therefore cause it to disappear, and that the figure of the Creator, Sustainer, and Judge of the world will recede behind the figure of the Redeemer, "Jesus Christ." This seems to be obvious as God is rarely spoken of except in the incidences of admonition of punishment or repudiation, i.e., warning of punishment or cast out and forgotten, left to one's own vices. While the Holy Spirit is at times associated with a gust of wind.

The Holy Spirit seems to have lost its true identity from Christianity as it is taught in modern-day views. The Holy Spirit, in Christian belief, is considered to be the third person of the Trinity. Numerous aspects of the Spirit are mentioned in the Acts of the Apostles, which encompasses healing, prophecy, the expelling of demons, and the speaking in tongues; these qualities are associated with the activity of the Spirit. The Holy Spirit will be discussed further in chapter 13.

People are truly arrogant. Why do I say so? Because we have always believed that we are the center of everything or at least something. I mean, we must be very special for God to send his only begotten Son to us? Is that not a strange thought? At first, centuries ago, mankind believed that the planet was the center of the universe, and we were proven wrong. Mankind then believed that our planet must surely be in the center of our galaxy, and yet again we were proven wrong. Our planet is actually on the outskirts of the galaxy. Yet mankind continues to believe that we must be at the center of something in one way or another. The other strange aspect is that numerous people believe that humans are the only intelligent life forms in the universe. Can you see the depth of arrogance that is required to see aspects that way? How could you think, even for a moment, taking the vastness of the universe into consideration, that humans must be central to God's design?

Imagine for a moment that we find intelligent life in the universe; most of these religious organizations would feel it is their religious duty to save these beings and would try to force their religious beliefs and doctrines onto them. Do you not see that the Inquisition has never truly left? The Inquisition was a tool for religion that has successfully transformed and conditioned millions of people's minds into the inquisitorial mind that exists today. How many cultures have not been forced into religion like Christianity? There are numerous examples throughout history, such as the Indians, the Mayans, etc., not to mention the path of devastation and unnecessary bloodshed of billions of people across the world over the centuries simply because they practiced their own religion and traditions. Why, you might ask? The inquisitorial mind sees nothing wrong with trying to ensure compliance and adherence with one's so-called version of the truth, even if it be by brute force. Religion has a deeply vested interest in that type of mind-set. At the end of the day, how people picture God is not the real God. For centuries, religious structures have created various distorted images of God and Jesus. They have perfected it to an art, manipulated and distorted it to suit the needs of these religious organizations at certain times in history, as they continue and will indefinitely still continue to do.

Be still for a moment and ponder on: "Who is God, and what is God?" Who is it that we pray to?

Most believers would define God as Creator, Sustainer, and Judge. If we as humans had the right to depict God in our own personal way, how would you describe him?

Everyone interprets God as wonderful; however, in general, it sounds as if God is a harsh old man. I thought that God is love, patient, and tolerant, sees no evil, speaks no evil, and does no evil. He is the self-control, the strength, and wisdom in the midst of mankind. God forgives. If this were true that God is all these things, everything which is positive, why would he then punish you if you make a human mistake? Is this not the same God that has no interest in the transitory, i.e., all that temporary? Is it God that intends punishing mankind, or is it perhaps mankind that wants to judge and punish and make it out to be the will of God? Or is this what you would want to portray as the love of God that he wants to better you?

In Genesis, our ancestral parents, Adam and Eve, are depicted in an absolute state of bliss because there is no suffering, pain, or disease. However, there was a catch; they were commanded by God not to eat the fruit of the tree of knowledge, knowledge of good and evil. Why would God prohibit his creatures from evolving and acquiring knowledge? You would expect that God would want his children to advance in wisdom, knowledge, and understanding. Would a parent prohibit their own child from learning and advancing? Obviously not. It even goes against what the Bible says about investigating everything and to chase after the truth. We all know what happens next; forbidden fruit is an impossible temptation to resist, the snake tempts Eve, and Eve tempts Adam. Wait a moment, who created the snake? Is God not the creator of all things? In any case, as the story goes, Adam and Eve were cast out of paradise after they had sinned. They were now exposed to suffering, disease, and pain because they sought for the knowledge of what was good and evil.

This depiction of God is rather bizarre because it seems as though he is insecure or afraid of his position. Why did God give us the capability of inquiring and being curious if we were not meant to be that way? The God that is portrayed from the Old Testament is psychotic, vengeful, insecure, neurotic, and an unstable entity. Nobody can deny these traits; have a look for yourself in your Bible. This is the God that the Jews managed to foster in Christianity. This is not who God is.

You will only find God in truth. Is that not what your Bible teaches you?

This brings us to another impasse, "Where is God; where does he live?" The most general response encountered is that God is in heaven, and his spirit is with us on earth. Most people generally believe that God lives up in the heavens and that Satan lives down below in hell, purgatory, and limbo. When people pray, they instinctively tend to look up, while the people on the opposite side of the globe are looking in the opposite direction. I have read in the Bible that is says that the kingdom of God is with humankind. God himself says in the Bible, who would search for him in the heavens and over the waters, do you not know that God came so close to you that he wants to live on your tongue and in your heart.

Let us summarize: If the kingdom of God is by mankind as God states himself and the Son of God is by his Father, where is the Son of God? Is the kingdom of God and heaven not the same place? This concept will be discussed in depth in chapter 7.

The question is sometimes asked, "Where does God come from?" The briefest answer to this would be to say that God is from eternity until eternity. He is the beginning and the end, the Alpha and Omega.

My thoughts instinctively go to a particular verse in the Bible, which is not read so often. Habakkuk 3 verse 3 says, "God came from Teman, and the Holy one from Mount Paran, Selah. His glory covered the heavens, and the earth was full of his praise." What would Teman and Paran possibly mean? Because other beliefs do not believe in the Trinity God, and they solely believe in a single God, would that mean that they worship another God?

We are referring to the Muslim belief. They name their god "Allah" which when translated means "the highest god of all the gods." According to their belief structure, they pray to their god through Abraham, Elijah, Moses, Jesus, and Mohammed. Does it not sound similar to the God that you worship? Due to their culture and the one other prophet that are part of their religion, Muslims are considered to be Gentiles by Christians who damn them and hate them. Who created them and who gave them life?

How can you say that you love God but you hate his creation? Is it not true that everything that God created was good? Or did God not create them? Therefore, I ask you again, "Who is God; what is God?" According to the Bible, everything that was created was created by God because the earth was without form and void; darkness was upon the face of the deep. God created each and every creature in the sea and on the land, from every bird to every tree and even man; and God saw that it was good.

God warns humankind not to judge because those who judge have already been judged.

Is God spirit? Does he look like the human race because God made us in his image and after his own likeness? Does God have a form up there in heaven or here on earth? What is God?

If you proclaim that you love God with your whole heart, soul, and being, then you should know who or what you love. How does this love we have for God appear to him?

I read in the First Epistle to John verse 3, "Behold, what manner of love the Father hath bestowed upon us, that we should be called the sons of God: therefore the world knoweth us not, because it knew him not" (King James Version 1611) and 1 John 3:4, "Whosoever committeth sin transgresseth also the law, for sin is the transgression of the law" (King James Version 1611). How do these laws of God look like? Would these laws not perhaps be the ten commandments of Moses?

Then I realize that those laws cannot be the Ten Commandments because in the scriptures, it says that people that hang on the Ten Commandments of Moses cannot enter the kingdom of God. I recall how these Ten Commandments where imprinted in the minds of all the worshippers of Christianity. Who is truly misleading who? Who is lost? Did God also simply become a myth or a symbol in your mind, just as the religion that you are chasing after? Blind faith without the right to question or even ask?

This brings us to a point in question that needs to be discussed, the church and religious structures which is in the next chapter.

Chapter 3

The Church and Its Religious Structure

A cursory glance at the suppressed history of religion reveals that even the foundational myths themselves are emergent culminations developed through influence over time. For example, a fundamental doctrine of the Christian faith is the death and resurrection of Christ. This notion is so important that the Bible itself states, "And if Christ be not risen, then is our preaching vain, and your faith is also vain" (1 Corinthians 15:14, King James Version 1611).

Yet it is very difficult to take this account literally, for not only is there no primary source that exists today, proving this supernatural event in nonreligious history, awareness of the enormous number of pre-Christian Saviors who also died and were resurrected immediately puts this story in mythological territory by association.

Early church figures such as Tertullian went to great lengths to break these associations, even claiming that the devil caused the similarities to occur. As stated in the second century, "The devil, whose business is to prevent the truth, mimics the exact circumstances of the Divine Sacraments. He baptizes his believers and promises forgiveness of sins . . . he celebrates the oblation of bread and brings in the symbol of the resurrection. Let us therefore acknowledge the craftiness of the devil, who copied certain things of those that be Divine" (Tertullian, AD 155-222 from *The Prescription against Heretics*, Chap XL).

What is truly sad, however, is that when we cease the idea that the stories from Christianity, Judaism, Islam, and all others are literal history and accept them for what they really are, which are purely hidden spiritual meanings that transcend the literal sense of a sacred text, which are expressions derived from many faiths. We see that all religions share a common thread. There are many wise words in the scriptures, but it is this unifying imperative that needs to be recognized and appreciated as well.

When there is talk concerning "church," it is immediately a holy aspect. The church is referred to by some as the house of God, and immediately it is seen as a Christian establishment and that its mere existence originated from the will of God.

Some individuals refer to the church building as a house of prayer, temple, or place of worship. It does not matter what it is called or referred to because the concept remains the same.

The concept of the church is a human-formulated concept which is not an authentically Christian invention. Churches and places of worship existed before Christianity existed. The so-called holiness associated with the church is a human established concept that includes the activities that are performed within it.

Not any of the proceedings were formulated or passed from God. Then you might ask, how could I make such a statement? Let us have a look.

We revisit the origin of religion and the inception of numerous beliefs by touching on a few points. First, one way of thinking, then two, and today there are more than ten thousand views or ways of thinking. Religion brought belief structures and in turn manifested in a church structure, everything in a humanly orientated perspective.

As it was in the beginning of religion, yet still the church fathers decide what makes sense to them to the advantage of the church and its religious structures. This in turn is passed off as the will of God through unexplainable happenings or miracles.

Aspects concealed from humankind helps to add to the mystery and so cannot be questioned. I thought then, according to the Bible, that nothing will be concealed from the children of God. In other words, if the religious institutions, i.e., churches proclaim that certain things are concealed, then they acknowledge that they are not children of God. This would be according to their Bible.

Many things are done today in the name of the Lord. Then I wonder which Lord are they talking about?

The laws of Moses are upheld as the true and only way in most of the churches. They speak of mysteries and occurrences that they cannot explain or comprehend are said to be miracles. The part in the Bible where it says that the wisdom of God is foolish by man has become a very useful tool for most Christian religious institutions. These days, however, you hardly hear of mysteries and miracles because it has all become the unseen, and only after the grave will these mysteries be opened for you to see.

Another confounding aspect from the church, that aids it in avoiding answering it, where they say that you will see and understand but you will only fully understand and see one day. Nowhere in any scripture is it mentioned that this day they speak of is after the grave.

Is it not these so-called unseen happenings that you need to see and understand fully to keep the darkness away? Why will each of us only see it when our soul comes to rest? Do you only need after the grave?

Let us be completely honest with each other. It is said in the Bible that "everyone that is weary and burdened should come to me." Who is this speaking of? The church fathers preach that everyone should go to church because your questions and answers are there. Everything that you desire to know you must gather from the church; however, the questions that truly bother you cannot even be answered successfully by your church leaders because they do not even know where the kingdom of God actually is. The church is believed to exist only to introduce you to God, but they tell you only what is written in the Bible; this you could have done at home for yourself.

Churches are filled with myths, symbols, traditions, rituals, and habits that were formulated by humans purposefully to give the churchgoers a mysterious, mystical, godly feeling. As soon as the church starts running slightly empty, they devise new ways to make it more appealing for the religious community to return to their church services.

Drought in a prayer is associated with the undisciplined church community and/or their children; they therefore conduct prayer sessions to help rectify this problem experienced by society. Has it not rained yet; should there be more prayer until rain falls? When it rains, the community is thanked for their honorable intentions with regard to the church and their beliefs; religion in turn gains strength again and again.

The most effective weapon predominantly used by the churches is natural psychological manipulation. They create and foster fear by their followers and worshippers of going to hell and by being punished by God or cast out by him when you sin or go against the church and their teachings. The church promises to give you forgiveness and a place for you in the kingdom of God. There are certain things you must do in the church first before you can get there. This religious quest requires a lifetime of perseverance. Your entire life actually belongs to the church because the church directs you as to the way you live your life, how to live your life, what form of prayer you are to follow, and the church leader must still know everything about your life. The Christian faith batters you to believe that you can only get closer to God through or in your church leader because according to them, God placed the church leader in the church for you. I thought the church chose its own leaders, the church council, or the community. In some religions, the churches use dreams from the congregation to appoint church leaders. Everyone one of these institutions have alleged grounded reasons to justify their actions; these might even sound reasonable at times. Sections from the Bible are used to make their actions and deeds seem even more righteous.

The Bible was compiled by a group of individuals that were handed down the knowledge through traditions and was jotted down on paper in their own views and perceptions of their traditions. Have a look at the four evangelist books in the New Testament. Not one of them explains the story of Jesus in the same way. Further discussion will be done in chapter 12.

It is so easy to say that this or that was inspired by God. Is this because it fits into the thinking of the church?

All the Christian entities state that their beliefs of the Christian religion and of God are the only true religion, and they judge the other churches as sects. There are more than ten thousand registered churches in the world. Each has their own form of worship and rituals.

All of these churches state that their existence emerged due to the will of God. All of them also promise you a path to salvation and heaven.

The Bible says it differently. Read Ephesians 4:5-6: "One Lord, one faith, one Baptism, One God and Father of all, who is above all, and through all, and in you all" (King James Version 1611).

There is not one church's baptism that is the same as the next. Some baptize adults while others baptize children. Holy Communion and their points of view also differ greatly. There is no unity between the Christian faiths, yet they state that it does not matter how you worship God. In the same breath, they also say that other sects are completely off track and are called false worshippers.

If I look at the different sects points of view, they do tell a similar story but from different perspectives. Who is wrong, and who is right? The Christian sects declare that they view the teachings and scriptures in a spiritual manner, but there is a warning in the Bible that says "God is spirit; serve him in spirit and in truth." They also refer to Jude verse 10, "But these speak evil of those things which they know not: but what they know naturally, as brute beasts, in those things they corrupt themselves" (King James Version 1611).

These sects that have all these different church leaders and duties do not always follow the structure that is spoken of in the Bible. Very few churches have this structure. It is stated in Ephesians 4:11 "And he gave some, apostles; and some, prophets; and some, evangelists; and some, pastors and teachers" (King James Version 1611).

In the First Epistle to the Corinthians 12:8-28, "For to one is given by the Spirit the word of wisdom; to another the word of knowledge by the same Spirit; to another faith by the same Spirit, to another the gifts of healing by the same spirit; to another the working of miracles; to another prophecy; to another discerning of spirits; to another diverse kinds of tongues; to another the interpretation of tongues: But all these worketh that one and the selfsame Spirit, dividing to everyman several as he will. For as the body is one, and hath many members, and all the members of that one body, being many, are one body: so also is Christ" (King James Version 1611).

Nowhere in the Bible is there any mention of a reverend, minister, or pope. A few people—intellectuals, academics, doctors, and professors, etc.—do not believe in the return of Jesus. The churches think they are strange because it does not align with what the Bible says.

Some church leaders have an answer for why they see it this way. The section in the Bible that says that those who believe that Christ is and came in the flesh are born from God; however, those who believe that he must still come are the Antichrist and the misleader. That is why they do not wait for the coming of Christ. For them, it is also not a natural happening. The graves will open is also not a natural thing that will happen but instead a spiritual occurrence.

Some Christian religious groups believe in the Trinity God while others do not. Would you think that they worship a false god, just because their views are different from yours? Why do you discriminate against the other churches and say that they are off track? Their baptism and Holy Communion differs from yours. Who is right and who is wrong, or is everyone wrong who believes in the stories of the Bible because they are filled with lies such as the wonderful Moses story: read chapter 15. Also about Noah and the ark: read chapter 18, or John the Baptist: read chapter 16, and so on. If there is one lie in a story, does that not make the entire story a lie? Can lies be holy or made holy?

Is plagiarism not also a form of a lie or even fraud? In the chapters that follow, you will be shown the lies, plagiarism, and fraud found in most of the Bible scriptures and stories. Do you think that half-truths will get you to heaven? Just because you believe, trust, and hope? Perhaps your best deeds, actions, and works would be rejected in the face of God?

Let us have a look at all the known registered churches in the world. They are all either registered as a company or a nonprofit organization. The general law of companies states that companies must have a bookkeeping system, and they must show a profit or money flow. It goes against what the Bible says in Matthew 6:24, "No man can serve two masters: for either he will hate the one, and love the other; or else he will hold to the one, and despise the other. You cannot serve God and Mammon [material wealth or possessions] at the same time" (King James Version 1611). It also says that for nothing you received it and for nothing you will hand it out.

The minister pays an outrageous sum of money to learn how to preach. Logically, they cannot give this knowledge out for nothing. The minister receives his wages in return for his knowledge. However, the Bible talks about this knowledge that you received for nothing, you will share for nothing; but if you receive wages for that that you did not pay for, you will receive nothing after the day, i.e., when you pass on.

Are we not in the circle of the mockers, or do we stand in the advice of the godless? Do you think God will be where there are lies? Or there where there are crooked dealings with his word? Yet they have an answer to overcome their transgressions by saying that it is their tenth that they are giving to the church when they serve God; therefore, they believe they should still be paid a salary. The church is filled with thieves, corrupters, and philanderers.

With the knowledge that the Bible is filled with lies, I do not think that it would be wise to defend anything that is written within the Bible. What is true and what is not? What is the will of God, and what is the will of humankind?

God wants us to discover what is good, i.e., what is helpful, needed, helpful for spiritual growth, etc. It is the truth that is good? Can lies, fraud, and deception make you free? Or is it the truth that will make you free?

The truth is not always pleasant to hear, and sometimes it is even painful. It is at times easier to live in a lie than it is to live in the truth. We have all experienced this at some stage in our lives. Therefore, you will understand what I am talking to you about.

This truth that I am showing you is not pleasant to hear, but yet you know deep within yourself that this is the truth. To break away from the lies is not simple and effortless because it is all that you have ever known, and it has become your comfort zone. You will experience conflict within yourself, and thoughts will emerge, such as "What will people say?" or "What if?"

The deeply entrenched fears that you will go to hell if you should decide to leave the church, or if you research, learn, or discover anything that will undermine your beliefs, religion, or your church in any way. Has religion become a tradition or an institution? Has it got to do with norms or views of others, or does it concern your relationship with God? Is it more important to you to be obedient to what others say and think than it is to discover and realize your spiritual journey and your relationship with God?

God cannot possibly be wrong. God is devoted, trustworthy, and without error. Why must the churches now apologize for the unjustified actions that they have done to others? If God was in control of the church, there would not have been discrimination within the churches or the Christian religion. The churches would also not have to change their establishment to suit the times. God is unchangeable and transcendent, as the churches proclaim, but it does not appear as if God is in charge because the churches continue to change. The church has become the model device invented as part of religion for the purpose of making mankind stupid.

The church leaders will unequivocally express the truth I unveil to you as the work of the Antichrist. There will even be reference made from sections of the Bible because they will attempt to destroy my credibility and what is written in this book. For example, a section out of the Bible that says that in the last days, there will be false teachers that will bring you other wisdom and that you should not believe them.

It is time to investigate and discover the truth. You have been misled for long enough through lies that have become intricate and refined over time into an attractive jewel that shines like pyrite (fool's gold).

Many will hear this and not accept a word of it; these are the people that follow norms and allow darkness to dwell in their consciousness in the name of their fictitious gods.

The church is strewn with myths, traditions, rituals, symbols, and habits. Ask yourself the question, will these things make me holy? The churches will be unable to exist without all these elaborate aspects. Do you honestly want to be part of it all?

Rather, go forth and investigate everything and retain only that which is good. Do not seek goodness in the darkness; you will not find anything good there. This is what God commands of all of us. The truth is good, even though it may not seem so. You will find God in the truth.

Has it become vitally important for you to be labeled or categorized as a Lutheran, a Mormon, a Pentecost, a member of any of the sister churches or a member of the Apostolic Church, etc.? Has the feeling of being one of the norms or to be with the in crowd kept you enslaved by their doctrines, or is it perhaps that you fear they might have something of relevance to teach you that keeps you in your place within the church?

Show me any church that was created and established by God or his Son. Jesus founded a religion, and mankind crowned him with the name Christ, which means "messiah" in Greek.

The Catholic religion places statues and imagery in their churches in the name of piety, and their pope is supposed to represent God in human form. Have a look at the pope's Episcopal miter or high hat that he wears; it is the shape of a fish head, which is a symbol of the fish god Dagon.

Go back in history and see for yourself why certain churches broke away from others. There is always disagreement when it concerns rituals, symbols, or traditions that they do not approve of; tension usually arises, and this is where groups tend to separate from the parent religious body to form their own doctrine. Then they proclaim to the world that it was the will of God. Which God brings division and estrangement between his children?

It is costly and expensive to build a new church; let us use a well-known example in South Africa, a well-known individual that started an American-based church.

He was unrestrained by convention or morality, and he lived a dissolute life. He came into conflict with the law and fled to America. He returned to South Africa after twelve years as a larger-than-life evangelist and started to lay the foundations of his church in the typical American style. Within a relatively short time span, his financial position strengthened, and he was able to erect an eight-million-rand church building. He divorced his wife that endured years of struggle and strife and married a young blonde woman; he said it was the will of God. Everything revolves around money, and he requests its congregation and followers to pray for considerable success and income.

God has no interest in transient things, as the churches will confirm and as the Bible tells us.

Read through all the chapters and explore, inquire, and probe through it all to find the truth that will reveal itself unto you within these pages. Then you are able make a rational deduction for yourself. Do not allow people to influence you with unfounded wisdom or deception because this matter is between you and God.

All I can offer you is advice and show you the facts; I have tried throughout this book to be as helpful as I can. I worship God entirely and live my life to the fullest, as God gives it to me because I am not bound to any particular institution of religion.

The following chapter discusses astrotheology and the origin of the Bible.

Chapter 4

Astrotheology and the Origin of the Bible

In order to understand theology, it is imperative that we go to where theology began and investigate the myths, symbols, and mysticism that formed the foundations of astrotheology. It would not be beneficial to shy away from the truth. The absolute and striking similarities that will be discussed in this chapter are not mere coincidences. For the very first time, you will come to see for yourself how precise the belief structures have been planned and forged to be able to stand the tests of time.

Contrary to common belief, there was never a onetime truly universal decision as to which books should be included in the Bible. It took over a century of the proliferation of numerous writings before anyone even bothered to start picking and choosing, and then it was largely a cumulative, individual, and happenstance event, guided by chance and prejudice more than objective and scholarly research, until priests and academics began pronouncing what was authoritative and holy, and even they were not unanimous. If it was inspired by God as many proclaim, would God make his children argue and differ on what his word is and was? Every church had its favored books, and since there was nothing like a clearly defined orthodoxy until the fourth century, there were in fact many simultaneous literary traditions. The illusion that it was otherwise is created by the fact that the church that came out on top simply preserved texts in its favor and destroyed or let vanish opposing documents. Hence, what we call "orthodoxy" is simply "the church that won." Can you still not see that everything you have been told by your church leaders has been a lie, that there were hidden agendas and human greed that formed the foundations of Christendom?

In this chapter, you will not be given blind faith and conviction, but rather the hard facts which are at times difficult to accept. We will sift through the order and forming of the Old and New Testaments of the Bible, the compilation of only certain books that formed the Bible as we know it to be today and why where other books left out completely.

To be able to understand the context, we will have to look at the writers of these books and the source of the information. For far too long have generations of our descendants blindly accepted that the information in the Bible is accurate and correct. It is human nature to make sure that certain aspects of our lives are trusted realistic versions of how we live our lives, what is true and correct. However, when it comes to religion, a mystical insanity overwhelms us, and the people accept it blindly without question. People are too scared to investigate because of the deep-rooted fear for hell, its eternal fire, and the wrath of God.

Ironically, the Bible says investigate everything and behold the good. The church fathers forbid you to look left or right. They tell you that there exists no other truth, but only that which they proclaim to you to be the truth. When the words "God" or "holy" are used in a sentence, it evokes fear by people; and because they are under the disguise of the holy cloak and they walk the "righteous way," people trust and accept without question everything that they are told by these church fathers. This comes forward as if people that are part of a church or congregation fear their church fathers' warnings more than the orders and commandments that God has given. I assure you and give you my guarantee that these writings are not satanic in any way, and that it is only the true hard facts that I have collected over many years to be able to compile this first book.

I would assume that it is the truth that you are searching for. You will be disappointed if you are looking for mystical wonders because you will see not only the reality with all the sordid and bizarre elements that the truth will bring with it, but also the enlightening and powerful understanding of knowing the truth. There is unfortunately no one as blind as those who look and do not want to see. Such also as those who hear and do not want to listen.

The Old Testament: Where does the Old Testament originate from?

The Septuagint, or simply "LXX," is an ancient Greek translation of the Hebrew Bible. It is referred to in critical works by the abbreviation "G." It was originally the designation for the Koine Greek translation of the Pentateuch but came in time to refer to the Greek translation of the Old Testament adopted by Christians, incorporating the translations of all the books of the Hebrew Bible and books later considered apocryphal or deuterocanonical, some composed in Greek and some translations. The translation process was undertaken in stages. It began by the third century BC and was completed by 132 BC, initially in Alexandria, but in time possibly elsewhere too.

It incorporates the oldest of several ancient translations of the Hebrew Bible into Koine Greek, the lingua franca of the Eastern Mediterranean from the death of Alexander the Great (323 BC) until the development of Byzantine Greek (c. 600 AC). Other versions are now preserved only in fragmentary form.

The Septuagint was held in great respect in ancient times; Philo and Josephus ascribed divine inspiration to its translators. Besides the Old Latin versions, the LXX is also the basis for the Slavonic, the Syriac, Old Armenian, and Old Georgian and Coptic versions of the Old Testament. Of significance for all Christians and for Bible scholars, the LXX is quoted by the New Testament and by the Apostolic Fathers.

According to the legend first recorded in the (anonymous) letter of Aristeas, and repeated with embellishments in Philo, Josephus, and various later Jewish and Christian sources, Jewish scholars first translated the Torah (the first five books of the Bible) into Koine Greek in the third century BC. The traditional explanation is that Ptolemy II sponsored the translation for use by the many Alexandrian Jews who were fluent in Koine Greek but not in Hebrew. According to the record in the Talmud,

"King Ptolemy once gathered 72 Elders. He placed them in 72 chambers, each of them in a separate one, without revealing to them why they were summoned. He entered each one's room and said: 'Write for me the Torah of Moshe, your teacher.' God put it in the heart of each one to translate identically as all the others did."

The date of the third century BC is confirmed for the Pentateuch translation by a number of factors, including the Greek being representative of early Koine, citations beginning as early as the second century BC, and early manuscripts datable to the second century.

Further books were translated over the next two to three centuries. It is not altogether clear which was translated when or where; some may even have been translated twice into different versions, and then revised. The quality and style of the different translators also varied considerably from book to book, from the literal to paraphrasing to interpretative.

As the work of translation progressed gradually and new books were added to the collection, the compass of the Greek Bible came to be somewhat indefinite. The Pentateuch always maintained its preeminence as the basis of the canon; but the prophetic collection (out of which the Nevi'im were selected) changed its aspect by having various Hagiographa incorporated into it. Some of the newer works, those called Anagignoskomena in Greek, are not included in the Jewish canon. Among these books are Maccabees and the Wisdom of Ben Sira. Also, the Septuagint version of some works, like Daniel and Esther, are longer than those in the Masoretic Text. Some of the later books (Wisdom of Solomon, 2 Maccabees, and others) apparently were not translated but composed in Greek.

The authority of the larger group of "writings," out of which the Ketuvim were selected, had not yet been determined, although some sort of selective process must have been employed because the Septuagint did not include other well-known Jewish documents, such as Enoch or Jubilees or other writings that are now part of the Pseudepigrapha. It is not known what principles were used to determine the contents of the Septuagint beyond the "law and the prophets," a phrase used several times in the New Testament.

The Lost Books of the Bible: Human history has allowed precious few ancient religious writings to survive the onslaught of the more aggressive and powerful religious forces, which seek only to gain territory and wealth. Genocide and cultural eradication always go hand in hand with missionary zeal. In many cases, every trace of the conquered society's religious writings, practices, icons, and even buildings were destroyed, in the name of conversion from worship of gods were considered evil and religious customs labeled as heresies. What generally results from past crusades is the conqueror's religion replacing or predominantly blending with the conquered culture's former religious practice, making its religion almost unrecognizable. Christianity falls into the latter category, having been the victim of the Roman Empire under the Emperor Constantine, who blended the Christian Church with the institutionalized "pagan" practices of Rome and eliminated any resemblance of either the Jewish religious influence or the first church Jesus established during his ministry.

The first reformation: After solidifying his position to gain complete control of the western portion of the empire in 312, the Emperor Constantine instituted the Edict of Milan, a "Magna Carta of religious liberty," which eventually changed the empire's religion and put Christianity on an equal footing with paganism. Almost overnight, the position of the Christian Church was reversed from persecuted to legal and accepted. Constantine began to rely on the church for support, and it on him for protection. The church and the empire formed an alliance, which remains to this day. Very rapidly, the laws and policies of the empire and the doctrine of the church became one with Constantine as the interpreter of both law and policy. This was accomplished by eliminating hundreds of books thought to be against "church" doctrine and watering down what remained by blending Christian beliefs and practices with long established Roman-sanctioned pagan worship.

Constantine believed that the church and the state should be as close as possible. Constantine tolerated pagan practices, keeping pagan gods on coins and retaining his pagan high priest title "Pontifex Maximus" in order to maintain popularity with his former subjects. In 330, he began an assault on paganism but used a clever method of persuasion to force people to follow the laws by combining pagan worship with Christianity. He made December 25, the birthday of the pagan Unconquered Sun god, the official holiday now celebrated as the birthday of Jesus. He also replaced the weekly day of worship by making rest on Saturday unlawful and forcing the new religion to honor the first, not the seventh day, as a day of rest. As a way of defining his concept of the new universal religion, he simply classified everything "Jewish" to be an abomination. Considering almost every aspect of the Bible is "Jewish" by association, every doctrinal biblical principle was changed or eliminated. After 337, Constantine increased his purging of the more obvious aspects of paganism.

Through a series of universal councils, he and his successors completely altered doctrine without regard to biblical edict, set up a church hierarchy of his own design, and established a set of beliefs and practices, which are the basis for all mainstream Bible-based churches. The separation of the Protestants and the Roman Church caused a physical split, but the beliefs and practices established by Constantine remained almost identical. Very little has changed since the fourth-century councils changed the face of Christianity. An effective practice instituted was the purging of any book in the formerly accepted biblical works, over 80 percent of the total, that church leaders felt did not fit within their new concept of Christianity. The doctrines and practices remaining in the surviving books were effectively eradicated by simply changing them by replacing clear scripture with church-sanctioned doctrine.

Books that Became Forbidden and Not Lost: Constantine began what was to become a century-long effort to eliminate any book in the original Bible that they considered unacceptable to the new doctrine of the church. At that time, it is believed there were up to six books, which comprised the work we now know as the Bible. Through a series of decisions made by the early church leadership, all but eighty of those books, known as the King James Translation of 1611, were purged from the work, with a further reduction by the Protestant Reformation bringing the number to sixty-six in the Authorized King James Bible.

What we now have in Bible-based religion, whether labeled as "Catholic" or Protesting Catholic, known as "Protestant," is unrecognizable from either the Hebrew religion, now known as the Jewish religion, or the church established at Jerusalem by the apostles and disciples of Jesus. The practices of this first church are not practiced by any major religion, and they are almost unknown, despite being clearly outlined in the existing New Testament, replaced by doctrines and practices first established in the first "true" Reformation of Christianity, which Constantine began. A man and not God made these decisions. Is this what you cling to? You religion that is based on lies, you make holy?

There is much controversy over how many books the Bible should actually contain but considering the depth and scope of those few works remaining in the "accepted" Bible, we see but a fragment of incredible wisdom and history. A study of the Lost Books of the Bible is incomplete without a clear understanding that this is not a matter of simple loss but a campaign by the Roman Catholic Church to purge books variously classified as heretical, dangerous, and corruptive. To the public, they are "lost"; to the church, they are "forbidden." Although the exact number of books purged is known only to the church and not shared knowledge, some can be determined by the discovery of their presence in the church prior to the reformation resulting in what became known as the Roman Universal Church.

One of the more obvious forms of discovery comes from the surviving books themselves, which sight works not present in the existing collection. Also many do not know that the Apocryphal books were actually included in the King James translation until they were officially purged by the Archbishop of Canterbury in

1885. Other writings also connect many books to the first church. Whatever the number before the purge by the formation of Catholicism by Constantine; even one lost book is a great loss indeed.

I claim no expertise concerning the authenticity of any of the lost books and leave this judgment to the reader. I do, however, strongly reject the self-proclaimed authority of any dogmatically motivated and church-controlled mortals who think themselves qualified to make such decisions. One of the most logical and realistic concepts in the Bible is the caution that one should prove all things. I believe that proving the veracity of a given thing is an individual responsibility, which must not and should not be the duty of those who think themselves better judges.

The Apocryphal or Deuterocanonical Books: The fifteen books, known as the Apocrypha, were not officially removed from the English printings of the King James Bible until 1885 by the Archbishop of Canterbury, leaving only sixty-six books from the original eighty-one. Why remove a book from the Bible that formed part of it for more than 1,800 years?

The Real New Testament: The books of the New Testament of the Bible were chosen by one man who was a servant of the Emperor Constantine and did that choosing to satisfy Constantine's agenda to completely reform early Christianity. Would you say that was inspired by God? It is actually the will of man for power, control, and wealth.

Books Mentioned but Not Found: Besides the Apocryphal books eliminated from the Bible used by the Protestant Church, there are at least twenty-eight other books mentioned in scripture, which do not appear in the Bible. Why are these books not included if they are mentioned in the Bible? If they are mentioned, then they are relevant.

There are those that cling to a singular view of all things biblical. If it is not in the King James Bible exactly the way he had it translated, it is a fake, a forgery, or an insidious plot by Satan to corrupt the minds of men. Those works mentioned here are mentioned in the Bible and are associated with it. It should be noted that the books mentioned in this chapter require individual research on the books because I will not spoon-feed you as your church fathers do to you. If you need to know the truth, then take what I give you and investigate. You will not get salvation by sitting the church benches through.

I have mentioned a few books that have been associated with the Bible either through archeological research, historical documentation, or mentions of books as referenced in the Bible.

The twenty-eight books mentioned in the Bible but not included

Book of Jasher (Found)

Joshua 10:13 "And the sun stood still, and the moon stayed, until the people had avenged themselves upon their enemies. Is not this written in the book of Jasher? So the sun stood still in the midst of heaven, and hasted not to go down about a whole day."

2 Samuel 1:18 "Also he bade them teach the children of Judah the use of the bow: behold, it is written in the book of Jasher."

Book of Enoch (Found)

Jude 1:14 "And Enoch also, the seventh from Adam, prophesied of these, saying, 'Behold, the Lord cometh with ten thousands of his saints.'"

The Manner of the Kingdom/Book of Statutes (Missing)

1 Samuel 10:25 "Then Samuel told the people the manner of the kingdom, and wrote it in a book, and laid it up before the Lord. And Samuel sent all the people away, every man to his house."

Book of Samuel the Seer (Missing)

1 Chronicles 29:29 "Now the acts of David the king, first and last, behold, they are written in the book of Samuel the seer, and in the book of Nathan the prophet, and in the book of Gad the seer . . ."

Nathan the Prophet (Missing)

1 Chronicles 29:29 "Now the acts of David the king, first and last, behold, they are written in the book of Samuel the seer and in the book of Nathan the prophet, and in the book of Gad the seer . . ."

2 Chronicles 9:29 "Now the rest of the acts of Solomon, first and last, are they not written in the book of Nathan the prophet, and in the prophecy of Ahijah the Shilonite, and in the visions of Iddo the seer against Jeroboam the son of Nebat?"

The Book of the Acts of Solomon (Missing)

1 Kings 11:41 "And the rest of the acts of Solomon, and all that he did, and his wisdom, are they not written in the book of the acts of Solomon?"

Shemaiah the Prophet (Missing)

2 Chronicles 12:15 "Now the acts of Rehoboam, first and last, are they not written in the book of Shemaiah the prophet, and of Iddo the seer concerning genealogies? And there were wars between Rehoboam and Jeroboam continually."

Prophecy of Abijah (Missing)

2 Chronicles 9:29 "Now the rest of the acts of Solomon, first and last, are they not written in the book of Nathan the prophet, and in the prophecy of Ahijah the Shilonite, and in the visions of Iddo the seer against Jeroboam the son of Nebat?"

Story of Prophet Iddo (Missing)

2 Chronicles 13:22 "And the rest of the acts of Abijah, and his ways, and his sayings, are written in the story of the prophet Iddo."

Visions of Iddo the Seer (Missing)

2 Chronicles 9:29 "Now the rest of the acts of Solomon, first and last, are they not written in the book of Nathan the prophet, and in the prophecy of Ahijah the Shilonite, and in the visions of Iddo the seer against Jeroboam the son of Nebat?"

Iddo Genealogies (Missing)

2 Chronicles 12:15 "Now the acts of Rehoboam, first and last, are they not written in the book of Shemaiah the prophet, and of Iddo the seer concerning genealogies? And there were wars between Rehoboam and Jeroboam continually."

Book of Jehu (Missing)

2 Chronicles 20:34 "Now the rest of the acts of Jehoshaphat, first and last, behold, they are written in the book of Jehu the son of Hanani, who is mentioned in the book of the kings of Israel."

Sayings of the Seers (Found)

2 Chronicles 33:19 "His prayer also, and how God was intreated of him, and all his sin, and his trespass, and the places wherein he built high places, and set up groves and graven images, before he was humbled: behold, they are written among the sayings of the seers."

Book of the Covenant (Missing)

Exodus 24:7 "And he took the book of the covenant, and read in the audience of the people, and they said, all that the Lord hath said will we do, and be obedient."

There are those that believe the Book of the Covenant is found in Exodus chapters 20 through 23. There are no authoritative sources for this text.

Book of the Wars of the Lord (Missing)

Numbers 21:14 "Wherefore it is said in the book of the wars of the Lord, What he did in the Red sea and in the brooks of Arnon . . ."

Certain sources believe that this is to be found by drawing text from several Old Testament books. There are no authoritative sources for this text.

Book of Gad the Seer (Missing)

1 Chronicles 29:29 "Now the acts of David the king, first and last, behold, they are written in the book of Samuel the seer, and in the book of Nathan the prophet, and in the book of Gad the seer . . ."

Epistle to Corinth (Found)

1 Corinthians 5:9 "I wrote unto you in an epistle not to company with fornicators . . ."

Epistle to the Ephesians (Missing)

Ephesians 3:3-4 "How that by revelation he made known unto me the mystery; as I wrote afore in few words. Whereby, when ye read, ye may understand my knowledge in the mystery of Christ."

Epistle from Laodicea to the Colossians (Missing)

Colossians 4:16 "And when this epistle is read among you, cause that it be read also in the church of the Laodiceans; and that ye likewise read the epistle from Laodicea."

Nazarene Prophecy Source (Missing)

Matthew 2:23 "And he came and dwelt in a city called Nazareth: that it might be fulfilled which was spoken by the prophets, He shall be called a Nazarene."

Acts of Uziah (Missing)

2 Chronicles 26:22 "Now the rest of the acts of Uzziah, first and last, did Isaiah the prophet, the son of Amoz, write."

The Annals of King David (Missing)

1 Chronicles 27:24 "Joab son of Zeruiah began to count the men but did not finish. Wrath came on Israel on account of this numbering, and the number was not entered in the book of the annals of King David."

Jude, the Missing Epistle (Missing)

Jude 1:3 "Beloved, when I gave all diligence to write unto you of the common salvation, it was needful for me to write unto you, and exhort you that ye should earnestly contend for the faith which was once delivered unto the saints."

Chronicles of King Ahasuerus (Missing)

Esther 2:23 "And when inquisition was made of the matter, it was found out; therefore, they were both hanged on a tree: and it was written in the book of the chronicles before the king."

Esther 6:1 "On that night could not the king sleep, and he commanded to bring the book of records of the chronicles; and they were read before the king."

Chronicles of the Kings of Media and Persia (Missing)

Esther 10:2 "And all the acts of his power and of his might, and the declaration of the greatness of Mordecai, whereunto the king advanced him, are they not written in the book of the chronicles of the kings of Media and Persia?"

The Other Chronicles

The Chronicles of King David (Missing)

1 Chronicles 27:24 "Joab the son of Zeruiah began to number, but he finished not, because there fell wrath for it against Israel; neither was the number put in the account of the chronicles of King David."

The Chronicles of the Kings of Israel (Missing)

1 Kings

14:19 "And the rest of the acts of Jeroboam, how he warred, and how he reigned, behold, they are written in the book of the chronicles of the kings of Israel."

15:31 "Now the rest of the acts of Nadab, and all that he did, are they not written in the book of the chronicles of the kings of Israel?"

16:5 "Now the rest of the acts of Baasha, and what he did, and his might, are they not written in the book of the chronicles of the kings of Israel?"

16:14 "Now the rest of the acts of Elah, and all that he did, are they not written in the book of the chronicles of the kings of Israel?"

16:20 "Now the rest of the acts of Zimri, and his treason that he wrought, are they not written in the book of the chronicles of the kings of Israel?"

16:27 "Now the rest of the acts of Omri which he did, and his might that he shewed, are they not written in the book of the chronicles of the kings of Israel?"

22:39 "Now the rest of the acts of Ahab, and all that he did, and the ivory house which he made, and all the cities that he built, are they not written in the book of the chronicles of the kings of Israel?"

<u>2 Kings</u>

1:18 "Now the rest of the acts of Ahaziah, which he did, are they not written in the book of the chronicles of the kings of Israel?"

10:34 "Now the rest of the acts of Jehu, and all that he did, and all his might, are they not written in the book of the chronicles of the kings of Israel?"

13:8 "Now the rest of the acts of Jehoahaz, and all that he did, and his might, are they not written in the book of the chronicles of the kings of Israel?"

13:12 "And the rest of the acts of Joash, and all that he did, and his might wherewith he fought against Amaziah king of Judah, are they not written in the book of the chronicles of the kings of Israel?"

14:15 "Now the rest of the acts of Jehoash which he did, and his might, and how he fought with Amaziah king of Judah, are they not written in the book of the chronicles of the kings of Israel?"

14:28 "Now the rest of the acts of Jeroboam, and all that he did, and his might, how he warred, and how he recovered Damascus, and Hamath, which belonged to Judah, for Israel, are they not written in the book of the chronicles of the kings of Israel?"

15:10 "And Shallum the son of Jabesh conspired against him, and smote him before the people, and slew him, and reigned in his stead."

15:15 "And the rest of the acts of Shallum, and his conspiracy which he made, behold, they are written in the book of the chronicles of the kings of Israel."

15:21 "And the rest of the acts of Menahem, and all that he did, are they not written in the book of the chronicles of the kings of Israel?"

15:26 "And the rest of the acts of Pekahiah, and all that he did, behold, they are written in the book of the chronicles of the kings of Israel."

15:31 "And the rest of the acts of Pekah, and all that he did, behold, they are written in the book of the chronicles of the kings of Israel."

The Chronicles of the Kings of Judah (Missing)

<u>1 Kings</u>

14:29 "Now the rest of the acts of Rehoboam, and all that he did, are they not written in the book of the chronicles of the kings of Judah?"

15:7 "Now the rest of the acts of Abijam, and all that he did, are they not written in the book of the chronicles of the kings of Judah? And there was war between Abijam and Jeroboam."

15:23 "The rest of all the acts of Asa, and all his might, and all that he did, and the cities which he built, are they not written in the book of the chronicles of the kings of Judah?"

22:45 "Now the rest of the acts of Jehoshaphat, and his might that he shewed, and how he warred, are they not written in the book of the chronicles of the kings of Judah?"

2 Kings

8:23 "And the rest of the acts of Joram, and all that he did, are they not written in the book of the chronicles of the kings of Judah?"

12:19 "And the rest of the acts of Joash, and all that he did, are they not written in the book of the chronicles of the kings of Judah?"

14:18 "And the rest of the acts of Amaziah, are they not written in the book of the chronicles of the kings of Judah?"

15:6 "And the rest of the acts of Azariah, and all that he did, are they not written in the book of the chronicles of the kings of Judah?"

15:36 "Now the rest of the acts of Jotham, and all that he did, are they not written in the book of the chronicles of the kings of Judah?"

16:19 "Now the rest of the acts of Ahaz which he did, are they not written in the book of the chronicles of the kings of Judah?"

20:20 "And the rest of the acts of Hezekiah, and all his might, and how he made a pool, and a conduit, and brought water into the city, are they not written in the book of the chronicles of the kings of Judah?"

21:17 "Now the rest of the acts of Manasseh, and all that he did, and his sin that he sinned, are they not written in the book of the chronicles of the kings of Judah?"

21:25 "Now the rest of the acts of Amon which he did, are they not written in the book of the chronicles of the kings of Judah?"

23:28 "Now the rest of the acts of Josiah, and all that he did, are they not written in the book of the chronicles of the kings of Judah?"

24:5 "Now the rest of the acts of Jehoiakim, and all that he did, are they not written in the book of the chronicles of the kings of Judah?"

To understand what is written in these pages, you only need to have an open, sober mind and to be able to exercise careful judgment that God has given each of us. There are no messages or symbolism brought forward from these chapters but only those that will be explained from the belief structures point of view to be able to understand each one's perspective.

Old Testament Apocryphal Writings: "The Apocrypha"

The term "apocrypha" comes from a Greek word meaning hidden or secret, and the books were originally considered by the early church as too exalted to be available to the general public. As time progressed, the exalted nature of the books was lost and the books were deemed by some as false. Between the book of Malachi and Matthew, there is a gap of approximately 450 years. It is these books that fill that gap and, in the time of Jesus, these books formed part of the Septuagint Greek Bible that was in circulation at that time.

What is missing from most Bibles, and our understanding of it, is what happened in that 450-year gap. Prophets were still writing and reflecting on life in the Holy Land right up until the Romans destroyed the temple of Jerusalem in AD 70. The world that Jesus entered in 4 BC is not the world that Daniel and Malachi experienced. One of the values of these books is how they reflect the mind-set of Judaism and a Roman world that the New Testament writers faced. Malachi and Daniel leave us in Persia; Matthew brings us into a Roman world. The Apocrypha bridges that gap and gently nudges us into the reality of Roman Palestine. It was only in the fourth century AD that Christians first started to question the "canonicity" of the works, although most survived to be included in the King James translation of the Bible in 1611. Why did the other books not survive? Why were most destroyed, altered, deleted, and changed? To empower religious institutions, increase their wealth, and brainwash Christians to make them ignorant and obedient to the institution and in turn to the state.

Unknown to almost all of the over two billion people who claim the Bible as their spiritual foundation is that there are several books and two sections missing from all but a few modern versions of that Bible. Perhaps one of the best-kept secrets of the modern Protestant Church is that the Bible used by that church is not the original King James Bible. That translation, completed in 1611, and the Bibles published for the use of the clergy and the church members until late in the nineteenth century, contained eighty books. Although attempts to remove the fifteen books, known as the Apocrypha, from the Bible began immediately after the King James translation was completed, they remained in the Bible until the end of the nineteenth century. There is no doubt that the fifteen books of the

Apocrypha were controversial, but it cannot be denied they were included in the original King James Bible.

The concept of the Protestant Church about the Apocrypha is virtually nonexistent, with the general understanding that only the Catholic Church uses it. One would be hard-pressed to find any members of the clergy even aware that these books were ever included in the King James Bible. There are 155,683 words and over 5,700 verses contained in 168 chapters now missing from the King James translation of the Bible due to the exclusion of the Apocrypha. Although this only happened just over a hundred years ago, their existence as fully accepted scripture is virtually unknown.

A clear history exists of the inclusion of the Apocrypha in the King James Bible:

- In the year 1615, Archbishop Gorge Abbott, a High Commission Court member and one of the original translators of the 1611 translation, "forbade anyone to issue a Bible without the Apocrypha on pain of one year's imprisonment."

- "It should be observed that the Old Testament thus admitted as authoritative in the Church was somewhat bulkier and more comprehensive than the [Protestant Old Testament] . . . It always included, though with varying degrees of recognition, the so-called Apocrypha or Deutero-canonical books. The use made of the Apocrypha by Tertullian, Hippolytus, Cyprian and Clement of Alexandria is too frequent for detailed references to be necessary." (Early Christian Doctrines, J. Kelly)

- "In 405, Pope Innocent I embodied a list of canonical books in a letter addressed to Exsuperius, bishop of Toulouse; it too included the Apocrypha. The Sixth Council of Carthage (419) reenacted the ruling of the Third Council, again with the inclusion of the apocryphal books . . . The Sixth Council of Carthage repromulgated in Canon 24 the resolution of the Third Council regarding the canon of scripture and added a note directing that the resolution be sent to the bishop of Rome [Boniface I] and other bishops: 'Let this be made known also to our brother and fellow-priest Boniface, or to other bishops of those parts, for the purpose of confirming that Canon [Canon 47 of the Third Council], because we have received from our fathers that these are the books which are to be read in church.'" (The Canon on Scripture, F. F. Bruce)

- "The holy ecumenical and general Council of Trent . . . following the example of the orthodox Fathers, receives and venerates all the books of the Old and New Testament . . . and also the traditions pertaining to faith and conduct . . . with an equal sense of devotion and reverence . . .

If, however, any one receive not, as sacred and canonical, the said books entire with all their parts, as they have by custom been read in the Catholic Church, and as they are contained in the old Latin Vulgate, and knowingly and deliberately rejects the aforesaid traditions, let him be accursed." (Decree of the Council of Trent in 1546)

- "In the name of Holy Scripture we do understand those canonical books of the Old and New Testament, of whose authority was never any doubt in the Church . . . And the other books [as Jerome saith] the Church doth read for example of life and instruction of manners: but yet doth it not apply them to establish any doctrine." (Articles of Religion of the Church of England, 1563, Sixth Article)

Two introductory sections were also removed from the original King James Translation. There was a preface written for the original King James Bible, which is mysteriously missing from that work, called "The Translator's Preface." There was also a dedication written for the original King James Bible called "The Epistle Dedicatory." These two sections can be accessed on the Internet or through the library system.

The most disturbing verses in the Bible in Revelation 22:18-19, "For I testify unto every man that hereth the words of the prophecy of this book, If any man shall add unto these things, God shall add unto him plagues that are written in this book: and if any man shall take away from the words of the book of this prophecy, God shall take away his part from the book of life, and out of the holy city, and from the things which are written in this book" (King James Version 1611King James Version 1611).

These individuals and groups that have torn the word of God up into shreds and placed what they saw as fit where arrogant enough to insert this verse while knowing full well that they themselves have transgressed this warning. These are the people that you look up to; consider to be holy and righteous? They taught the descendants that followed the same teachings are taught by your church leaders. Do lies and falsifications become truth?

The First Book of the Bible: Let us look at the beginning of the Bible and show you a few problems and later delve deeper into the origins of astrotheology.

Genesis 1:1 "In the beginning God created the heaven and the earth." (King James Version 1611)

With the first sentence from the Bible comes the first question. I am also going to ask certain questions to open your third eye. If God created the heavens first and then the earth, where did God live before the heavens existed? I would understand that the Spirit of God wandered on the waters as is written in Genesis 1:2 "And the earth was without form, and void; and the darkness was upon the face of the deep. And the Spirit of God moved upon the face of the waters." Remember that

God is the Alpha and the Omega. He was and always has been there. Do you want to tell me that God just wandered aimlessly over the waters before he created earth? According to the biblical texts, the earth is only six thousand years old. Is this also how old the heavens are? You and I know that the earth is much older because there is evidence that proves it.

Within the writings, you will get explanations on these questions.

Let us move on. In Genesis 1:3-1:9, God created the first day, called the light day and the darkness night. God divided the waters from the waters, the waters under and above the firmament. You and I know that there is no water above the clouds; therefore, between the waters above and below, the earth God called heaven. Heaven is in the atmosphere of the earth.

God also made all the plants and grass, yielding seeds and fruit, and God saw that it was good. On the fourth day, God then only made the sun, the moon, and the stars. Therefore, the earth is older than the sun, moon, and stars. These celestial bodies such as the sun are now also in the earth's atmosphere. Is it because God is almighty and all knowing?

Let us look further. On the sixth day, God created man. Genesis 1:26, "And God said, Let us make man in our image, after our likeness: and let them have dominion over the fish of the sea, and over the fowl of the air, and over the cattle, and over all the earth, and over every creeping thing that creepeth upon the earth" (King James Version 1611).

There are questions that glare out here. God made all the plants, their seeds and fruits. God saw that it was good. Read Genesis 2:5, "and every plant of the field before it was in the earth, and every herb of the field before it grew: for the Lord God had not caused it to rain upon the earth, and there was not a man to till the ground" (King James Version 1611). What did God see that was so good if it was not there yet?

On the sixth day, God created man, a living soul, not in the form of man but in his image and likeness. God is the strength and the wisdom. If God is Spirit and does not have the image of man, how did man look that he made in his image and likeness? We proclaim that God is almighty and all knowing. God created mankind, so is humanity also almighty and all knowing, do we share the same traits as God? Some people have theories that it was a shadow figure of God's image, and that it was only some of his likeness. Would God then not have said instead that he has made man as a shadow figure of himself? Nowhere in the scriptures does it say that man is a shadow figure of God with only some of his likeness. Therefore, the only assumption is that which was written was meant in the way it was written. Or is it symbolical with a deeper meaning? Or is it written in such a way that every church group can interpret the scriptures in their own way and include the interpretations into their doctrine?

There was a certain religion that made me understand that the scriptures must be seen in a purely spiritual way. This aspect does not make sense either because the Bible says, such as in nature so also in spirit. In other words, as things happen in nature, so too it will be in spirit. Have you not noticed that when something is unexplainable from the Bible, that it is then understood in a spiritual way? Or that the wisdom of God is foolish by man? If it was so, then we could not have been formed in his image or likeness because we would have been able to understand God's word.

According to the Bible, we are here to learn and grow, but how can we learn or grow if we are being spoken to in symbols? Symbolism brings a certain amount of confusion because it can be understood in a number of different ways. No wonder there are so many religions.

Let us leave religion for a moment and have a look at the Bible as it is written. Let us have a look at translations, the kernel of everything, how the scriptures came into existence from astrology, the study of how stars may affect people's lives. The astrological gods were humanized and given human characteristics. There are events that are noted as miracles but are instead astrological myths. Today, humankind makes it holy and rejects any other explanation.

Think for a moment, are all these holy myths, symbolisms, rituals, and traditions "holy," or can they make you holy?

Is astrology the devil's work? How can it be if it forms part of the Bible?

Let us have a look: John 14:2, "In my Father's house are many mansions: if it were not so, I would have told you" (King James Version 1611).

This does not seem to make sense nor does it? God lives in the heavens. We know of at least twelve astrological houses, i.e.,

♈ Aries (Ram): March 21-April 19   ♌ Leo (Lion): July 23-August 22

♉ Taurus (Bull): April 20-May 20   ♍ Virgo (Virgin): August 23-September 22

♊ Gemini (Twins): May 21-June 21   ♎ Libra (Balance): September 23-October 23

♋ Cancer (Crab): June 22-July 22   ♏ Scorpius (Scorpion): October 24-November 21

♐ Sagittarius (Archer): November 22-December 21   ♒ Aquarius (Water Bearer): January 20-February 18

♑ Capricornus (Goat): December 22-January 19   ♓ Pisces (Fish): February 19-March 20

Let us walk a path together, and you will see that I have shown you only the truth to this point. Let us go back to the Egyptian religion to see how far these views have come.

The Sphinx that is in front of the pyramids has the head of Virgo and the back quarters of a lion (Leo). The Sphinx symbolizes the entire zodiac, all twelve houses. It starts by Virgo and ends with Leo. (Zodiacal constellations varied in antiquity and became fixed only with the development of mathematical astronomy.) Isis the Virgin was impregnated by Osiris, the eternal Father, and the end is the son that will come; the son of Osiris is Horus the Lion. This cycle is called the Great Year which takes approximately twenty-five thousand years for the earth to pass in turn through the influence of all the signs of the zodiac.

The same story plays out in the Bible. The beginning by the Virgin Mary, which is impregnated by the eternal Lord God and the end will be when with the coming of Jesus, the Son of God, which he is known as the Lion. Is it mere coincidence? Let us look further.

Read Mark 14:13-14: "And he sendeth forth two disciples, and saith unto them, Go ye into the city, and there shall meet you a man bearing a pitcher of water: follow him.—say ye to the goodman of the house" (King James Version 1611).

The entire story of Jesus is associated with the zodiac house Pisces. Jesus feeds the masses with two fish, the fishermen, etc. This is correct because for the last two thousand years, we have moved through the house of Pisces.

It takes the earth approximately two thousand years to move through each zodiac house. During the transition from one house to the next, there are certain events that occur, i.e., earthquakes, disasters, temperament changes that cause war, etc. These are all signs that indicate the end of a zodiac house's time span. The transition phase from one zodiac house to another takes approximately twenty years. During this time is when these events occur. Let me explain why this occurs.

The earth's axis is on 23.5 degree angle; however, it does change due to the precession of the equinoxes and influences by celestial bodies including the planets. It matches what was discussed earlier in terms of the Great Year. While the Greek astronomer Hipparchus was compiling his star catalog, which was completed in 129 BC, he noticed that the positions of the stars shifted in a systematic way when compared to earlier Babylonian measures. This implied that it was not the stars that were moving but that it was the earth. This motion is called precession and consists of a cyclic wobbling in the orientation of the earth's axis of rotation, which has a period of approximately twenty-six thousand years. Precession is caused by the gravitational influence of the sun and the moon acting on the earth's equatorial bulge. To a lesser extent, the planets exert influence as well.

Today, the north celestial pole points to within just 1° of the arc of Polaris. It will point closest to Polaris in AD 2017. In twelve thousand years, the north celestial pole will point about 5° from Vega. Presently, the south celestial pole does not point in the vicinity of any bright star.

When these shifts occur, it is related to the transition from one zodiac house to the next. In 1998, the solar system began to move away from the Pisces house and is now moving into Aquarius. In 2018, our solar system will be predominantly in the house of Aquarius. The house of Pisces will no longer have an effect on the earth, and the natural balance will return to some normalcy once it has moved over completely.

Can you see that the end that is spoken of is not the end of the earth or existence as we know it, but instead that it is the end of a period, the period of Pisces? The sun has gone ahead of us to prepare a place for us in our new house. as did the Son also go ahead to prepare our new house for us.

Jesus, the Son of God, who is the Son of righteousness, is the same as Ra. Ra, the Son of God, is the Son of righteousness from the old Egyptian mythology.

The whole story is based on natural happenings, but the human race transformed the natural powers into humanlike gods.

Perhaps you may perceive me as lying. Let us first have a look at who we deem to be holy.

- The birth of the Savior Jesus is on December 25.

- The holy Sabbath is on Sunday, the day of rest and going to church; it is a holy day.

- After each prayer, it is empowered and confirmed with the word "Amen." In the name of the Son, in his name you ask for these things in your prayer.

Why December 25? Let us have a look. In the Northern Hemisphere of the earth where the religion originated from, December is winter. On December 21, the sun reaches its lowest point south and lies on the equinox cross. This is the cross of the zodiac. The sun does not move north or south during the time of the winter solstice; this is the shortest day and the longest night. The sun is on the cross, and it dies for three days. On December 25, the sun moves northward; this is the beginning of summer. That is why December 25 is the birth of the sun that comes to give his life to humankind. Everything comes to life, and as long as the sun shines, there will be eternal life on earth. The sun offers us eternal life. Sunday is named after the sun, and we as human beings made this day holy.

Many will tell you that the word "Amen" means so shall it be if you translate it into Greek. They are right, but I have a problem with it if that is the way to end a prayer.

Prayer means an earnest request or wish. You ask.

Amen means so it shall be. This is a command.

In other words, you ask God for things in your prayer and end it off with a command. The holy ones will tell you that it is a spiritual form of asking or saying. Do you actually believe them?

Let us move on to the twelve houses. Jesus, the Son of God, had twelve disciples. Horus had twelve Har-Kutti or Kin-Hurr or disciples. The twelve star signs or houses will lead and teach us the lessons which are there to learn.

The Bible speaks of astrology in the book of Job which is the oldest book in the Bible. Read Job 38:31-38. This is astrology.

Have a look at what the churches or religious structures make you believe. Everyone is waiting for the end of the world. This is not even what the Bible describes. The Bible also speaks of the end of the time that is coming. The man in the city with the pitcher of water is the water bearer, Aquarius.

A few months ago, I walked into a charismatic church as a visitor, and there was an announcement that they will be placing water pitchers in front of the church for the offerings. I found the same in forty-five different churches. Do the church fathers know something that they are not telling us, or is natural instinct that makes it happen?

I have taken photos of church windows with lead inlay that have the two fish portrayed in it; the two fish symbolizes Christianity. Below the image was the word "Pisces." This particular church was built in 1832.

Who are the misleaders? Who speaks untruths and declares falsities? Are you still going to sit among the mockers and listen to the advice of the godless people?

Have a look at the cross above most old churches; it is a circle on a cross. It is not a human being; it is the sun on the equinox cross.

The images of the Savior, saints, and holy individuals, there is a light or sun disc that shines its rays in the picture. Even in the Bible, there is mention of a large majestic light in the heavens. Again, this is reference to the sun. For example, in Genesis 1:16: "And God made two great lights; the greater light to rule the day, and the lesser to rule the night: he made the stars also."

Can you see that these balanced stories have a natural aspect? However, it is the humanizations of these elements that have made mankind idolize them. God gave us instruction and warning that we shall not create an image of him up in the heavens or down on earth.

If Jesus is God as humans make him to be, then we are sinning by creating images of him. You as a human being expect a human man on a natural cloud that will come to console you. Let us have a look at two pieces from the Bible.

It is stated in the Bible that the kingdom of God is by man. God himself states in the Bible and says who would search for him on the highest mountains or over the waters because he has come so close to us that he wants to live on our tongues and in our hearts.

If it is correct that the kingdom of God is with mankind, then God is by humankind because remember, God is spirit. The Son went to his Father, so where is the Son of God? Is he in heaven? We know by now that heaven is here by man on earth according to the Christian Bible.

This means that the Son must also be here with mankind. Why would you then wait for the Son of God to fetch you one day and take you to God if he is already by mankind?

Keep in mind, if the Son is also God, then he will no longer have the form of man. Is that perhaps the meaning of where it is written that he is the way, the truth, and the life that will lead us to God which is the strength and the wisdom in our midst? This is written in the scriptures. Why does mankind not proclaim it this way? Or do they not believe what is written in the scriptures? Do people only read what pleases them and decide to leave the rest?

What is true and trusted in the scriptures? What makes these aspects holy when they are actually natural elements?

Yes, God created everything but not in the fairy-tale story that people wish to believe in. Go to the beginning with the truth, and then only will you truly realize how magnificent God truly is. Not the mental image developed by the church of what and who God is, those if you just believe, then you are saved.

The Bible states that belief without action is dead. The churches tell you that you must simply believe and profess. So who is lying to you now?

Who are the misleaders? Just pray, but to who are you praying to? Are you praying to the sun? It is after all the origin and foundation of your Christian religion.

Why do you still cling to the humanization of natural elements and make it out to be holy? Has belief and stories bound you to such an extent that you are unable to see what you actually dealing with?

There are numerous other examples in the Bible that reveal that it is based on the worshipping of astrology and astrotheology.

The next chapter is "Old Scriptures: The Naked Truth."

Chapter 5

Old Scriptures: The Naked Truth

While doing research for this book, I stumbled upon old authenticated documents that you will never see in any bookshop. These documents contain essential information; just their mere existence will force your church leaders to act and do everything in their power to prevent it from seeing the light of day. The information in these documents will be revealed to you in this chapter. These matters were not described in this age, and I do not believe that the meaning of these documents was to influence you. It is the naked truth that has been removed by so-called holy individuals that left the remains of a fairy-tale Christian religion.

If you are not prepared to receive the truth with all the bizarre and displeasing aspects that form part and parcel of the bigger picture, then I would suggest you put this book away and only open it again when you are ready to receive it. Stay in your safe wonder world where you will wait for your savior to fetch you on a natural cloud and take you up into heaven where there are streets of gold and mansions made of gemstones. There you will live as kings and priests with earthly things in a spiritual world. You will use streets that only humans need in a heaven above the earth, sun, moon, and stars. You will be far away from the earth and all its feeling, away from the kingdom of God and from God himself that made his home by mankind.

Wait on your Jesus that will come to fetch the righteous and leave the unrighteous behind. You will not hear the gnashing of teeth and strictly according to the Bible those that stay behind will seek their death but it will not come. This stands in your Bible. Perhaps you should give me a chance to explain.

It does not make sense. This same Jesus proclaims that he will capture the devil and imprison him for a thousand years. Think about it for a moment; for a thousand years, there will be no temptation, but this will only be for those who stay behind because you and others will be saved, along with those that come from the opened graves—you will go to heaven. The people that stay behind will have their own heaven without the devil.

Only after a thousand years will the same Jesus return to release the devil for a brief moment. Then it will be the end. Why would Jesus return to earth if he has already taken those that were meant to be saved? It is supposed to be the end of the world. Perhaps the end of the world will be without churches because all the church people would have been taken to heaven. There are no more struggles because the devil is imprisoned. A new world without the six thousand fanatical

Christian religions that judge each other and that use the same Bible to promote thousands of conflicting views and opinions.

I can hear those people that are protesting and say, "I do not understand." There is nothing to understand. This that I have shown you comes from the Bible. Does it sound ridiculous to you now? It did not sound ridiculous when you were blindly clinging to it though. Perhaps you simply never thought about it that way before. You have the life that God has given you to live, you have prayed it away, and you had absolute unwavering conviction that the heavens were paved with gold and filled with material things. You even believed that you were going to rest in the lap of Father Abraham and that you will all be kings and priests. I do not know who you were going to be kings and priests for. What are kings without their subjects and priests without their members? According to your scriptures, there will only be kings and priests residing together in heaven.

That makes me wonder how many people will protest concerning the next point; in the Bible, it states that only the 144,000 sealed souls will inherit the kingdom of God.

Do you want to tell me that in the last two thousand years, there have not been true believers of the faith that have lived better lives than you and me? What chance do we have in our time with all the sin and temptation in our world?

As Christians, you are told repeatedly to blindly believe in the Bible and what is written in it. Perhaps these 144,000 sealed souls that are mentioned in the Bible have a symbolic meaning. Yes, you already have your place in the church; you have your religion and would feel that you do not need to listen to what is in these pages. Many of you have already labeled me as the Antichrist in your minds because the Bible warns you against the Antichrist.

Jesus: Did he exist? Yes, Jesus truly did exist; there are shreds of proof to confirm his existence. Below is a brief sample of suggested evidence of which many are thought to be forgeries. The concept and the man known as Jesus will be discussed in more depth in chapter 11. There are numerous ancient texts that have been destroyed and others that are kept secret.

Main Article: Josephus on Jesus

Josephus's writings, which document John the Baptist, James the Just, and Jesus, are of the most interest to scholars dealing with the historicity of Jesus

Flavius Josephus (c. 37-c. 100), a Jew and Roman citizen who worked under the patronage of the Flavians wrote the Antiquities of the Jews in AD 93. In these works, Jesus is mentioned twice, though scholars debate their authenticity. The one directly concerning Jesus has come to be known as the Testimonium Flavianum.

In the first passage called the Testimonium Flavianum, it is written: "About this time came Jesus, a wise man, if indeed it is appropriate to call him a man. For he was a performer of paradoxical feats, a teacher of people who accept the unusual with pleasure, and he won over many of the Jews and many Greeks. He was the Christ. When Pilate, upon the accusation of the first men amongst us, condemned him to be crucified, those who had formerly loved him did not cease to follow him, for he appeared to them on the third day, living again, as the divine prophets foretold, along with a myriad of other marvellous things concerning him. And the tribe of the Christians, so named after him, has not disappeared to this day."

Mara bar Sarapion

Mara was a Syrian Stoic. While imprisoned by the Romans, Mara wrote a letter to his son that includes the following text:

For what benefit did the Athenians obtain by putting Socrates to death, seeing that they received as retribution for it famine and pestilence? Alternatively, the people of Samos by the burning of Pythagoras, seeing that in one hour the whole of their country was covered with sand. Or the Jews by the murder of their Wise King, seeing that from that very time their kingdom were driven away from them? For with justice did God grant a recompense to the wisdom of all three of them. For the Athenians died by famine; and the people of Samos were covered by the sea without remedy; and the Jews, brought to desolation and expelled from their kingdom, are driven away into every land. Nay, Socrates did "not" die because of Plato, nor yet Pythagoras because of the statue of Hera, nor yet the Wise King because of the new laws which he enacted.

Composed sometime between AD 73 and the third century, some scholars believe this describes the fall of Jerusalem as the gods' punishment for the Jews having killed Jesus because they infer that Jesus must be "the wise king" referred to by Mara.

Main Article: Lucian on Jesus

Lucian, a second century Romano-Syrian satirist who wrote in Greek, wrote the following: "The Christians, you know, worship a man to this day—the distinguished personage who introduced their novel rites, and was crucified on that account . . . You see, these misguided creatures start with the general conviction that they are immortal for all time, which explains the contempt of death and voluntary self-devotion which are so common among them; and then it was impressed on them by their original lawgiver that they are all brothers, from the moment that they are converted, and deny the gods of Greece, and worship the crucified sage, and live after his laws."

Celsus wrote about 180 books against the Christians, which is now only known through Origen's refutation of it. Celsus apparently accused Jesus of being a magician and a sorcerer and is quoted as saying that Jesus was a "mere man." F. F. Bruce noted that Celsus, in seeking to discredit Jesus, sought to explain his miracles rather than claim they never occurred.

The Acts of Pilate is purportedly an official document from Pilate reporting events in Judea to the Emperor Tiberius (thus, it would have been among the *commentarii principis*). It was mentioned by Justin Martyr, in his First Apology (c. 150) to Antoninus Pius, Marcus Aurelius, and Lucius Verus. He said that his claims concerning Jesus's crucifixion, and some miracles, could be verified by referencing the official record, the Acts of Pontius Pilate. With the exception of Tertullian, no other writer is known to have mentioned the work, and Tertullian's reference says that Tiberius debated the details of Jesus's life before the Roman Senate, an event that is confirmed by Eusebius, but today it is almost universally considered to be absurd. There is a later apocryphal text, undoubtedly fanciful, by the same name, and though it is generally thought to have been inspired by Justin's reference (and thus to postdate his Apology), it is possible that Justin mentioned this text, though that would give the work an unusually early date and therefore is not a straightforward identification.

Who is so blind that they look and do not see? Who is so deaf that listens and cannot hear?

Has the church told you from who Jesus took over as the high priest of Melchizedek? Have they ever mentioned to who Jesus sold his priesthood to?

Jesus and his older brother Thomas, firstborn of Mary, started the Qumran religion next to the Dead Sea. They later broke up because of differences of opinion and points of view. Jesus started his own ministry with 144,000 anointed people, and they accepted members from all walks of life including Jews and Gentiles. During this time, his members crowned Jesus the Christ.

These are not lies but rather the naked truth.

In the scriptures of the old governors, it is noted that Jesus the Nazarene did a favor for one the governors and in turn Jesus was rewarded the position of high priest of Melchizedek in place of his brother Thomas who held the position.

Jesus sold his priesthood to three Gentile brothers and went with Thomas to the Qumran Mountains where they started the Qumran religion. The Qumran region were the Dead Sea Scrolls were found in 1947, the region on the northwestern shore of the Dead Sea. What do the Dead Sea Scrolls say about Jesus? This is a common question asked by those not familiar with the dates of the scrolls. The body of literature known as the Dead Sea Scrolls predates the time of Jesus by approximately eighty years and as a consequence of this, there are no direct references to his life and teachings.

The two brothers had combined knowledge of various religions, and with this knowledge, they simplified the evangelic teachings and appealed to the people.

There were differences of opinion and views between the brothers, and a division was incurred in their ministry. Thomas maintained the original Qumran religion while Jesus left with 144,000 of their members and started his ministry, his religion. This religion was more lenient and fundamental. This religion also declared that the kingdom of God can only be attained by those who are impoverished and humble of heart. This religion was open to everyone.

Jesus promised his 144,000 anointed members of his ministry a place in the kingdom of God and promised that they would rule as kings and priests.

On the strength of the permission from Jesus, his followers named him the Christ. In other words, Jesus was their Messiah.

Rumors started to spread regarding the extensive wonders that Jesus had done and that he was a mighty ruler. Jesus was declared the king of all kings by his followers.

The government had disfavor over this behavior, and Jesus was brought before the council to defend these rumors. He managed to talk his way out of trouble by saying that he would not be the king in this life but in the lifetime thereafter. This was not considered a threat to the state in those days, and Jesus was released. It was rather the behavior of his followers that kept getting him into hot water because his followers believed that they did not need to be obedient to the government and their laws. The governors attempted to force Jesus to stop preaching his evangelistic religion.

It astounds me that other people who know the truth remain silent. Why should I be afraid of the truth?

I am not afraid of disapproval from people because I proclaim only the truth. I am not part of the new era groups. I have a profound relationship with God and do not go around disseminating an ancient evangelistic belief or religion; I live my life in my own spiritual way.

I publicly accept and promote patience and tolerance; I see no evil, hear no evil, and speak no evil. I love God's creation in its totality, and my family prays with sincerity at the table and during the day to God. We do not call on the names of the elements and ask for everything "in the help of God." We do not worship many gods that are declared as one. Our service is in the almighty God. It is my task to destroy the lies that devastate souls. Part of my duty and responsibility is to end the eternal judging and bring true love to humanity.

Many of the old scriptures that I have are labeled as myths by many churches, but it is astonishing that these are true accounts of the true story. In some instances, it is only names and places that differ while others are taken over word for word.

So as not to jump around and create confusion, each aspect is discussed under headings pertaining to it. This will aid in building your understanding in a logical order.

Do not blindly believe but instead investigate these aspects of truth for yourselves. Do not make a fool of yourself by searching for answers in the Bible. The absolute and enlightening truth is out there for anyone who searches for it. I am available at all times to discuss any aspects further and share information. There is nothing holy about these writing within the pages of this book. This truth will only free you from the mysticism, symbolism, and myths.

God wants each of us to search and investigate the truth. Do not allow yourself to be misled by people or mystical feelings because you will destroy yourself. Think critically and logically about everything that you will discover. Life does not only focus on material things, and religion will not take you very far. Get out of the groove you are used to, live the life God has given you, and find your true purpose that each of us has been given.

Wake up from your deep slumber. Yesterday is history, tomorrow is only a dream, and today is your present from God because you can change now. Why wait for tomorrow or some day? How would you benefit if in your thoughts you start to make a change but your actions hold you back due to fear?

Do you honestly believe that God will punish you for seeking the truth? Your only obstacles are your fears, your religion, and the warnings from the blind that have no idea of what they are saying, and those who think they know because they have studied the Bible, and those who are captivated by the lies.

Break out and call out your victory cry to the world and be proud of your victory. You lose nothing, except empty promises that have in any case smothered your life. However, I caution you to have restraint and preserve your moral values. God is a god of logical order and does not condone chaos and barbaric actions. Observe nature and learn. Everything lives and functions in harmony.

Be the best you that God has made because we are all unique in the eyes of the Creator. There are no copies of people; we are not the same because God wanted it that way. Why do you want to be a Moses or a David as in the scriptures? God made you who you are; do not try and be someone else, instead be the best that you can be.

Do not be afraid that you no longer have a title or label. You are no longer an apostolic, Methodist, Catholic, etc. You are free from the dictatorship of the church. Do not blemish and taint your thoughts with myths, traditions, symbols, rituals, and mystical nonsense.

Your God is a true and existing God of today. He is not a dream god of after the grave. Become blessed and content, even within your soul. Allow the pressure to be lifted off you so that you are able to enjoy a joyous and fortunate life in peace. It is your life, and God gives you the strength to transform the desert in you into a paradise.

Do not hinder your life any further by praying it away or by waiting for a better life after this one. Know happiness so that you are accustomed to happiness before you move on from this life.

Do not allow your life to revolve around fear. Satan has no power over you. You give him power when you allow him to have power over you. Do not walk around with his name on your lips or by telling him how powerful he is. He has no power over you when you are free.

Let me show you who he really is.

End of chapter 5.   Chapter 6 follows: Satan, the Devil, Lucifer, or the Prince of Darkness

Chapter 6

Satan, the Devil, Lucifer, or the Prince of Darkness

There is probably not a nation that does not know who the devil is. It is ironic that parents educate their children about the devil, and so doing they scare the children. It is true that everything that is negative and evil comes from the devil, the negative energy. Let us have a look at where people are almost manically obsessed with Satan. How could I make a statement like that? Let me explain.

Every child that I know has an image of a devil burned into their minds. It originates with the parents from their view of protecting their children; it is their duty to inform their children of the devil. The child should know that anything that is wicked comes from the devil, such as naughty children come from the devil. Do you recall the story that was always told to children that the devil sits on their shoulder? Therefore, the child must have Jesus in their heart so that they do not to listen to devil. The devil always has a tail and horns, dressed in black. Jesus is dressed in a white robe, and angels have wings.

These images are warped and distorted images that are implanted in children's minds. Images of little devils that carry pitchforks and stab people. Children are told to love Jesus, even though children have no inclination of what love is, but you will hear little children say that they love Jesus. One of the main reasons children accept this concept is because they do not want to be rejected by their parents or by Jesus.

The devil is a man, to be exact, or is he? The devil is spoken of as a "he."

Let us have a look at what is written about where the devil comes from.

According to the Bible, Lucifer was an angel of God, and he did not want to do the will of God. God cast him out of heaven. The devil or Satan is the Prince of Darkness as Jesus is the Prince of Light. Therefore, the devil is everything that is evil and negative, while God is everything positive and good.

Just as we cannot create an image of God, so too we cannot create an image of Satan because he is not human. As God is the strength and wisdom in our midst, so the devil or Satan is the weakness and ignorance in our midst.

As the strength and wisdom is of God and is always present in our midst, so too is the weakness and ignorance of the devil is always with us and in our midst. These are energies and powers that we have mentioned, not people.

Satan or the devil is the Prince of Darkness and is associated with darkness which is linked to incomprehensibility. Light is linked to comprehensibility. The reason why these aspects are related to one another is because we are not dealing with people but instead with immense powers and energies. The best description would be that they are positive strengths and negative powers. These strengths and powers do not need physical space to occupy, therefore the original concept of heaven and hell is incorrect. A spirit is a condition of being; and therefore, a spirit does not need a physical place to exist.

Let us have a look at where Satan first was mentioned and where his name comes from. We need to revisit the ancient Egyptian time period of Horus, who is the son of Osiris. Horus ruled over the south while his uncle Seti ruled over the north. Seti was a brutal and violent ruler who was ruthless and merciless toward his citizens. Seti would use cruel methods to enforce order by burning those who were not obedient. Horus was, however, the complete opposite of Seti because he was honorable and fair toward his people and kept order and harmony among his people. It came to be that these two rulers stood up to one another. The one was evil and wicked, while the other was good and wise. These two men resembled the positive and negative powers. Seti is compared to Satan as Horus is compared to Jesus.

The good things and everything that is positive has become God. The evil and negative things in life became Satan. Many names are given to Satan. He is known as the devil, Satan, Lucifer, and the Prince of Darkness; and in the last few years, another label has cropped up, demons. Demons are actually the devil's helpers, but they are also brought forward as the powers of darkness. I care not what labels these powers of darkness have but that there are discussions about the forces of darkness are correct as it is important to know and understand. However, I have an issue with the fact that these energies are being humanized by mankind, and so it is being perceived as human. Just as mankind humanizes God, so too do they humanize Satan.

At times, humans do incorrect or wrong actions through their own will. Then it is instead labeled as the devil's work. So my will has now become that of the devil? God proclaims that he has given mankind free will, and that he leaves his will with us.

People and especially the church are obsessed with what is right and wrong. They play word games, but they justify the fact that they humanize God.

The Christian religion has certain measures in place to ensure that they are protected and that the religion will not be dismantled. That is why when anyone reveals the fraud and corruption of the Christian religion, they are immediately labeled as a blasphemer and seen as a demonic power. For the last two thousand years, the church leaders ensured that deep-rooted fears are instilled about the devil. These fears are so immense that people are petrified to read material that goes against their religious beliefs or their religious institutions.

Most people are not prepared to listen or investigate. This blind faith in their religion is ignorantly just accepted without question irrespective of the lies and fraud that is revealed. Is that how you see God? There are so many people who worship many versions of false gods, but it is these people that condemn freely and haphazardly without a grain of evidence.

I am not condemning anyone. This is the truth that I believe everyone is entitled to know and have access to. However, I also believe that God walks in the truth and not in man-made myths.

The struggle that I have and many other people should have is with lies and misrepresentation that the churches portray and sell as holy truths.

I am not the destroyer of souls, but rather I am trying to help souls. My aim is to save souls from the clutches of a godless giant that misleads souls through godless lies. I am not here to mislead any souls because the truth does not mislead or misinform. Truth is proven, but stories they make you believe.

Our endeavor is to strive against the evil powers of the light, those that are perceived as angels that display great wonders. Those individuals and institutions who continue to feed you with maliciously concocted dreams of golden streets, empty promises of kingship and priesthood after the grave; they must be toppled and eradicated. What I have to offer you is not sugarcoated or there are no promises of great things. On the contrary, you should not follow me; you should follow God. I am merely showing you the light and the actual truth, and it is up to you to take the responsibility and make your own decisions and have God in prayer. This is not a collective decision; it is a decision between you and God.

Do not call on the name of the devil or Satan in your life. Live without him and the grief he brings. Equip yourself with love, patience, tolerance, and all the other fruits of the soul. You should discontinue taking part in man-made rituals and do not see life in a symbolic fashion.

Invigorate yourself in the true God, and he will keep you from the forces of darkness. Not a hair on your head will be harmed if you wonder in the truth.

Live in God and remove the thoughts of wickedness from your life. Distance yourself from the negative aspects you encounter in your life because then you do not need to talk about the devil. As long as you mention the devil's name, he hears you, and he is present. Rather, build your thoughts on the positive elements and the steadfastness of the truth that you will have in your possession.

How is it then that I hear the name of the devil in more conversations than that of God? Everything that does not go according to your plans is simply the work of the devil. Sometimes God withholds certain things from coming to realization or prevents us from doing certain things, but then we are so childish that we are unhappy about it. It is ironic that the devil's name comes up again because it is his fault.

How easy it is to mistake the discipline of God as the work of the devil. God allows that certain things happen to us, so that we are equipped and experienced to deal with a future task. There have been many things that have occurred in my own life that I previously did not understand, until I came across a situation that required my past experiences to enable me to work through it. Sometimes through suffering, we acquire wisdom.

For the conclusion of this chapter, become still within yourself and contemplate for a moment if you are able to discern between the works of the devil and the works of God. Are you aware if it is the deceptiveness of the darkness or when it is the actual truth that presents itself to you?

More often than not, it is our own will enforced as the will of God, and the will of God is mistaken for the will of the devil. When something pleases you and you perceive it as good, it is then logically associated with the will of God. However, when information or knowledge challenges your belief or does not meet your distorted ideas, then it is perceived as the work of the misleader. Some of you will ask: Is my wisdom then so warped? The church fathers will show you a method to see the devil, but have a close look; it has more to do with protecting the church than actually protecting your soul.

When you have read through the next chapter, which discusses the concept of heaven and hell, you will have a better understanding of the forces of darkness.

The devil is very real, and he does exist but ensure that you are able to comprehend the difference between your will and the will of the devil. Keep in mind that the forces of darkness will portray itself as an angel of light. Verify and test that spirit or apparition; establish if the entity is able to speak the truth on what it says. Prohibit yourself from being like the grass in the wind that turns left or right according to every teaching that is brought forward.

When you have the truth within you, then you do not need to fear the devil. When you wonder in the truth, you will not find the devil there because he will not be able to enter the truth. If your refuge is by God, the darkness cannot attack you.

Which father would give his child a rock if the child has asked for bread? Think for a moment; which father would allow his child to be attacked by the darkness?

People have this concept that God is far away in a heaven which nobody knows where it is. Therefore, because God is far away, the darkness is capable of stealing souls. It is only those people that believe this nonsense that commit sin and want to be misled. These individuals or groups perceive the will of the devil as easier and more favorable in terms of revenge, sinning, and the like when compared to the will of God. The will of the devil appears to some to be without detriment or disadvantage, so insignificant and small. A sperm cell is so small, but yet it forms a much larger being; this is the same concept.

Be aware and pray that you who stand in the name of God are not already in the counsel of the devil. The will of the church is shown as the will of God. Try to conceive for yourself, who established all the thousands of churches? Is it not at the end of the day a group of people that have the same opinions and views? Who says that they bring forward the actual will of God? They use a handbook that is based on myths, traditions, symbols, rituals, and habits. They even commit plagiarism. Truth is based on facts and not on symbolic viewpoints. I inquire with you to think with a sober mind and not with blind faith.

Would you go about a multimillion contract haphazardly without looking at all the facts? Then why are you so careless when it concerns your eternal life and your soul?

God commands you to investigate everything but also to behold only the good from everything. Only the truth can be good.

The Bible does contain many wise words, and it makes people aware of God or at least a god. Unfortunately, lies and truth cannot work together in harmony in one book.

Chase after the truth and reject the lies because lies are associated directly to the forces of darkness. You, the reader who has been given the truth from these pages, cannot simply go back and say now that you do not know these things. People are either cold (uneducated in terms of the truth), or they are hot (educated in terms of the truth, and their deeds are performed accordingly), but those that are lukewarm (know and understand the truth but do nothing) will be spat out of his (God's) mouth.

Behold your belief in God and read further in the following chapters to see and understand the truth.

Chapter 7

The Concept of Heaven and Hell

In order to understand the concept of heaven and hell, you should be able to know the difference between good and evil. The question of whether heaven and hell are places or states of being has caused many disputes between religions.

<u>Concept of Heaven</u> is thought of by most as the dwelling place of God, gods, or other spiritual entities which is also the home or state of being of the "saved" when they pass over to the afterlife or when the time comes after the last judgment.

The concept of heaven is interpreted in various ways in the different religions of the world. In the Old Testament, heaven is regarded as the dwelling of Yahweh, the God of the Israelites because he was also known as heaven's creator. Until the third and second centuries BC, Israelites generally did not believe that heaven was the dwelling of those who died, but rather they believed that all men (good and evil) slept in Sheol, the underworld, which was a place of neither pain or pleasure, punishment or reward. However, in later Judaism, heaven came to be viewed as the ultimate destination for the righteous souls that entered the afterlife; after death, they would then be resurrected to live with God.

Christianity, which has its origins from Judaism, views heaven as the destination of the true believers and followers of Christ. Some of the more recent interpretations by Christians is their view that heaven is considered to be symbolical, as a state of life with God rather than as a place to which the saved go after death.

Islam, which was influenced by Judaism and Christianity, views that heaven is a place of joy and bliss where faithful Muslims go, according to the will of Allah (God). In the Quran, the Islamic scriptures, there are references in their scriptures to the belief that everyone must go through or pass by hell before reaching heaven.

In Eastern religions, their concepts of heaven vary considerably, some being similar to Western religious views and others being very diverse. The Chinese heaven, T'ien, is the guardian of the moral laws of man and the physical laws of nature. T'ien is also synonymous with divine will. In Hinduism, there are many and varied concepts of heaven. Worshippers of Vishnu the Preserver, for example, believe that they will go to a heaven in which there is no suffering, fear, or even death and that they will be able to live in the glory of Vishnu's eternal light. In some Mahayana Buddhist sects, such as the Pure Land sect, heaven is a Western Paradise for those who have received the saving grace of Amitabha, a Buddha who vowed to save all living creatures. Orthodox Buddhists, especially those of the Theravada (Way of the Elders), do not usually speak of heaven, but rather of Nirvana which is the state of existence where there is an extinction of desires.

Concept of Hell: the place or state of being of evil spirits or souls that is damned to punishment after death. The word "hell" is derived from an Anglo-Saxon word meaning "to conceal," or "to cover." The term "hell" originally was associated to the scorching and fiery regions of the underworld; though in some religions, the underworld is believed to be cold and dark.

The concept of a state of being or of a place that separates the good from the evil or the living from the dead are found in most religions of the world. In religions of ancient and primitive people, the dwelling place of the dead as the destiny of the soul might be a gloomy subterranean realm or a distant island such as the Greek Hades, who was the ruler of the underworld; a deep abyss in the lower world in which the souls of persons are punished, it was called, in the Greek religion, Tartarus; a dark region in the lower world in which both good and evil souls continue to exist as shades in constant thirst, it was referred to as the ancient Israelite Sheol; an underworld of cold and darkness, reference made to the Norse Niflheimr, which was also called Hel; the Pueblo Indians believed in a celestial dwelling place in which the souls of the departed resided, and upon their death, they became clouds, bringers of rain; the North American Indian hunting tribes believed that there was an existence in which the soul might eventually fade into nonexistence.

Western prophetic religions hold the view that hell is the final dwelling place of the damned after the Last Judgment. These religions are as follows: Zoroastrianism, Judaism, Christianity, and Islam. In Zoroastrianism, it is believed that the soul at death waits three nights to be judged and on the fourth day goes to the Bridge of the Requiter (Rashnu), where his deeds in life are weighed. If the good outweighs the evil, the soul crosses the bridge; it broadens, and the soul goes to heaven. If the evil deeds outweigh the good, the bridge becomes too narrow to cross, and the soul falls into a freezing and foul-smelling hell to suffer torment and punishment until the resurrection. For those whose good and evil deeds are equal, they are sent to "hamistagan" which means "the place of the mixed," where these souls suffer from both extremes of heat and cold. Hamistagan corresponds to the Christian concept of purgatory.

Islam bases its concepts of hell, Jahannam, on Zoroastrianism, Judaism, and Christianity. Hell is described as a huge crater of fire beneath a narrow bridge that all souls must pass over to go to paradise. The damned fall from the bridge and suffer torments, unless Allah (God) wills otherwise.

In Hinduism, hell is only one stage in a career of the soul which it must go through and experience. In their religion, it is believed that all actions have consequences, and due to reincarnation, the time spent in one or more of the twenty-one hells beneath the netherworld are not of any real significance. Eventually, the soul will return to the "world soul," even though it takes many lifetimes to do so. The Jaina hell (*bhumis*) is a place where demons torture sinners until any evil which was accumulated during their lives has been completely exhausted.

Buddhism denies the existence of both the individual and the World Soul; multiple hells correspond to *karmavacara*, the cosmic realm in which the five senses may be experienced in a variety of bodies and perceptions.

Judaism, as it developed from Hellenistic times, viewed hell in terms of Gehenna, which is an infernal region of punishment for the wicked. The Christian view of hell, based on Jewish concepts, regards hell as the fiery domain of the devil and his evil angels, a place of eternal damnation for those who have lived a life of sin and who thereby deny God. However, most of the Christian thinkers believe that hell is a state of punishment for those who die unrepentant of their sins. Some modern theologians still hold that hell is, at least, a state of separation of the wicked from the good.

In China, a primarily Buddhist concept of the realm of punishment and atonement after death was accepted and modified by Taoists. Popular views of hell are based on fictional accounts of journeys to the netherworld and on Buddhist scriptures describing the journeys of mercy taken there by the bodhisattva (one who is destined to be enlightened), Ti-ts'ang. At the moment of death, the dead are supervised by messengers to the god of walls and moats, Ch'eng Huang, who gives the dead a preliminary hearing. The righteous may go straight to one of the Buddhist paradises; to K'un-lun Mountain, the dwelling place of the Taoist immortals; or to the tenth court of hell for immediate rebirth. After forty-nine days, the sinners descend to the realm of hell, located at the base of Mount Meru. The courts of the ten kings are in the chief town, Feng-tu. The sinners undergo a fixed time span of punishment in one hell or in a series of hells, which can be changed by the merciful Ti-ts'ang. In preparation for their rebirth, the dead drink the broth of oblivion and climb onto the wheel of transmigration, which carries them to their next existence.

Discussion: The word "place" when used in "It is not my place to pass judgment" does not relate to a physical place but instead that it is not appropriate to judge. Perhaps it seems inappropriate due to religion, belief, circumstance, etc.

The question most frequently asked relating to one's spirit or soul, "Does a person's soul require a place to stay?" This question obviously receives many reactions. There are religious institutions that see everything in a natural and human way; therefore, they believe that heaven and hell are actual physical places that exist. Whereas others see heaven and hell as a state of being because God is spirit and when one passes over, the soul is considered as a state of being.

The Bible promises golden streets and mansions; however, these are all materialistic things, and why would a soul require these human or man-made things? There is also mention that there is eternal rest in the lap of Father Abraham. So which of these two would it be because it could not possibly be both instances?

More promises come forward from the Bible, such as everyone will rule as kings and priests. If everyone is kings and priests, over whom will they rule? What are kings without their subjects and priests without their members? If people believe that these kings and priests will rule over the people that are left behind on earth, then I do not understand the concept of eternal rest.

The people who are left behind are those that God has rejected and they will inherit hell, then they would belong to the devil.

There is written in the Bible that God is by mankind, God himself proclaims that he lives by mankind. Another question, is there a difference between heaven and the kingdom of God?

There is mentioning in the Bible of the ascending to the heavens. There is also mention that Jesus ascended to the height of a man. Jesus proclaims to some of those that are present during his ascent to the heavens that some of them will not see death until the Son of God has returned from his Father in heaven. Where are these people who are more than two thousand years old? Or was it a lie? Perhaps the Son is already by mankind?

If the kingdom of God is by mankind and God himself is by mankind, the Son is said to be by his Father, and then where is the Son? Then he should also be by mankind, is it not? If this is true, then why does mankind wait for the Son to come and fetch them and take them to God if God and his Son are already by mankind?

Where did the concept originate of heaven and hell?

When people were in their earliest stages of development in prehistoric times and they associated the elements with gods. When there was a sun god, fire god and so on; this was pure astrotheology. It was decided that there must be a high god that rules the others; that seemed logical back then. This high god had to live in the heavens such as Amen-Ra from Egypt that lived in the heavens.

If God lived in the heavens, then logically speaking the devil had to live in another place; this is where up in the heavens and down in hell came into the equation. To simply accept this concept does not actually make sense. Those of us who know that the earth is round and that it rotates will be able to tell you that there is no actual up or down. What is up and what is down? Because what might seem up now will be down over the next twelve hours.

Perhaps it could be suggested that hell will be or already is on earth. However, there is written that there is already an existing heaven and hell. If this is truly the case, then hell cannot be a physical place. The confusion comes from the incident where Jesus fell down to hell; this indicated that the hell must be down somewhere.

Where it speaks of the fires of hell, I wonder if that does not perhaps relate to the earth's core. Even this would not seem scripturally correct because God would not build his kingdom which is on earth on top of the foundations of hell.

Before we delve any deeper, let us go to the beginning of the Bible. Genesis 1:1 "In the beginning God created the heaven and the earth" (King James Version 1611). This means that heaven and earth were created at the same time. In Genesis 1:3-1:9, "God created the first day, called the light day and the darkness night. God divided the waters from the waters, the waters under and above the firmament" (King James Version 1611). The space between the waters above and the waters below, God called heaven.

When you look at the scripture that Jesus raised to the height of a man, on the contrary, it does not stand in the scriptures that he ascended but instead that he was taken up.

There are some who believe that the heaven that is mentioned in Genesis is not the same heaven that the souls of God go to. There is more than one heaven because there is mention of the fourth and seventh heaven in the Bible. Where would the other heaven then be? The only heaven that I read about is the one on earth. Is it not strange that God lives in the one on earth, his kingdom which is also on earth and earth, among humanity is where he lives?

Even the Bible says that God is not one which is far, but people get stuck with materialist and human, carnal views. There is proclaimed that the kingdom of God does not come with any visible signs and that flesh and blood cannot inherit the kingdom. Therefore, this heaven and kingdom cannot be a physical place.

If heaven cannot be a physical place, then hell can also not be a physical place. Is there perhaps something behind this concept that would be more like a state of being or a condition? In the importance of religion, I would reckon that it would be necessary to do further detailed research into this matter, instead of blind faith and conviction. We should listen to what God tells us, that we must investigate everything and behold what is good.

Perhaps you would reckon that it would be better to listen to your preacher, pastor, or church leader.

Some people would claim that the heaven mentioned in the Bible is that which Jesus is preparing for us, that it is a spiritual heaven. Whereas the heaven mentioned in Genesis is a natural heaven. Then the scriptures in the Bible also say that as it is in nature, so it is in spirit.

My conclusion is that most, if not all, the church fathers do not actually know where God or heaven is. Review what is written in Revelations 21. It sounds like these church leaders are trying to sell the concept of golden streets and beautiful homes that await the people who inherit the kingdom of God. Then there is still the title that everyone will have of being either kings or priests that will be bestowed upon everyone who enters this kingdom, and they will also have the right to rule. To rule over what or who?

To be able to rule, there must be people who are subservient to those kings and priests. I wonder who or what that would be. This is utter dribble because several conflicting promises are made when it comes to the eternal rest. There is talk about reuniting with your loved ones, then that you will rest in the lap of Father Abraham and then more promises of a New Jerusalem with golden streets, beautiful houses, and titles for every one of kingship and priesthood. This sounds more like hard selling than truth because why do they contradict one other?

These are all carnal things that mankind cling to, this is human wisdom. Do you not know that the wisdom of man is foolish by God and that the wisdom of God is foolish to man?

Therefore, I ask you again, why would God make a carnal heaven or kingdom and give it to his children? Souls do not need streets or houses.

If God is as it is written that he is the wisdom in our midst, why would he make a carnal and materialistic heaven? Is heaven also where you sit in a corner and I sit in mine? I was under the impression that we would all gather in glory. Then why would I go to a certain house to be alone? Will there be husband, wife, and children together in their homes as it was on earth? Then by which ex-wife or ex-husband will you live with? Will you all live together? That really makes no logical sense because that will have to be one massive house to accommodate for all of your forefathers and descendants.

When we look at the opposite, what is hell? It is also known as the kingdom of the devil. Are there also streets? What are the houses made of? Is it a place where there are eternal burning pools of fire that everyone is enveloped in where you will burn forever? This would come forward to be more of a spiritual fire because natural fire has no effect on a spirit or soul.

A person is so accustomed to accept without question and not to actually listen to what you are being told. As long as the wonder of the mysticism is present, then it is all in order. When you are told of this wonderful place that you will go to when you pass on, then people forget to live their life that God gave them. God warns us that we must not live in the past and neither in the future of dreams, but instead that we live now in the present, the present that God gave us.

Why do you wish and pray your life away? Why do you long for a life after this?

God offers you contentment and bliss. People interpret this phrase into the idea that you will experience bliss, joy, and contentment after the grave only; that wonderful soul bliss and contentment. Bliss means complete happiness; blessedness means enjoying happiness and content means to be satisfied. To be content is when you have eternal soul happiness within yourself that you experience. This experience takes place now in the land of the living, not one day when you have passed on.

Religion is supposed to fulfill you now with happiness and peace, not a heap of promises of one day. In what state is your soul currently? Does your soul have inner peace, or is your soul experiencing a hellish sufferable period with all your problems?

You are either in a heavenly state or in a hellish state of an internal fight with questions that go unanswered. Do you have true peace within yourself, or is there a touch of fear that makes you wonder if your soul is well. Do you truly have complete peace?

This is not the sort of question that is asked that will receive an audible answer because only you can answer this question.

If you answer is no, then you have a problem. You must ensure that it becomes a yes answer. How will you benefit if you believe that you will inherit the kingdom of God irrespective of how you live? You cannot lie to your own conscience. You cannot blame anyone else for it. God gave you life; God commanded you to investigate everything and behold the good. Alone you entered this world, and alone you will leave this world.

Allow me to ask you this question, "Do you know God?" I am not talking about the image that many people have of an old man with the white beard. "Do you honestly know your creator?"

Then there is an even harder question, "Does God truly know who you are?" It is easy to say yes, but how do you really know? What surety do you have? Are you told to simply believe? To know someone is to live with someone. There is a difference when you know someone and when you know of someone.

You cannot say that you know someone or love them if you have only read about them.

What is religion without action? Even if you were able to speak all the languages of man, the language of the angels, and you knew all the secrets that there is to know, all your efforts would be in vain because if you do not have love, you have nothing.

What is this love that is talked about? Is it to sit on the church benches or grovel on your knees? The Bible gives more clarity on this in the First Epistle of John 5:3 "For this is the love of God, that we keep his commandments: and his commandments are not grievous" (King James Version 1611). This does not concern Moses and the Ten Commandments, neither does it mean that you should go around and announce the Bible in a certain view point or perspective. Ultimately it means that you need to live the Gospel instead of preaching it.

Allow your life to speak volumes of your love, patience, tolerance, and self-control. Why do you want to walk around and talk about the Bible to others? I am sure these people read it as well.

Build on heavenly aspects and restrain yourself from wasting away your God-given life, for one day when you pass on. Focus your energy and attention on your task that you have to fulfill in this life. Not everyone has the same task because not everyone can be a David or a Moses. You were created in your own right; you are unique with your own task. Live it and become holy through your own works. By holy I mean that you should be devoted to your task and the work of that task by having heavenly qualities such as those mentioned previously. God never placed you in a group and commanded you to work as a team toward your spirituality. Your religion cannot give you inner peace, strength, and contentment because you need to find these qualities within yourself, through the truth and through God. What might be good for one person does not mean that it would necessarily be good for you.

This is a brief overview concerning the concept of heaven and hell and the aspects relating to it.

To enable you to get a deeper understanding of this concept, it is imperative that you read through the following chapters. These are only facts, and it does not draw strength from blind faith, conviction, or carnal, human wisdom.

Bring everything together that you read, and you will see that God truly does exist today for all of us while we are living.

Read the next chapter that deals with a story that has been glorified and see how you also believe in myths. The chapter deals with "Eternal God: the Mortal Virgin and the Holy Child."

Look at the similarities and save your judgment until you have read through the chapter.

Chapter 8

Eternal God: The Mortal Virgin and the Holy Child

It does not matter how you look at the following aspects because it stands out like a sore thumb. Something is definitely going on.

Mary also called Saint Mary, Virgin Mary the mother of Jesus, a figure worshipped in the Christian Church since the apostolic age. Mary is known from biblical references, which are, however, too few and scattered to construct a consistent biography. The development of the doctrine of Mary can be traced through titles that have been ascribed to her in the history of the Christian religion, such as guarantee of the incarnation, virgin mother, second Eve, mother of God, ever virgin, immaculate, and assumed into heaven.

Every Christian child knows the story of the eternal God the Father that took favor over the Virgin Mary and an angel impregnates her, and from her a child is born that is divine and human. This sounds wonderful, but the story is not as holy as it is made out to be. This story is ancient and has been used in various religions before Christendom existed.

The eternal transcendent immortal God, which does not have the form of man but is spirit, finds favor with a mortal virgin woman and from her a child is born that is half human and half god. Obviously a son, and he is the Savior of the entire human race. If this tale was new and limited only to the Christian religion, with the single birth of the child Jesus, then it would have been a truly wonderful event.

Even if there were only one or two similar events, it would probably still have been considered to be a credible event. However, there are more than sixteen identical stories with the same life sequence as lived by Jesus. Along comes this last account or story, and the Christians accept it as the only truthful account, and they label the others as myth.

Let us stand still for a moment by the Eternal Transcendent God.

The Bible proclaims that God is spirit and does not have the form of man. The scriptures also claim that God has no interest in carnal things. This God is proclaimed to be the strength and the wisdom among mankind. This comes from the Bible; if I understand it correctly, there is also written that everything that is written is true and correct. No person will add or remove anything from what is written in the Bible. It is a pity that more than half the original Bible has been altered and modified by church fathers. These are the people you admire, and these are the people that you trust by believing blindly in everything that they say.

Let us have a look at history. Osiris, who is the eternal father of the underworld, the transcendent god, finds favor over the mortal Isis and impregnates her through an angel. From Isis, Horus is born part human and part god. This son knows no evil and performs miracles. One of his first miracles was the healing of the lepers. Unfortunately, even with all his power and might, mankind rejects him. He is crucified and goes to Osiris to weigh the heart of humanity.

Here is another example of the same story that comes from another period and a different religion, the Greek religion of Zeus. Zeus is the transcendent immortal upper god who resides on the mountain of Olympus. He finds favor over a mortal virgin and impregnates her; from her, a son is born by the name of Hercules who is half god and half man. The son had immense powers but was rejected by mankind. Hercules now also resides with his father on Mount Olympus.

There are still sixteen saviors that follow the same trend as those mentioned above. You can read about them in chapter 11.

How is it possible that the same story comes up through the ages over and over again? Is man then so ignorant that he does not realize that he is being fed the same regurgitated story over and over again? There is just a touch of mysticism here and there that gives the story another flavor, but the core remains the same. How is it possible that all the previous stories are labeled as myth, but the newest version that appears in Christianity is regarded as the one and only truth? Do not even attempt to defend your view or opinion by using the same dribble that Tertullian claimed. Tertullian went to great lengths to break these associations, even claiming that the devil caused the similarities to occur. As stated in the second century: "The devil, whose business is to prevent the truth, mimics the exact circumstances of the Divine Sacraments. He baptizes his believers and promises forgiveness of sins . . . he celebrates the oblation of bread and brings in the symbol of the resurrection. Let us therefore acknowledge the craftiness of the devil, who copied certain things of those that be Divine" (Tertullian AD 155-222 from *The Prescription against Heretics*, Chap XL). Tertullian was only one of the many church fathers that either attempted or was successful in destroying, altering, removing or adding to their perceptions and versions of the truth.

Mary the mortal human being has been raised above all other humans because she has been upheld to a godlike status. There are even religions that pray through her to reach the Son, so that the Son can pass the prayer onto his Father. There are alleged witnessed accounts of people seeing Mary and claiming that she now possesses healing powers.

Even worse is the fact that many more people idolize the Son to such an extent that he is given a higher position than God himself. Many declare that the Son is God. He is portrayed as the good one that will forgive all your sins and trespasses, but God will punish you, and you will therefore not enter the gates of heaven. When God is presented in this way, people make him seem as if he cannot forgive, that he is strict and cruel. It seems as if he has little love for his creation; well, that is how people make it seem. The Son on the other hand is viewed as the one that is full of love and that he forgives all. These two personalities cannot possibly be of one god. In chapter 10, we discuss the Trinity God, where this belief originated, and how it is interpreted.

It is easy to say that God makes everything possible, but God is a god of logic and order. Do you not learn this from nature? How it is possible that a spirit could possibly impregnate a human woman and manages to give birth to a human baby? Refrain from labeling everything which does not make sense to you as miracles, especially the story of the virgin birth that has been accepted by Christianity; that is older than the hills and has been retold over the ages.

It should be realized that God is the one and only God; he is the master, creator, and ruler. Why do you feel the need to pray to other gods?

Contemplate on this for a moment; God is the creator of everything and created everything that needed to be created. He also created man. Why would God use an angel to impregnate a human woman of his choosing? Why not simply create his Son as he created everything else? Everyone knows that God is mighty; if he wanted his Son to be born all, he needed to do is place his Son's soul into a human baby, as he has done throughout time with all of our predecessors and with us and as he will continue doing with our descendants.

This melodramatic story is created to portray immense danger and utter struggle to get the spiritual message to mankind.

Over and over throughout time, the same story has been claimed as the holy truth, and man has been clinging on to it. Mankind has murdered and burned their own species because they dared to go against their beliefs or gods. Are you not doing the same today? You laugh at the religious myths of others, but you believe your own concocted ancient religion's myths.

You who judge, speak about people that do not accept your mythical religion. Those individuals and groups that judge are the people who do not have the facts and only believe in the Bible, the book riddled with myths, rituals, traditions, and symbolism. The holy chosen figures, such as Moses, David, and many others are a bunch of murderers. Is the Bible not against murder, and does God not condemn murderers? Murderers will not inherit the kingdom of God. There is mention in the Bible that Moses commits murder and receives no punishment. King David desired another man's wife and ensured that he perished in the war, so that he could claim that man's wife. The laws of Moses were broken again; these were desires; a murder was planned and executed to satisfy that desire. These are the examples of holy figures that the church leaders preach to you about, and they want you to be like these holy murderers.

The following chapter deals with myths, traditions, rituals, habits, and symbolism. This chapter will reveal how myths are growing in their strength and support among half of the population around the world because the majority believe in these myths.

Chapter 9

Myths, Traditions, Rituals, Habits and Symbols

Since the existence of mankind when it evolved as a species that could rationalize and conceive ideas, myths, traditions, rituals, habits, and symbolism became part of the pattern of thought and behavior.

Within the context of Christian faith, Christian mysticism refers to the human being's direct experience or consciousness of a perceived ultimate reality, the experience is understood as being God. The essence of mysticism is the sense of some form of contact with the divine or transcendent, frequently believed to be the highest forms as involving union with God. Mysticism has played an important role in the history of Christian religion and today continues to have a noticeable living influence on its followers.

Mysticism became part of religion. Whereas myths, rituals, symbolism, and the like originated from mankind's curious nature in their attempt to find answers and tolerate their fear to a degree of the unknown. Mysticism is a factor employed to provide solace in a falsely perceived holy manner.

Mysticism conforms to fantasy because it deals predominantly with beautiful ideas that instill calmness over the mind and heart while being perceived as holy and automatically in turn is associated with God. However, when mysticism infers or instills fear and restlessness, it is considered unholy, and therefore it is perceived as that of the devil.

These factors that have formed the basis of human nature required a stronger ingredient, which was conviction.

Once a person is convinced of these factors mentioned above, it is not easy to change their point of view, and that is when we talk about religion. When a person has been convinced that myths, traditions, rituals, habits, symbolism, and mysticism is the true and only way, then that person is inclined to believe it blindly and wholeheartedly. All of these factors become a religion-oriented reality that is widely accepted.

When this reality becomes a belief, people's perceptions and points of view concerning certain aspects change, and these new perceptions affect behavior patterns, and another ingredient comes into the mix which is behavior.

A person's behavior, conduct, and attitudes are diverse. Culture and environment play an integral part when it concerns behavior. A person's temperament also has an effect on one's behavior.

Behavior and conviction are formed through the nature of the point or purpose. The manner and method that is used to convince a person needs to be adapted to that particular person's culture, behavior, and mind-set because that is where the success lies in terms of whether a person will accept or reject the notion. As soon as there is conflict in the mind or heart, it results in doubt and in turn manifests confusion and bewilderment.

Confusion determines the behavior and attitude of a person. At this point, we see the origin of acceptance or rejection of belief or disbelief. These are the basic principles of good or bad, right or wrong, and metaphorically also seen as the light or darkness.

When there is acceptance or belief in a certain standpoint, it is interpreted as light; whereas when disbelief, rejection, or doubt creep in, it is interpreted as darkness or night.

Through the formation of language and culture, behavior patterns were developed. For example, when an individual is in the dark about a certain aspect and someone provides an explanation to clarify any misunderstanding, then the response is usually "I see"; in other words, this individual now understands. This is where the interpretation of light and darkness derives from. When one does not understand, your mind is in darkness; but when you understand, then this implies light.

By using this concept of behavior, religion has formed the church service to get ideas and perceptions across to people, such as the so-called spiritual creation and origin that has taken hold of mankind's thoughts.

To bring a thought over to someone is usually said to plant a thought in someone's mind; to plant a seed. Obviously, this does not refer to the natural earth, but instead it refers to a person's mind. That is why a person's mind is interpreted as the earth. The manner that an individual's mind is prepared to receive a specific message or thought is interpreted as to prepare the earth. When your mind ("the earth") is not prepared to conceive the message ("seed"), then it will not be able to grow and flourish. If the message ("good seed") is planted in the mind ("earth") and there has been no preparation in terms of eradicating conflicting perceptions or ideas ("weeds"), then this new seed will be suffocated by these conflicting perceptions or ideologies ("weeds") and cannot take root and grow.

When a person is simply stubborn toward the thought or idea, then their mind is referred to as "hard ground." When the earth is spoken of metaphorically, it concerns the individual's mind-set or consciousness, and the "seed" becomes a thought.

This brings us back to what is understood and misunderstood in terms of light and darkness. More importantly, differences must be acknowledged between "good seed" and "bad seed."

Remember that the "seed" is a thought or an idea, and it does not mean that the seed or thought is always correct or "good seed." It depends on the method used to convey the thought or idea by using suggestion and illusion, which creates an acceptable perception by the person receiving the thought or idea; the thought is brought forward as either good or bad.

It is through myths, traditions, rituals, habits, symbolism, and mysticism being used over the years in the pursuit of mental manipulation that religion evolved into a church service pattern today and became one of the most powerful forms of psychological manipulation. The driving force is the inborn fear of the unknown, the search for explanations, and the satisfying solutions thereof.

The church fathers came to the conclusion; if they provided satisfying solutions strewn with mystic images and promises, when used in a successful method in combination with mystical fear and satisfaction, then it manifests subservience in mankind. Therefore, they were able to get a firm grip over mankind's behavior, which gave them power and control over the masses, the manipulative steering of people's thoughts and behavior patterns. It became an enduring and tenacious form of governance; they were able to overpower people's thoughts and conduct to their advantage.

Through the use of the right mystical forms, control is exercised over human thought, and certain suggestions are made to the submissive and obedient members of their strong yet submissive religion where a magnitude of powerful deeds and actions are performed and conducted. The immense power was utilized from total unity of thought and perspectives.

Oneness in thought, such as the gods that reside in the heavens which comes from astrotheology, the search for the unanswerable from the elements of nature, and the explanation that there must be one power and strength that rules over all the other powers or gods. This became known as the Upper God, and then all these other gods and powers became one God.

To make it easier for mankind to relate to this God, he and the other gods were given human characteristics and qualities. The upper strength was referred to as "he" because this God was immensely strong and associated with a strong man. God was then viewed as the beginning of mankind and the earth; he became the image of a father. God, which is the positive energy, and wisdom have now morphed into the image of an old man.

The humanization and imagery of this power was created on a mystical basis and instills hope within people. Manipulation and deception are used with the promises of wonderful events that will occur on the condition that you believe and remain subservient and obedient to the suggested patterns that have been established by church fathers. Ideologies were created that was referred to as the will of God.

Do not misunderstand me; many positive aspects have been borne from religion, but there has been more death, destruction, heart sore, and devastation committed in the name of religion even when compared to any natural disaster or event. What mankind exercises presently is nothing more than idol worship.

The image or blatant thought of God as a manly or father figure makes it idol worship. The man-made myths, traditions, rituals, habits, and symbolism in its mystical form confirm a cultural form of idolatry.

The desperate need to be part of a brotherhood or group instead of being alone has formed group-bound human beings. The personal growth of each person is being suppressed; they cannot grow to the best of their abilities because they are part of a belief structure as a sister or brother, as part of a group. Suggestions to be more like a Moses or a David destroys each person's personality and ensures that the control over the masses becomes easier.

The question of whether God exists can be confirmed by looking around; there is life, and no other being can create life except for the mightiest strength and wisdom which is in and around us. It is one power and energy that works harmoniously through everything.

Have you become so blinded and your mind clouded by your religion that you cannot understand the true reality? Have myths, traditions, rituals, habits, and symbolism become so integrated in your actual existence that all other truths do not make sense to you?

God is a god of order. Why then must there be these mystical forms of myths, traditions, rituals, habits, and symbols that are coupled with and form part of your life's pattern? Why did God create you as a certain entity if you constantly change to become like others, just to be accepted by them? Different churches have different methods and techniques which they perform and have set in place to bring so-called holiness to you.

In actuality, it is no longer a priority to gain control over you and your family nor your money because it is an established automated influence that no longer needs to be closely monitored all the way. These religious institutions are enriched from your fears and your desperate search for a better life. Show me a church that is not a proprietary limited or closed corporation. Or show me a church that does not subtly manipulate the scriptures in order to secure your tenth in the form of money. They place tremendous emphasis on obedience in order to guarantee that you will accept everything that they bring to you with no resistance and reluctance, the so-called order of God which only man has structured.

I need to ask you earnestly, whose order is it actually and whose will are you obedient to? How many religious church orders has God made? In South Africa alone, there are over six thousand registered church orders and more than fifty thousand in the world. The one is more attractive and seductive than the other, with beautiful buildings, the newest sound technology, comfortable plush seating, and air-conditioning. Music that is played before the service commences in order to create the most receptive ambience in the audience, whereas others still use choirs to create a holy and mystical experience to ensure that the audience is more receptive to the messages being brought to them by religious leaders.

There are religions that promote silence during segments of their service in order to allow the prophet to be free within their members so that the prophet can prophesy or speak in tongues. Which father would speak to his children in tongues and expect them to understand or listen to him?

How can you hold up your religion as true when it is scattered with numerous myths, traditions, rituals, habits, and symbols? Not any of these aspects can make you holy, even though it has an immense impact and influence on the members of the church.

Everything that is written in the scriptures within the Bible are proclaimed to be holy and given by God. How can lies and delusions be holy? How can myths or plagiarism be holy? In fact, it is these things that the Bible warns against that you should not do, but yet the Bible itself is infested with lies and deception. The Bible and religion have been sweetened and portrayed with wonderful ideas and delusions only to conceal the hideous and despicable truth of its history over the centuries since the beginning of its existence.

In actual fact, the truth has been twisted to such an extent that it is meant to display the so-called strength of the Jews' God. If this is what your religion has in store for me, then I am not interested in honoring God in such a false manner. I cannot honor God with lies and fraud simply because it is meant and committed with good intentions in mind. An infallible lie remains a lie, and a lie cannot be honored or made holy.

One lie in a book cannot make the entire book holy. There are no half lies or half-truths; it is either a lie, or it is the truth.

The history of Christian myth and legend from the early church claimed many mythological motifs and genres from the Greek and Middle Eastern cultures that were predominant during the Hellenistic age of 300 BC to AD 300. To mention a few, the supernatural birth of a deity from the virgin birth of a god or goddess;

this was a common theme in the mythology of the Hellenistic period. Another example, Mithra, the Iranian god of light and of sacred contracts, described as a divine child of radiant heavenly beams. Mithra was born from the rock of a cave; shepherds witnessed his birth on December 25 and later claimed by Christians as the birth of Christ.

Hellenistic Judaism had already reinterpreted many Gentile subject matter and ideas that were set within a biblical context. From Greek and Jewish sources, Christians took up and altered many favorite mythical themes, i.e., the creation of the world, the end of the paradise and the fall of mankind, that God assumes human form, the saved savior, the devastation and destruction at the end of time, and the final judgment. Christians merely adapted and altered these myths within their new views of history and added them to their doctrines concerning the nature of God, sin, and redemption. As it spread beyond Palestine and the Hellenistic world over time, Christianity continued to develop mythical themes that were important to the religious consciousness of their converted people.

The twentieth century continues to generate important Christian myths and legend-based practices, including pilgrimages to holy or biblical sites. Myth and legend express the fulfillment of religious desires and hopes that constituted religious traditions even before Christianity emerged.

Myths are fabrications of the truth. A myth is a popular belief or tradition retold through the ages and embodies the ideals and institutions of a society or segment of society based on an unfounded or false notion. These false notions are passed on as the truth. Myths are predominantly used in religions where a type of church or religious service structure is in place. In short, a myth is nothing more than a lie.

Traditions are an inherited, established, or customary pattern of thought, action, or behavior upon which certain cultures or social structures live their lives accordingly. Church or religious services are faithful to culture because their techniques on passing on ideology are altered to match with their institution or society's traditions to ensure that their ideas are accepted and understood by their members. Is God then a chameleon? With each culture, the portrayal and perception of God is different, i.e., a certain manner of dress, manners of worship, etc.

Rituals are the performance of ceremonial acts prescribed by tradition or by sacred decree and are acted out to honor the supposed historical acts as accurately as possible, such as Holy Communion and baptizing. These human constructed events were originally invented to appease the ancient gods and were maintained but later used to remind people of what once was. There is nothing holy about a ritual. The churches speak of the Holy Communion, baptizing, etc. Who made rituals holy? It was people who made rituals holy. Therefore, you are performing the will of mankind, and yet you expect God to bless you. Mankind attaches God to rituals and believe that if you do not take part in these man-made rituals, you are not part of the certain events that it culminates. Baptism with water is commonplace but whatever happened about baptism with fire? Chapter 22 discusses baptism.

Religious institutions such as churches will cease to exist without rituals. The entire religion is based upon rituals.

Habits are part of a person's mental makeup which is a custom or a practice of a way of acting fixed through repetition. Each religious structure has its own habits. Some congregations stand when there is prayer while others sit during prayer. The basic ways of serving the religion is unique to each sect with few similarities. Habits are bound to traditions, rituals, and even symbolic thought processes in religion. None of these aspects are holy in any fashion and cannot in turn make you holy. The church is incapable of existing as a separate entity with its own identity without these habits.

Symbolism is the art or practice of using symbols by bestowing things with a symbolic meaning or by expressing the invisible or intangible by means of visible or sensuous representations. Every religion is based on symbolism, such as the raising of outstretched arms when a blessing is conferred or when baptizing and Holy Communion is performed. There are hordes of many other symbolic rituals, habits, and myths of symbolic traditions. The entire religious institution is built on symbolism. The parables of Jesus were in the form of similarities because everything that he explained was symbolical, i.e., people who were planted as trees by streams of water. Water is symbolic for spiritual life. Symbols were used to speak in a type of secret language. Symbolism is the last thing that could possibly make you and me holy because it is intertwined with numerous lies. Confusion among mankind is predominantly caused by symbolical preaching, and the rifts in religion are created through the differing viewpoints of these symbolic meanings. Truth and straightforward language cannot cause misunderstandings. Symbolism is almost like a game; those that are able to unravel it win a prize. Unfortunately, the rules are impossible to adhere to and nobody stands a chance to win. Show me an individual who has no desire.

All these elements we mentioned are held together with the mysticism factor.

Services or proceedings are begun with prayer through the Trinity God. This brings us to the following chapter that deals with the concept of the Trinity God, which is present in Christianity.

Chapter 10

The Trinity God

Thus far, we have looked at a few various aspects of religion, and some of these aspects have created bewilderment in your heart and mind. Yet again your earth (your consciousness) has been shaken.

The Trinity has been an essential feature in the religion of many Oriental nations. The Holy Ghost was the third member under various appellations. In the Hindu trinity, it was Siva, the other members of the trinity being Brahma and Vishnu.

This notion of a third person in the deity was disseminated among all the nations of the earth. The Trinity doctrine forms part of antiquity. In the Hindu system, this third person was the Holy Breath, by which living creatures were made. The Holy Ghost became visible in the form of a dove, a tongue of fire, etc.

The Holy Ghost was sometimes the agent in immaculate conceptions. In the Mexican trinity, Y Zona was the Father, Bascal the Word, and Echvah the Holy Ghost, by the last of whom Chimalman conceived and brought forth Quexalcote. When Sesostris invoked the oracle to know who before him could subjugate all things, the answer was "First God, then the Word, and with them the Spirit." Plutarch, in his *Life of Numa*, shows that the incarnation of the Holy Spirit was known to the ancient Egyptians.

The doctrine of the word as the creative power is very ancient. The Chinese Bible states that "God pronounced the primeval Word, and his own eternal and glorious abode sprang into existence." According to the Zend-Avesta, it was the word, more ancient than the world, that Ormuzd created the universe. The ancient Greek writer Amelias, speaking of the god Mercury (Hermes), says "And this plainly was the Logos, by whom all things were made."

Plato taught a trinity of the soul, in which it is easy to see striking similarities pointing to a higher form of the doctrine.

It is said that there was an ancient Greek inscription on the great obelisk at Rome that had on it: (1) The Mighty God, (2) The Begotten of God, and (3) Apollo the Spirit.

The Christian religion promotes a three-in-one god. The Trinity in Christian doctrine is the unity of Father, Son, and Holy Spirit as three entities into a single god and is also referred to as the Godhead. However, neither the word "Trinity" nor the doctrine appears in the New Testament.

The Christian doctrine of the Trinity defines God as three divine entities meaning that God the Son and God the Holy Spirit have exactly the same nature or entity as God the Father in every way. The three entities are distinct yet coexist in unity and are coequal, coeternal, and consubstantial. Put another way, the three entities of the Trinity are of one being. Therefore, that implies that God the Son and God the Holy Spirit are also eternal, transcendent, infinitely wise, infinitely holy, infinitely loving, and possess universal and complete knowledge.

The Father: that resides in and rules from heaven.

The Son: that took the form of man, born from a mortal virgin, and went to his Father to prepare a place for his chosen people. He will return one day on the Last Judgment.

The Holy Spirit: depicted as a dove and is the comforter for mankind.

These three manifestations of one God are conveyed differently by each church structure.

Christianity which in itself has its origins from pagan Egyptian and Stoic sources, also having emerged from Judaism, is a monotheistic religion. Never in the New Testament does the Trinitarian concept become a "tritheism" (three gods) nor even two. God is one, and that the Godhead is a single being is strongly declared in the Bible:

The Shema of the Hebrew scriptures: "Hear, O Israel: the LORD our God, the LORD is one." (Deuteronomy 6:4)

The first of the Ten Commandments—"Thou shalt have no other gods before me" (Deuteronomy 5:7). and "Thus saith the LORD the King of Israel and his redeemer the LORD of hosts: I am the first and I am the last; and beside me there is no God" (Isaiah 44:6).

In the New Testament: "The Lord our God is one" (Mark 12:29).

The first recorded use of this Greek word in Christian theology (though it was not about the Divine Trinity) was by Theophilus of Antioch in about 170. He wrote: "In like manner also the three days which were before the luminaries, are types of the Trinity, of God, and His Word, and His wisdom. And the fourth is the type of man, who needs light, that so there may be God, the Word, wisdom, man."

Tertullian, a Latin theologian who wrote in the early third century, is credited with using the words "Trinity," "person," and "substance" to explain that the Father, Son, and Holy Spirit are "one in essence—not one in Person."

Reflection by early Christians on passages such as the Great Commission: "Go therefore and make disciples of all nations, baptizing them in the name of the Father and of the Son and of the Holy Spirit" (Matthew 28:19) and Paul the Apostle's blessing: "The grace of the Lord Jesus Christ and the love of God and the fellowship of the Holy Spirit be with you all" (2 Corinthians 13:13), while at the same time the Jewish Shema Yisrael: "Hear, O Israel: the Lord our God, the Lord is one" (Deuteronomy 6:4) led the early Christians to question which way the Father, Son, and Holy Spirit are in unity. Later, the diverse references to God, Jesus, and the Spirit found in the New Testament were systematized into a Trinity—one God subsisting in three entities and one substance—to combat heretical tendencies of how the three are related and to defend the church against charges of worshipping two or three gods. As you can see, it was not the will of God but instead the will and decision of men. Whose will are you obedient to at the end of the day?

The Trinity doctrine developed by varying degrees over several centuries and had to deal with many controversies. Initially, both the requirements of monotheism inherited from the Hebrew scriptures and the implications of the need to interpret the biblical teaching to Greco-Roman religions seemed to demand that the divine in Christ was to be referred to as the Word, or Logos, be interpreted as subordinate to the Supreme Being. Yet again, it was the decision and logic of man and not that of God. An alternative solution was to interpret the Father, Son, and Holy Spirit as three modes of self-disclosure of the one God but not as distinct within the single being of God itself. The first tendency recognized the distinctness among the three, but at the cost of their equality and hence of their unity (subordinationism); the second came to terms with their unity, but at the cost of their distinctness as "entities" (modalism). It was not until the fourth century that the distinctness of the three and their unity were brought together in a single orthodox doctrine of one essence and three entities. Eventually, human beings in power decided among themselves to form a widely accepted conclusion. This was certainly not inspired by God.

In 325, the First Council of Nicaea established the doctrine and crucial formula of the Trinity as orthodoxy and adopted the Nicene Creed, which described Christ as "God of God, Light of Light, very God of very God, begotten, not made, being of one substance with the Father," even though it said very little about the Holy Spirit. The doctrine of the divinity and personality of the Holy Spirit was developed by Athanasius in the last decades of his life and again was not given by God.

Saint Athanasius defended and refined the Nicene formula, and, by the end of the fourth century, under the leadership of Basil of Caesarea, Gregory of Nyssa, and Gregory of Nazianzus (the Cappadocian Fathers), the doctrine of the Trinity took substantially the form it has maintained ever since. It is accepted in all the historic confessions of Christianity, even though the impact of the Enlightenment decreased in importance over time.

Saint Athanasius, who was a participant in the council, stated that the bishops were forced to use this terminology, which is not found in scripture, because the biblical phrases that they would have preferred to use were claimed by the Arians to be capable of being interpreted in what the bishops considered to be a heretical sense. They therefore "commandeered the non-scriptural term homoousios ('of the same being') to safeguard the essential relation of the Son to the Father that had been denied by Arius." Therefore, in the Trinity doctrine, each entity is understood as having the identical essence or nature, not merely similar natures.

The being of Christ dominated theological discussions and councils of the church until the seventh century and resulted in the Nicene and Constantinopolitan creeds, the Ephesine Formula of 431, the Christological statement of the Epistola Dogmatica of Leo I to Flavianus, and the condemnation of monotheism in the Sixth Ecumenical Council (680-681). From these councils, the following Christological doctrines were condemned as heresies: Ebionism, Docetism, Basilidianism, Alogism or Artemonism, Patripassianism, Sabellianism, Arianism, Apollinarianism, Nestorianism, Eutychianism, Monophysitism, and Monothelitism. Why were these doctrines no longer relevant? Was it not inspired by God? Is it not perhaps strange that one doctrine is accepted and later altered or replaced completely? Why would God create vast differences in thinking among his children? God is a god of order. This is further proof that doctrines and ideologies are concocted by mankind and not created by God.

Trinitarianism, belief in the Trinity, is a mark of Roman Catholicism, Eastern and Oriental Orthodoxy as well as of the "mainstream traditions" arising from the Protestant Reformation, such as Anglicanism, Baptist, Methodism, Lutheranism, and Presbyterianism. The Oxford Dictionary of the Christian Church describes the Trinity as "the central dogma of Christian theology." Are you also like many church fathers who would stand up and proclaim that all of these doctrines and ideologies were inspired by God? What type of god will first mislead his so-called Christian children and only from the fourth century suddenly change? If it was true that the Trinity God was, is, and shall be forever more, why was it only introduced at a much later stage of Christianity and forced upon the priests?

In Genesis 1:1, "In the beginning God created the heaven and the earth" (King James Version 1611). Which God is present in this scripture? Is it the Father? Is it perhaps the Son? Or is it perhaps similarly conveyed as certain churches would say that it is the Trinity God? Most people would generally accept the Trinity God doctrine.

The Father comes forth and says that he will send his Son to earth in the form of sinful flesh. Why did God then not state that he himself will come to mankind in sinful flesh? How is it possible that God and the Son are one entity? The Father sends his Son to mankind, and he remains in his kingdom.

God states in the Bible that he does not have the form of man and that no image or statue will be made of him of either in the heavens or here on earth. God also states that he is spirit, and that he will be served in spirit and in truth.

His Son arrives in human form, and the Son states that if you see him, you also see his Father. John 14:10: Jesus says "Anyone who has seen me has seen the Father." According to this verse, God has the form of man.

When the term "father" is used to describe God, he is perceived as a human man. The Son who also has human form is implying that God also has human form. Could it possibly be that God has the form of man?

God and his Son look the same. God impregnated Mary. Only a man can impregnate a woman. For the first time, the Holy Spirit comes into the picture because it is actually the Holy Spirit that impregnates Mary. That would make the Holy Spirit also a man.

By depicting God as a man when using the word "father," we are creating a manly image in our minds. Yet that is what God warns us against.

Let us begin investigating as God commands us to do. Investigate everything and behold only the good. To enable us to follow the command of God, we must go back to the origins of the three-in-one God.

During the period when the Hebrews were in exile in Egypt, there was an Egyptian mediator known by the name Isis.

- *Isis* proclaimed that she was the eternal mother. She is the strength and the wisdom in the midst of the people. She stated that she *Is*.

- In the Bible, it states that *God* is the eternal Father. He is the strength and the wisdom in the people's midst. He states that he *Is*.

After the death of Isis, the Pharaoh orders the priests to search for an eternal mediator.

- *Amen-Ra* is born as a religion and as a god. He is the Son of God, the Son of Righteousness, and he gives his life to the world. As long as the sun is there, there will be eternal life on earth.

- *Jesus* is born as a Savior and a God; He is the Son of God and the Son of Righteousness. He gives his life and as long as you have Jesus in your life, you will have eternal life.

After the exodus of the Hebrews from Egypt when they lived under the Canaanites, they encountered another religious service and a Canaanite mediator, the god "El," who is the comforter.

- *El* is the comforter god who is associated with the planet Saturn which is in turn also associated with the dove.

- The *Holy Spirit* is the comforter which is associated with a dove.

As you can see, ancient myths and religions were used to create a new powerful and magnificent god. That is also how the Palestine partition became known as Israel, and this is how it got its name: Is from Isis, Ra from Amen-Ra, and El from the god El; when combined, it spells out Israel. This is discussed further in chapter 14, "Israelites—God's Chosen People."

Other religions are mocked and laughed at because the actual truth is not understood or sort after. It does not help to become enraged and defend your religion without knowing the facts and the truth behind your religion. Not everything that goes against your religion is from the devil. The truth may hurt at times, but it will set you free from the curse of lies which you are subservient to.

There is only one God. There is no father or mother. God will not come forth in the form of a man or a dove. God is the strength and the wisdom from which everything was created. God is the god of all life, as is also stated in your Bible. Why do you judge those who have divergent views on spiritual life and life in general? What is religion? It is an unwavering conviction in that which you believe but cannot see; whereas, if it was factual truth, you could no longer see it as a religion. Your religion originated from varying viewpoints of people that held it before you as the only truth and the only way to salvation. Did God not say that you should investigate everything and behold only that which is good? Alone you entered this world and alone you will depart. This means that you must strive toward your own salvation.

God presented you with this life and expects you to live it to its fullest. Then why do you pray your life away? You are squandering your life away due to individuals and groups that bring themselves forward as people from God. You live in fear because you believe that you will go to hell if you do not perform the will of their god. These people do not even know where the Kingdom of God is because nobody has even seen God but they claim to know him. They make you believe that by giving your all toward them that you are actually doing it for God in order to build the kingdom of God. They tell you that God does not need you, but that you need God. It seems to me that the god of these churches requires your money and support to exist.

The Bible states that God is a god of unconditional love. However, if you do not adhere to the church institution, then you will go to hell. In the Bible, it says in Matthew 7:9, "Which Father would give His child a rock if the child asks for bread, and which Father would give His child a snake if the child asked for a fish." Then I read the section in the Bible about the good shepherd that keeps watch over his sheep. He will never leave his sheep so that the wolves can steel his sheep. Jesus, the shepherd, leaves his sheep for more than two thousand years to prepare a place for his chosen people in the kingdom of God. In the same Bible, it says that the kingdom of God is by mankind. God resides in his kingdom by mankind.

The church leaders try and explain this by telling you that it is only the spirit of God that is by mankind. According to the Bible, I thought that God was only spirit. If the kingdom of God is by mankind and God or his spirit is by mankind, then where has Jesus disappeared to because people have been waiting for two thousand years for him to return, for him to take them to a wonderful place that has no heart sore or grief? I understand that it is not pleasant to see your religion in this light, but fortunately it is not too late.

Not everybody believes, serves, or is subservient and obedient to the same God. Some religions worship a god that is high above the moon and stars, while others believe that God is high above but that his soul is here among us. Others believe that God is here among us and will one day take us to another place, heaven.

I trust that all religions will at least agree with me that God is not a man and does not have human form. God also does not have a gender; he is not male or female, and therefore God cannot be referred to as he or she. To call God our Father, we make God to be a manly entity which is nothing more than idol worship. Others have the audacity to give God a name. Who named the planets in the galaxy? Mankind did. We even named all the plants and animals, but we are so arrogant that people decided to name God.

Here is an example of mankind giving God a name. Yahweh is the god of the Israelites; his name was allegedly revealed to Moses as four Hebrew consonants (YHWH) which is called the Tetragrammaton. From the third century BC onward, the Jews ceased to use the name Yahweh for two main reasons. As Judaism became more thought of as a universal religion through its numerous conversions throughout the Greco-Roman world, the more common name of Elohim, meaning "god," replaced Yahweh in an attempt to demonstrate the significant supremacy of Israel's God over all others' religious gods. At the same time, many Jews regarded their god's name to be far too sacred and divine to be uttered by anyone, and it was therefore replaced by the Hebrew word Adonai ("My Lord").

Clement of Alexandria in the second century had used a form like Yahweh, and this pronunciation of the Tetragrammaton was fortunately never lost. Various other Greek transcriptions also indicated that YHWH should be pronounced Yahweh. The Masoretes worked to reproduce the original text of the Hebrew Bible between the sixth and tenth century; they replaced the vowels of the name YHWH with the vowel signs of the Hebrew words Adonai or Elohim. This is where the artificial name Jehovah (YeHoWaH) came into being. Most biblical scholars began to use the form Yahweh (YHWH) again in the nineteenth and twentieth centuries.

If God is the creator of all life, then all life belongs to God. Then how can people state that those who do not follow their religion are not from God? Because someone decided to add a section in the scriptures that says if you do not proclaim that Jesus is the Christ, then they are not born from God. Whoever inserted that text into the Bible is surely the Antichrist and the misleader. If you love God, then how can you hate his creation, even if they are different from you?

When I talk frankly, keep in mind that I do so not out of harshness, not out of cruelty, not for the passion of my purpose, but because I want you to understand what I am saying. Your prejudices, your fears, your religious authorities new and old are all barriers to understanding. I cannot make myself clearer than this. I do not expect you to agree with me; I do not want you to follow me. I want you to understand what I am saying and to explore, inquire, and search for the truth. I have provided truths and facts within this book to provide a foundation for you to start your journey from.

This understanding is necessary because your religious belief has not transformed you but has only complicated you; and therefore, you are not willing to face the truth as it is. You want to have your own gods and religions which are all equally valueless that are all barriers and serve as limitations. You are all depending on someone else for your spirituality, your happiness, and your salvation. When you depend, you gradually become weakened; you become helpless and decrepit. You are incapable of thinking clearly, and this is a fact.

When I say that you must put all of these ideologies and doctrines away and look within yourselves for the enlightenment, for the contentment, for the happiness, and for the incorruptibility of the self, not one of you is willing to do it or at least very few. Religious organizations cannot make you free because they were built and formed on myths, lies, and deceit. No person from outside, form of worship, or organization can make you free from religion or its conditioning. Where there is conditioning, there is no freedom. You will achieve nothing by sacrificing yourselves for a cause.

You have the idea that only certain people, such as your religious leaders, hold the key to the kingdom of God. No one holds it; no one has the authority to hold that key because that key is within you. So you will see how absurd the whole structure is that your religious leaders have built, you keep looking for external help, depending on others for your comfort, happiness, and strength. These can only be found within yourselves and by searching for the absolute truth. You have become irresponsible because you are dependent, and that may be the root cause of all your confusion. Take responsibility for your spiritual life and your daily living.

In the following chapter and those that follow, there is factual proof that will certainly make you gain a deeper understanding of your religion. Many sections of the Bible are scrutinized due to facts; I leave it up to you to be your own judge concerning the aspects that are covered.

Every few years, a new leader appears that alters and adapts the Bible. The explanation is usually to ensure that the Holy Book is more understandable for people. Millions are spent to convince everyone that the Bible is the one and only truth from God, but instead the wool is being pulled tighter over the follower's eyes.

Who is your God? Is it the mythological Trinity or the one and only true God who is the creator of all life?

History is there, right in front of you; inquire and search in your own way. The Bible is certainly not the only place to look for the truth. People have tried to hide the truth; some have destroyed some parts of it and even altered and corrupted history. The truth is a funny thing; it always finds a way out. Prevent your conditioned mind and prejudices from clouding your vision.

The following chapter discusses Jesus and his predecessors, not from the Bible but from the pages of history. Let us see if Jesus is a true story or a fairy tale, or perhaps that you have been misled by a mythological religion.

Chapter 11

The Jesus Story and His Predecessors

As you have seen already from chapter 10, not everything is in place when it comes to the Savior as the church leaders and the Bible proclaim it to be.

There is no doubt however that Jesus the Nazarene lived, that he performed great feats and was the founder of Christianity.

Let us have a look at a few interesting views from stories that are brought from the Bible.

Such as the statement, "what good can be born from Nazareth," most Christians must have heard of this statement before, but there is never emphasis placed on this statement. What is it about the Nazarenes that would justify such a statement?

The Nazarenes were always regarded as the undisciplined and lazy people of the Jewish nation; they were also referred to as the black Jews. Yes, Jesus was a black Jew and not the blond, blue-eyed man that has always been depicted by church fathers. Most artists have portrayed images of Jesus as a tall, lanky, blond-haired and blue-eyed man. This is not what Jesus looked like.

If Jesus is God, the Bible forbids images be made of him in the heavens or here on earth. Therefore, every person who walks around with a crucifix that has the image of a man on it is committing the worst form of idol worship.

Was Jesus born from a virgin as the Bible tells you? Let us investigate the facts. Jesus had an older twin brother by the name Thomas. Thomas was well known by many, especially in the east, as Thomas the Apostle. Jesus had another younger brother, James, who was known as James the Just.

Does this mean that the scriptures are a lie or that they could be untrue? Not necessarily all the scripture; when we have a look at the oldest scriptures available which says God found Mary pure as a virgin, it does not mean that she was physically pure as a virgin.

Look at another story from the Bible where God lowers the sheet from heaven for Peter to slaughter and eat it. Peter refused and said unto God that the Jews do not eat such impure animals. God's answer to Peter was, "Who I find pure, who will find it impure." The new translations rather have it as "what" in place of "whom."

Therefore, God found Mary pure as a virgin, according to the old scriptures. She was not a physical virgin as the church leaders have made her out to be. The old scriptures never mentioned it in the same way as the more modern versions say, that no man entered Mary. This insert only appeared about six hundred years ago. The wonder and mysticism was created by having parts added such as this example.

Let us move further and see other bothersome points.

Jesus who is the Redeemer and Savior, to save us from what?

In the time of Jesus, he saved and redeemed the Jewish people from the laws of the Jewish religion that befell his followers. Even today, the Jewish religion is described as immensely strict, and their laws that appear in the Torah are almost impossible to live by and cannot possibly be from God of unconditional love.

The salvation that the Bible speaks of is not something that awaits you in another life, as the churches want to make you believe. It is something that you must experience in this life.

Salvation is liberation from ignorance or illusion for you to be blessed or in bliss and to be content, this promotes soul satisfaction. These are not things that wait for you in another life after you have died. It is at this very hour at this very day that you should be living your life and attaining soul satisfaction; it is even described in the Bible. The four canonical books in the Bible that tells the story of Jesus are very vague regarding numerous aspects concerning many important points relating to Jesus. In chapter 13, we will look at the scriptures of Matthew, Mark, Luke, and John.

Concerning Jesus the Lord, let us have a look at a few old myths that are attached and that are now suddenly considered to be holy.

The Sabbath, the day of the Lord, the overruling Christian religions accept the Sabbath to be on Sunday, the day of worship and the day that you attend church. When you pray, do you end off your prayer with the word "Amen"? Your church fathers tell you that it means let it be so. I do not know out of which language they derived that explanation from, but in Greek, "Amen" means "so shall it be"; this is a command. Prayer means an earnest request or wish; your asking is now ended off with a command. Or is there something else behind Amen that your church fathers have failed to reveal to you?

Year for year, the birth of Jesus is celebrated on December 25; what a holy day. Nowadays, it is celebrated as a family day, a day to reconcile with each other. The Christian religion has changed from what they originally promoted.

In ancient Egypt, a nativity story is related and recorded on walls at the Temple of Amon at Luxor, built by Amenhotep III (1411-1375 BC): First, the ibis-headed god

99

Thoth (this is a Greek word; the Egyptian word is Dwhuty). In this story, Thoth was the Egyptian equivalent of the Hebrew Gabriel. He hails the Virgin Queen, Isis, and informs her that she is to bear a son. Next, she is visited by Kneph (spirit) and becomes mysteriously impregnated when the ankh is held to her mouth. Later, the child is born. The god is given gifts and adored by gods and men. The wall painting shows three human figures, kneeling and offering gifts. Other ancient Egyptian stories complete the nativity story: Horus (Jesus) and his virginal mother, Mari (Mary or Isis) accompanied by Seb (Joseph), his foster father and protector, are forced to flee to the marshes of Egypt to escape from the evil serpent Herrut (Herod). Can you see any resemblance to your Christian nativity story?

Let us look at the three views of Christian belief with regard to the Sabbath, the use of Amen at the end of prayer and the birth of Jesus. Not one of these views originated solely from Christianity; these are predominantly Egyptian views that come from their Ra culture.

Ra, the sun god, his name is Amen-Ra. In the old Ra scriptures, it is stated that which you ask for in his name he will provide, Amen! Every time you pray, you confirm that in the name of the sun or do you give your Lord a command when you ask him something as it is described in Greek? Let us look at the next aspect; the Sabbath, which is the day of the Lord and the day on which you worship. This day is named after the sun god Ra, and the Egyptian priests named it the Sabbath, which is Sunday, and no one was allowed to work on this day.

This brings us to the other aspect mentioned earlier, the holy Christmas, the birth of Jesus on December 25. There are many Christians who are aware that December 25 was not the date of his birth, but they still celebrate this day and go to church. Whose birthday is it then? Let us again go to the old Egyptian religion of Amen-Ra.

It is winter during December in Egypt. Winter is associated with death because all plants are perceived to die during this time. On December 21, the sun reaches the lowest point south; this is the longest night and the shortest day in the Northern Hemisphere. A strange event occurs; the sun lies on the equinox cross and remains in that position for three days. The old Egyptian Ra priest proclaimed to the people that the sun had symbolically died on the cross for three days. On December 25, the sun turns and begins moving northward which is referred to as the birth of the sun god, Amen-Ra, who gives his life to the world. Everything grows, and new life appears. The old Egyptian priests held a great feast on December 25 because it was the birth of their mediator. Later in Christianity, the Christmas tree made its appearance and Santa Claus started playing a vital part in Christmas tradition. Only until relatively recently has this day become holy. Who made this day holy? Definitely not God; it is your church fathers that made this day holy. They have unfortunately lied to you.

This is a reasonably large plagiarism phenomenon by Christendom which comes from an old mythical religion.

THE HOLIEST LIE EVER

Who or what is it that you actually worship when you practice worship on the Sabbath, say Amen, and celebrate December 25?

Let us have a look at the life of Jesus and compare his life with other saviors who lived before him. All of these saviors that we will be talking about all shared some of the following traits: were either born in a stable, cave, or in horrible circumstances; their births were announced by the presence of a star; their parents had to flea because the earth's rulers wanted to murder the child; they taught a priest or priests at the age of twelve at a temple or sacred building; they announced and promoted their religion or beliefs at the age of thirty, performed miracles and raised the dead; they were either crucified or stoned at the age of thirty-three; they were resurrected and went to the heavens or to their father to prepare a place for their holy people and they would return to fetch their holy people on a later unknown date.

Before we go on, it is interesting that Jesus is seen as God or as having the same substance as God. According to the Bible, it takes God six days to create heaven, earth, and everything on and in it. However, it takes Jesus more than two thousand years to prepare a place for 144 thousand sealed souls that will inherit the kingdom of God.

A Brief Summary of Jesus:

Jesus Christ

- Born of the Virgin Mary on December 25 in Bethlehem
- Birth was announced by a star in the east
- Three kings or magi followed the star to locate and adorn the New Savior
- Was a teacher at the age of twelve
- Was baptized at the age of thirty
- Had twelve disciples
- Traveled around with his disciples performing miracles, such as healing the sick, walking on water, and raising the dead
- was known as
  - The King of Kings
  - The Son of God
  - The Light of the World
  - The Alpha and Omega
  - The Lamb of God
  - The Lion of Judah
- After being betrayed by Judas and sold for thirty pieces of silver, he was crucified.
- Placed in a tomb for three days and then resurrected.
- The birth sequence (three kings following bright star in the east) is because the three stars are called "the three kings" lined up with the

star Sirius, and on December 24 point at the place on the horizon where the sun will rise. (The three kings, Sirius, and the sunrise are collinear on December 25.)

- The Virgin Mary (or Myrra or Maya) represents Virgo, which is also known as Virgo the Virgin, and is represented by a modified letter M.
- Virgo is also known as the "house of bread," which represents harvest in the fall.
- Bethlehem literally translated means "house of bread."
- Right after the winter solstice, the sun appears to stand still in the same spot for three days before beginning to head north again.

<u>The Old Testament Joseph was a prototype for Jesus:</u>

Joseph (Old Testament)	Jesus (New Testament)
Immaculate Birth	Miracle Birth
Twelve brothers	Twelve disciples
Sold for twenty pieces of silver	Sold for thirty pieces of silver
"Judah" suggests the sale of Joseph	"Judas" suggests the sale of Jesus
Began work at the age of thirty	Began his work at the age of thirty

The story of Joseph is considered by many to be a carefully written piece of literary craftsmanship. Though it characterizes the personality of Joseph, it is introduced in Genesis 37:2 as the "history of the family of Jacob." Many religious authorities agree that parts of the story show reliance upon the ancient Egyptian "Tale of Two Brothers," but is written in a characteristic Hebraic fashion; the narrator in Genesis seems to have ignored the mythical and magical motifs in the Egyptian tale, and the main focus of the outcome of the story is placed on its meaning for the whole house of Israel.

Let us get back to the other mediators and saviors. All of these saviors or redeemers proclaimed that they were each the Son of God and were born from a virgin mother.

Here are the names, places, and periods of sixteen saviors who were before the time of Jesus. Seventeen people with similar life patterns and events, each one had a purpose to fulfill on earth, but only the last Savior is recognized and crowned as the true Lord by the followers of his religion. The other saviors are considered false, and other religious leaders alleged that they were from the devil. Others contend that their stories are fabricated or fictitious.

These saviors are listed in terms of most resemblance in comparison with Jesus.

Name	Also Known As or Identified With	Area Most Popular	Time Period Most Popular
Krishna	Vishnu	India	1200 BC
Hindu Sakia	-	India	600 BC
Tammuz	Dumuzi in Akkadian	Assyria and Mesopotamia	1160 BC
Wittoba	-	Telingonesic	552 BC
Iao	Jao and Yahweh	Nepal and Greece	622 BC
Hesus	Esus	Celtic	834 BC
Quexalcote	Quetzalcoatl	Mexico	587 BC
Quirinus	Romulus	Rome	506 BC
Prometheus (Aeschylus)	-	Greece	547 BC
Thulis	Zulis and Zhule	Egypt	1700 BC
Indra	Sakra	Tibet, India, and Syria	725 BC
Dionysus	Bacchus	Greece and Rome	600 BC
Atys	Attis	Phrygia and Rome	1170 BC
Crite	-	Chaldea	1200 BC
Bali	Baal, Mahabali, Maveli, and Pious	Orissa, Tibet, Canaan, and India	725 BC
Mithra	Mitra or Mithras	Persia and India	600 BC

Other saviors also claimed to have these characteristics:

- Salivahana of Bermuda
- Odin of the Scandinavians
- Zoroaster of Persia
- Xamolxis of Thrace
- Zoar of the Bonzes
- Adad of Assyria
- Deva Tat and Sammonocadam of Siam

- Thor, son of Odin, of the Gauls
- Cadmus of Greece
- Hil and Feta of the Mandates
- Gentaut of Mexico
- Universal Monarch of the Sibyls
- Ischy of the island of Formosa
- Divine Teacher of Plato

- Alcides of Thebes
- Mikado of the Sintoos
- Beddru of Japan
- Eros and Bremrillah of the Druids

- Holy One of Xaca
- Fohi and Tien of China
- Adonis, son of the virgin Io of Greece
- Ixion of Rome

Be honest with yourself. How is it possible that there were so many people that lived the same or similar lives and you proclaim the latest savior as the true Son of God?

Early church figures such as Tertullian went to great lengths to break these associations, even claiming that the devil caused the similarities to occur. As stated in the second century: "The devil, whose business is to prevent the truth, mimics the exact circumstances of the Divine Sacraments. He baptizes his believers and promises forgiveness of sins . . . he celebrates the oblation of bread and brings in the symbol of the resurrection. Let us therefore acknowledge the craftiness of the devil, who copied certain things of those that be Divine" (Tertullian, AD 155-222 from *The Prescription against Heretics*, Chap XL).

It is just strange that the devil's work happened before the events of Christianity. How is it possible that the devil makes things happen before God does? It makes you wonder who copied whom. It is more likely and logical that man concocted these ideas, events, and images of a significant part of Christianity, as shown in the previously mentioned undeniable facts and those that follow next.

Another interesting aspect was that the title of Son of God was very common among the ancients and at the commencement of the Christian era. Saint Basil says, "Every uncommonly good man was called the Son of God." When Apollonius, standing before Domitian, was asked why men called him a god, his reply was, "Every good man [chrestos] is entitled to that appellation."

What I have shown you thus far is history without the elements of mysticism or fabrication. It is there for you to research and not to accept blindly. How are your church fathers going to interpret the truth? As New Age nonsense? It is their way and style to reject unexplainable things because it is generally labeled as either New Age nonsense or it is considered demonical. Others will influence you by stating that it is the work of the Antichrist. Read your Bible; it says that the Antichrist sits in front of the church in the church benches. I am not busy selling you a viewpoint; these are facts, and they are true. How can you allow yourself to be blinded simply because you are afraid? It is most probably because you are afraid and concerned about what people would think or say about you. Why do you not have the courage then to get out of your comfort zone and search for the truth? At the end of the day, your soul is your responsibility and nobody else's responsibility.

Perhaps your parents and grandparent were Christians, but they were also lied to. You have the opportunity to investigate what the truth really is and which are only myths, rituals, traditions, habits, and symbolism because these aspects cannot make you holy.

The ancient story of a messiah, mediator, or savior has remained unchanged throughout the ages. The eternal God that finds favor with an immortal virgin impregnates her, and a child is born that is half god and half man. Or as a seasoned Christian would explain that the child is man but God. How great is God to you in your mind that you could compare the creator with a human being?

Have a look at what the churches and religion are busy doing to you. As mentioned previously in earlier chapters, they hold up a ridicules concept or idea of heaven in front of you that they state has roads of gold and magnificent homes. They go even further and promise that those who are humble of heart will become priests and kings. You will also rest in the lap of Father Abraham. These empty promises are only used to manipulate people psychologically. It happens to work so effectively that most people accept it blindly while only very few have noticed the many contradictions and discrepancies.

How would I benefit from misleading you? I have no hidden agenda, and I do not have any desire or belief in starting any form of religious organization either. As I have mentioned to you on numerous occasions throughout the book, you alone know yourself, and therefore you should take the time to investigate all these aspects that are mentioned and discussed. The truth is out there; you just need to have the will and desire to find the truth. I am not trying to convince anyone, and I do not intend for people to follow me. Keep in mind that it is better to either remain ignorant of any truth or to rather find the truth and do something about it than to know the truth and do nothing. Do not see it as a lecture; I am merely giving you facts and history so that you are able to understand and see for yourself.

In the Infancy Gospel of the New Testament, it tells of the holy family that had to flee into Egypt to escape the persecution of King Herod, the Antipas. King Herod the Great was an Arab and not a Jew. Herod was a puppet king who had been placed in this position by the Romans in the year 63 BC. We are told nothing as to what the holy family did in Egypt and nothing after the return of Jesus from Egypt. The next time we hear of Jesus is when he is in the temple at Passover for his bar mitzvah. Jesus most likely was a student at the Egyptian mystery schools during his time in Egypt because there are many sacred rites and rituals used by Jesus that are identical and similar to those of Egypt.

Let us have a look at a brief overview of Horus and then go through the similarities between Horus and that of Jesus from the Bible. We will also have a look at biblical scriptures regarding Jesus and also compare these with some of his predecessors. Pay attention to the similarities and decide for yourself.

Brief Summary of Horus:

- The twelve constellations represented places of travel for god's sun.
- The sun god of Egypt of around 3000 BC
- His life is a series of allegorical myths involving the sun's movement in the sky.
- Horus represents light, and his enemy, "Set," represents darkness or night.
- Born on December 25
- Born of a virgin
- Three kings followed a star in the east to find Horus's birthplace.
- Began to teach at the age of twelve
- Baptized at the age of thirty
- Traveled about with twelve disciples
- Horus and his disciples performed miracles, such as healing the sick and walking on water.
- Horus was known by these names:
  - "The truth"
  - "The light"
  - "God's anointed sun"
  - "The good shepherd"
  - "The lamb of god"
- After being betrayed, Horus was crucified, buried for three days, and then he was resurrected.

Comparison between Horus and Jesus:

1. Horus, the son of Osiris, the eternal father of the underworld, born from the virgin Isis = Jesus the Son of God, born from the Virgin Mary.
2. Horus, born in Annu, the place of bread = Jesus, born in Bethlehem, the house of bread.
3. Horus, the good shepherd with the crook upon his shoulders = Jesus, the Good Shepherd with the lamb upon his shoulder.
4. Horus, baptized with water by Anup = Jesus, baptized with water by John.
5. Anup, the baptizer, was the cousin of Horus = John the Baptist was the cousin of Jesus.
6. The seven on board the boat with Horus = The seven fishermen on board the boat with Jesus.
7. Horus as the Lamb = Jesus as the Lamb.

8. Horus as the Lion = Jesus as the Lion.
9. Horus, the black child = Jesus, the black child.
10. Horus identified with the tat or cross = Jesus identified with the cross.
11. Horus at twelve years of age was a teacher = Jesus at twelve years of age was a teacher.
12. Horus baptized at thirty = Jesus baptized at thirty.
13. Horus the Krust = Jesus the Christ.
14. Horus the manifesting son of (God) Osiris = Jesus the manifesting Son of God.
15. Horus and Set the same but are opposites = Jesus and Satan the same but are opposites.
16. Horus the sower and Set the destroyer in the harvesting = Jesus the sower of the good seed and Satan the sower of weeds.
17. Horus led off by Set to the summit of Mount Hetep = Jesus led off by Satan to a very high mountain.
18. Set and Horus contending on the mount = Jesus and Satan contending on the mount.
19. The star as the announcer of the child Horus = The star in the east that indicated the birthplace of Jesus.
20. Horus the chosen one = Jesus the chosen one.
21. Horus gives the life eternal = Jesus gives the eternal life.
22. Horus came to fulfill the prophecy = Jesus came to fulfill the prophecy.
23. Horus as Iu-em-Hetep, the child teacher in the temple = The child Jesus as teacher in the temple.
24. Horus came through water, blood, and spirit = Jesus came through water, blood, and spirit.
25. Horus of two horizons = Jesus of two lands.
26. Horus walked on water = Jesus walked on water.
27. Children of Horus = Children of Jesus.
28. Horus went inside the mountain at sundown to speak to his father = Jesus went inside the mountain at sundown to speak to his Father.
29. Horus ascended from the mountain = Jesus ascended from the mountain.
30. Twelve followers of Horus as Har-Khutti = Twelve followers of Jesus as the twelve disciples.
31. Tat-Aan made the secrets of Horus's mysteries known = John made the secrets of Jesus's mysteries known.
32. Anup and Aan were the two witnesses of Horus = Two Johns were the witnesses of Jesus.
33. Horus as the morning sun = Jesus as the morning sun.
34. Horus who gives the morning star (sun) to his followers = Jesus who gives the morning star (sun) to his followers.
35. The trinity of Atum the Father, Horus the Son, and Ra the Holy Spirit = The trinity of the Father, Son, and Holy Spirit.
36. The Paradise of the Pole Star—Am-Khemen = The Holy City lighted by one luminary, which is neither the sun nor the moon: the Pole Star.

37. Horus the avenger = Jesus who brings the sword.
38. Horus as Iu-em-Hetep, who comes with peace = Jesus the bringer of peace.
39. Horus the afflicted one = Jesus the afflicted one.
40. The Har-Seshu or servants of Horus = The servants of Jesus Christ.

These are only a few comparisons that are mentioned from the lives of Horus and Jesus.

These are all aspects of Egyptian ideas long predating Christianity and Judaism:

- Baptism
- Afterlife
- Final Judgment
- Virgin Birth
- Death and Resurrection

- Crucifixion
- The Ark of the Covenant
- Circumcision
- Saviors
- Holy Communion

- Great Flood
- Easter
- Christmas
- Passover

Let us have a look at a few similarities between the lives and scriptures of the Buddha Gautama and Jesus.

1. Buddha is born from the virgin Maya, impregnated by an angel. Without carnal intercourse. = Jesus is born from the Virgin Mary, impregnated by an angel. Without carnal intercourse.
2. The becoming of flesh of the Buddha is noted as the impregnation of the virgin Maya through a wonderful power that is called the Holy Spirit. = The becoming of flesh of Jesus is noted as the impregnation of the virgin Mary through a wonderful power that is called the Holy Spirit.
3. Buddha willed himself into becoming flesh in the body of the virgin Maya, and she accepted him in her belly; her belly glowed like a clear transparent crystal; Buddha appeared as beautiful as a flower = Jesus willed himself into becoming flesh in the body of the virgin Mary, and she accepted him in her belly; her belly glowed like a clear transparent crystal; Jesus appeared as beautiful as a flower.
4. The birth of Buddha was announced in the heavens by an astrological star that appeared on the horizon, the Messianic star. = The birth of Jesus was announced in the heavens by an astrological star, "his star," that appeared on the horizon.
5. According to tradition, Buddha was born on December 25 = According to tradition, Jesus was born on December 25.

6. Buddha was visited by wise men, and they accepted him as the Holy Savior, and he was surely called the God of All Gods before the end of that day. = Jesus was visited by wise men, and they accepted him as the Holy Savior, and he was surely called the God of All Gods before the end of that day.

7. When Buddha was an infant, just born, he spoke to his mother and said: "I am the greatest among men." = When Jesus was an infant in his cradle, he spoke to his mother and said: "I am Jesus, the son of God."

8. Buddha was baptized with water; the spirit of God was present; the Holy Spirit recognized him as the one sent through the virgin Maya. = Jesus was baptized with water by John in the Jordan River; the spirit of God was present; the Holy Spirit recognized him as the one sent through the Virgin Mary.

9. Through prayer in the name of the Buddha, his followers expect the reward of paradise. = Through prayer in the name of the Jesus, his followers expect the reward of paradise.

10. Buddha ascended in flesh to the highest heavens when his work on earth was fulfilled. = Jesus ascended in flesh to the highest heavens when his work on earth was fulfilled.

11. Buddha is the Alpha and the Omega, the beginning and the end, the eternal. = Jesus is the Alpha and the Omega, the beginning and the end, the eternal.

12. Buddha will return to the world again at a later stage for his followers. = Jesus will return to the world again at a later stage for his followers.

These are a few comparisons between the lives of the Buddha and Jesus. There are numerous ancient sources that parallel the teachings of Jesus, especially eastern traditions. Jesus integrated sacred rituals and symbology from various traditions including parallel teachings totally outside the Jewish religion. Jesus did not quote the sources of his teachings because it was not customary for him to do so. Most of the famous parables of Jesus come from the teachings and sayings of the Buddha Gautama.

The essence of the teachings of the Buddha Gautama is that all of mankind are related to one another; that charity should be extended to all, even to one's enemies; that good work should not to be done openly but rather done in secret; that the dangers of riches are to be avoided; that mankind should love truth and hate the lie; that mankind should strive for the highest purity in thought, word, and deed, since the higher things are pure. Does is not sound like the teachings of Jesus?

List of teachings and sayings of Jesus and the Buddha:

1. Buddha: "Consider others as yourself." (Dhammapada 10:1)

   Jesus: "And as ye would that men should do to you, do ye also to them likewise." (Luke 6:31) King James Version 1611

2. Buddha: "If anyone should give you a blow with his hand, with a stick, or with a knife, you should abandon any desires and utter no evil words." (Majjhima Nikaya 21:6)

   Jesus: "And unto him that smiteth thee on the one cheek offer the other . . ." (Luke 6:29) King James Version 1611

3. Buddha: "Hatreds do not ever cease in this world by hating, but by love: this is an eternal truth. Overcome anger by love, overcome evil by good . . . Overcome the miser by giving, overcome the liar by truth." (Dhammapada 1.5 and 17.3)

   Jesus: "But I say unto you which hear, love your enemies, do good to them which hate you, bless them that curse you, and pray for them which despitefully use you. And unto him that smiteth thee on the one cheek offer the other; and him that taketh away thy cloak forbid not to take thy coat also." (Luke 6:27-30) King James Version 1611

4. Buddha: "If you do not tend one another, then who is there to tend to you? Whoever would tend me, he should tend the sick." (Vinaya, Mahavagga 8:26:3)

   Jesus: "Then shall he answer them, saying, Verily I say unto you, Inasmuch as ye did it not to me of the least of these, ye did it not to me." (Matthew 25:45) King James Version 1611

5. Buddha: "Abandoning the taking of life, the ascetic Gautama dwells refraining from taking life, without stick or sword." (Digha Nikaya 1:1:8)

   Jesus: "Then said Jesus unto him, Put up again thy sword into his place: for all they that take the sword shall perish with the sword." (Matthew 26:52) King James Version 1611

6. Buddha: "Just as a mother would protect her only child at the risk of her own life, even so, cultivate a boundless heart towards all beings. Let your thoughts of boundless love pervade the whole world." (Sutta Nipata 149-150)

Jesus: "This is my commandment, that ye love one another, as I have loved you. Greater love hath no man than this, that a man lay down his life for his friends." (John 15:12-13) King James Version 1611

7. Buddha: "The body of the Buddha is born of love, patience, gentleness and truth." (Vimalakirtinirdesha Sutra 2)

   Jesus: "Grace and truth came by Jesus Christ." (John 1:17) King James Version 1611

8. Buddha: "The faults of others are easier to see than one's own; the faults of others are easily seen, for they are sifted like chaff, but one's own faults are hard to see. This is like the cheat who hides his dice and shows the dice of his opponent, calling attention to the other's shortcomings, continually thinking of accusing him." (Undanavarga 27:1)

   Jesus: "And why beholdest thou the mote that is in thy brother's eye, but perceives not the beam that is in thine eye? Either how canst thou say to thy brother, Brother, let me pull out the mote that is in thine eye, when thou thyself beholdest not the beam that is in thine own eye?" (Luke 6:41-42) King James Version 1611

9. Buddha: "Giving is the noble expression of the benevolence of the mighty. Even dust, given in childish innocence, is a good gift. No gift that is given in good faith to a worthy recipient can be called small; it affects us so great." (Jatakamala 3:23)

   Jesus: "And he looked up, and saw the rich men casting their gifts into the treasury. And he saw also a certain poor widow casting in thither two mites. And he said, Of a truth I say unto you, that this poor widow hath cast in more than they all." (Luke 21:1-4) King James Version 1611

10. Buddha: "Those who have sufficient faith in me, sufficient love for me, are all headed for heaven or beyond." (Majjhima Nikaya 22:47)

    Jesus: "And whosoever liveth and believeth in me shall never die." (John 11:26) King James Version 1611

11. Buddha: "During the six years that the Bodhisattva practiced austerities, the demon followed behind him step by step, seeking an opportunity to harm him. But he found no opportunity whatsoever and went away discouraged and discontent." (Lalitavistara Sutra 18)

    Jesus: "And when the devil had ended all the temptation, he departed from him for a season." (Luke 4:13) King James Version 1611

12. Buddha: "Anyone who enters into meditation on compassion can see Brahma with his own eyes, talk to him face to face and consult with him." (Digha Nikaya 19:43)

    Jesus: "Blessed are the pure in heart, for they will see God." (Matthew 5:8) King James Version 1611

13. Buddha: "Let us live most happily, possessing nothing; let us feed on joy, like the radiant gods." (Dhammapada 15:4)

    Jesus: "Blessed be ye poor: for yours is the kingdom of God." (Luke 6:20) King James Version 1611

14. Buddha: "As a man with eyes who carries a lamp sees all objects, so too with one who has heard the Moral Law. He will become perfectly wise." (Udanavarga 22:4)

    Jesus: "The light of the body is the eye: therefore when thine eye is single, thy whole body also is full of light; but when thine eye is evil, thy body also is full of darkness. Take heed therefore, that the light which is in thee be not darkness." (Luke 11:34-36) King James Version 1611

There are many more teachings that are similar; I have only mentioned a few. There is so strong a resemblance between the characters and teachings of Jesus and of Buddha that it cannot have been purely accidental. It is important to draw attention to the fact that there is Buddhist influence in the Christian canonical Gospels. This gives credible evidence that Jesus was a student at many mystery schools of the ancient masters during the gaps of the life of Jesus that are evident in the canonical Gospels. Since more than a hundred years, Buddhist influence in the Christian Gospels has been known and acknowledged by scholars from both sides. There is noted that there are over a hundred parallels between the Buddha and Jesus.

More examples can be given of other saviors that are similar to Jesus. There are claimed similarities noted between Krishna and Jesus.

Krishna is one of the most widely revered and most popular of all Indian divinities, worshipped as the eighth incarnation (avatar) of the Hindu god Vishnu and also as a supreme god in his own right.

Similarities between Krishna and Jesus:

1. Krishna's presence on earth and his death were to atone for the sins of man. = Jesus's presence on earth and his death were to atone for the sins of man.

2. Krishna was crucified to appease God. = Jesus was crucified to appease God.
3. Krishna was worshipped by his disciples. = Jesus was worshipped by his disciples.
4. Krishna has often been depicted in drawings with a divine halo over his head. = Jesus has often been depicted in drawings with a divine halo over his head.
5. Krishna has often been depicted in drawings as having a "sacred heart." = Jesus has often been depicted in drawings as having a "sacred heart."
6. Krishna—the cross became a religious symbol and icon after his death. = Jesus—the cross became a religious symbol and icon after his death.
7. Krishna preformed miracles, including healing of the sick, curing lepers, restoring sight/sound/speech, raising the dead, and casting out demons. = Jesus preformed miracles, including healing of the sick, curing lepers, restoring sight/sound/speech, raising the dead, and casting out demons.
8. Krishna—a book which claimed to be divinely inspired, the Bhagavad Gita, told of his coming and his miraculous works. = Jesus—a prophecy which claimed to be divinely inspired told of his coming and his miraculous works.
9. Krishna was born of a virgin, and the mother and child were visited by shepherds. = Jesus was born of a virgin, and the mother and child were visited by shepherds.
10. Krishna spent a period of reflection in a desert. = Jesus spent a period of reflection in a desert.
11. Krishna was baptized in a river. = Jesus was baptized in a river.
12. Krishna once miraculously enabled his hungry followers to catch many nets full of fish. = Jesus once miraculously enabled his hungry followers to catch many nets full of fish.
13. Krishna taught by parable and sermon. = Jesus taught by parable and sermon.
14. Krishna—his mother was named Maia. = Jesus—his mother was named Mary.
15. Krishna was said to be born on the equivalent of December 25. = Jesus was said to be born on the equivalent of December 25.
16. Krishna had an earthly adoptive father. = Jesus had an earthly adoptive father.
17. Krishna proclaimed to his followers, "I am the Resurrection." = Jesus proclaimed to his followers, "I am the Resurrection."
18. Krishna had a last supper with his disciples before being crucified. = Jesus had a last supper with his disciples before being crucified.
19. Krishna was crucified between two thieves. = Jesus was crucified between a thief and a murderer.
20. Krishna was crucified at the age of thirty-three. = Jesus was crucified at the age of thirty-three.
21. Krishna rose from the dead three days after being buried. = Jesus rose from the dead three days after being buried.

22. Krishna physically ascended into heaven. = Jesus physically ascended into heaven.
23. Krishna taught "Seek and ye shall find." = Jesus taught "Seek and ye shall find."
24. Krishna spoke of "the blind leading the blind." = Jesus spoke of "the blind leading the blind."
25. Krishna regarded carnal and earthly pleasures as evil. = Jesus regarded carnal and earthly pleasures as evil.
26. Krishna taught "faith can move mountains." = Jesus taught "faith can move mountains."
27. Krishna taught his followers to love their enemies. = Jesus taught his followers to love their enemies.
28. Krishna prophesied his return to Earth, which he referred to as the "second coming." = Jesus prophesied his return to Earth, which he referred to as the "second coming."
29. Krishna taught "It is better to give than receive." = Jesus taught "It is better to give than receive."
30. Krishna is depicted and worshipped as a small child. = Jesus is depicted and worshipped as a small child.
31. Krishna is light, and his opposite is Putana, which is darkness. = Jesus is light, and his opposite is Satan, which is darkness.
32. Krishna was called a god and the son of God. = Jesus was called a god and the Son of God.
33. Krishna was the Savior and referred to as the second person of the Trinity. = Jesus was the Savior and referred to as the second person of the Trinity.
34. Krishna was called "the lion of the tribe of Saki." = Jesus was called "the lion of the tribe of Judah."
35. Krishna referred to himself as having existed before his birth on earth. = Jesus referred to himself as having existed before his birth on earth.
36. Krishna is without sin. = Jesus is without sin.
37. Krishna born human and divine. = Jesus born human and divine.
38. Krishna was criticized for associating with sinners. = Jesus was criticized for associating with sinners.
39. Krishna descended into hell and was resurrected. Many people witnessed his ascension into heaven. = Jesus descended into hell and was resurrected. Many people witnessed his ascension into heaven.
40. Krishna is considered to be omniscient, omnipotent, and omnipresent. = Jesus is considered to be considered omniscient, omnipotent, and omnipresent.

In Hindu, the Lord Krishna says "I am the letter A. I am the beginning and the end." While in the Christian book of revelation, Jesus the Christ says, "I am the Alpha and the Omega." Both Krishna and Jesus also tell their disciples that he will dwell with them and them in him. Other similarities are noted between Catholic, Buddhist, and Hindu, such as the rosary, celibate clergy, veneration of relics, etc.

The Gospel of John begins with the statement, "in the beginning was the word and the word was with God." The Vedas says, "in the beginning was Brahman who was the word and the word was Brahman." This is a direct quotation that appeared centuries before Jesus was born. Krishna was born, lived, and died at least fourteen centuries before Jesus. Estimates of the birth date of Krishna vary; some stated dates of the birth of Krishna: 1477 BC, 3112 BC, 3600 BC, 5150 BC, and 5771 BC. Below, I provide you with a few sayings of Krishna. See if you can find the similarities.

- Lord Krishna declared himself as the Only God: "Those who are devotees of other gods and who worship them with faith actually worship only me, O son of Kunti, but they do so in a wrong way. I am the only enjoyer and master of all sacrifices. Therefore, those who do not recognize my true transcendental nature fall down" (Bhagavad Gita 9.24).

  Krishna: "Abandon all varieties of religion and just surrender unto Me. I shall deliver you from all sinful reactions. Do not fear." (Bhagavad Gita 18.66) = Jesus: "And whosoever liveth and believeth in me shall never die . . ." (John 11:26) King James Version 1611.

- Lord Krishna declared himself as the Supreme Father: "It should be understood that all species of life, o son of Kunti, are made possible by birth in this material nature, and that I am the seed giving father" (Bhagavad Gita 14.4).

- Lord Krishna declared himself as the Supreme Creator: "Furthermore, O Arjuna, I am the generating seed of all existences. There is no being, moving or unmoving, that can exist without me" (Bhagavad Gita 10.39).

- Lord Krishna declared himself as the Supreme Controller: "I give heat, and I withhold and send forth the rain" (Bhagavad Gita 9.19). "With a single fragment of myself I pervade and support this entire universe" (Bhagavad Gita 10.42).

- Lord Krishna is omnipresent: meaning he is present everywhere. "I am the supersoul, O Arjuna, seated in the hearts of all living entities, I am the beginning, the middle, and the end of all beings" (Bhagavad Gita 10.20).

- Lord Krishna is omnipotent, meaning he is the greatest: "There is no truth beyond Me. Everything rests upon Me, as pearls are strung on a thread" (Bhagavad Gita 7.7).

- Lord Krishna is Omniscient: meaning he knows the past, present, and the future: "O Arjuna, I know everything that has happened in the past, all that is happening in the present, and all things that are yet to come. I also know all living entities" (Bhagavad Gita 7.26). "Many, many births both you and I have passed. I can remember all of them, but you cannot!" (Bhagavad Gita 4.5).

Correspondences between Hinduism and some branches of Christianity: At least some branches of Christianity share the following beliefs with Hinduism.

- Free will.
- Fasting.
- Being born again.
- Salvation requires faith in the Savior.
- God is considered the "Word of Logos."
- A day of judgment.
- A general resurrection.
- The need for repentance for sin.

- A belief in angels and of evil spirits.
- A future reward in heaven or punishment in hell.
- A past war in heaven between good and bad angels.
- A belief that disease and sickness is caused by evil spirits.
- Hinduism and Catholicism share the concept of purgatory.

In light of all the similarities between the religions and their teachings, it is absolutely tragic that the religions that grew up around those teachings became the heart of the division and conflict that exists among them.

Jesus is portrayed as a magnificent being who performed many miracles, but yet there were numerous historians that lived in and around the Mediterranean during or shortly after the life of Jesus that made no mention of him at all. Below is a list of these historians.

Historians that lived in or around the Mediterranean during or shortly after Jesus Christ but who made no mention of him:

- Aulus Persius (60)
- Columella (first cent.)
- Dio Chrysostom (40-112 CE)
- Justus of Tiberius (80 CE)
- Phaedrus (15 BC-50 CE)
- Philo Judeaus (20 BC-50 CE)

- Livy (59 BC-17 CE)
- Marcus Annaeus Lucanus (63 CE)
- Lucius Florus (first, second CE)
- Petronius (d. 66 CE)
- Quintilian (35-100 CE)
- Seneca the Younger (4 BC-65 CE)

- Phlegon (first cent.)
- Pliny the Elder (23-69 CE)
- Plutarch (46-119 CE)
- Pomponius Mela (40 CE)
- Quintus Curtius Rufus (first cent.)
- Silius Italicus (25-101 CE)
- Caecilius Statius (first cent.)
- Theon of Smyrna (70-135 CE)
- Gaius Valerius Flaccus (first cent.)
- Valerius Maximus (20 CE)

Four historians are commonly cited to support the historical Jesus. The first three only mention the word "Christ" and are only a couple of sentences long at best. "Christ" is a title meaning "the anointed one" and is not a name.

The three historians who only mention the word "Christ" are the following:

- Pliny the Younger
- Suetonius
- Tacitus

The fourth historian is Josephus, and this source has been claimed by some scholars to be a forgery for hundreds of years.

Thomas Paine (1737-1809) once said, "The Christian religion is a parody on the worship of the sun, in which they put a man called Christ in the place of the sun, and pay him the adoration originally payed to the sun."

A bit of background on the next character in our discussion: Saint Justin Martyr was a pagan and was reared in a Jewish environment. Justin studied Stoic, Platonic, and other pagan philosophies and became a Christian in 132 at Ephesus, near modern-day Turkey. Soon after the year 135, he wandered from place to place proclaiming his newfound Christian philosophies to convert educated pagans. However, after debating with the cynic Crescens, Justin was denounced to the Roman prefect as subversive and condemned to death. Authentic records of his martyrdom survive. He was declared a saint after his death.

What Justin Martyr (AD 100-165) wrote concerning Jesus:

. . . wrote: "When we say that he, Jesus Christ, our teacher, was produced without sexual union, was crucified and died, and rose again, and ascended into heaven we propound nothing different from what you believe regarding the sons of [the god] Jupiter."

. . . also wrote: "He was born of a virgin. Accept this in common with what you believe of [the god] Perseus. The devils . . . craftily feigned that Minerva was the daughter of Jupiter not by sexual union."

Although he was converted, he maintained many of his own beliefs because they were very much aligned with Christianity in some instances.

Have you ever heard of the Notovich Scrolls? Nicolas Notovich is an important character in the history of studies surrounding the theory of Jesus in India. He was a Russian aristocrat; he became most famous for his book, *The Unknown Life of Jesus Christ* or as earlier titles, *The Life of Saint Issa*, that was published in 1894.

Notovich had set out on his journey in 1878 after the Russian-Turkish War to explore Eastern Europe, the Middle and Far East. Notovich reached India, Nepal, Tibet, and little Tibet called Ladakh in the year 1887. The main reason for his journey was to study the culture and customs of the people and the geography of the landscape. Notovich heard various times during his journey that there were scrolls in existence that spoke of Jesus. Notovich arrived at the monastery of Hemis in Kashmere; it was hidden in a remote valley.

Notovich claimed that he was shown a copy at Hemis of an ancient Buddhist manuscript which described the life of Jesus from his teenage years up to the age of twenty-six and that this section of his life he lived in Tibet. These scrolls contained accounts of what Jesus did during those years. After a period of time and an accident, when the Lamas felt that they could trust Notovich they eventually showed these scrolls to Notovich. The lamas told Notovich that the scrolls were translations and not the original which was in the ancient language of Pali, the language of the Buddha Gautama. Notovich had the sections relevant to Jesus translated into French. The account of the life of Jesus in those scrolls was allegedly written down three to four years after the crucifixion of Jesus and was based on the testimony of merchants from India who had witnessed the event personally.

There was immense drama once the book was published in 1894; the attacks began almost immediately. There were many people who were against the publication of the book such as the Archbishop of Kiev who was a cardinal in Rome, and another unnamed cardinal tried to persuade Notovich for him to buy his notes. Another individual, Cardinal Rotelli from Paris, also tried to discourage the publication of the book and even said that the church had suffered enough hostile criticism and what this would do to Christianity if it became public knowledge. Why would these types of reactions and arguments have occurred if the documents were regarded as false?

People such as Prof. Max Muller, Prof. J. Archibald Douglas, Edgar J. Goodspeed, and others tried to discredit Notovich and the scrolls. You must understand, India has experience many terrifying attacks from Westerners in the past, and they have grown weary toward any strangers that would want to deal with them in any way. As a nation and people, they have lost thousands of lives and numerous irreplaceable writings and relics. However, there were individuals who claimed to have either heard of or seen the scrolls themselves.

Name of Visitor	Year	Reported
Nicholas Notovich	1887	Saw the scrolls at Hemis; translated sections pertaining to Jesus and published the book in French and English. There is proof of his visit in the Mission Diary at Leh.
Henrietta Merrick	1921	Visited and later wrote in her book, *In the World's Attic*. In Leh is the legend of Jesus who is called Issa, and the Monastery at Hemis holds precious documents fifteen hundred years old which tell of the days that he passed in Leh where he was joyously received and where he preached.
Swami Trigunatitananda	1895	Visited and confirmed Notovich had spent time there. This is cited in *Swami Trigunatitananda: His Life and Works* by Marie L. Burke
Swami Abhedananda	1922	Lamas confirmed that Notovich was at the monastery and was shown the scrolls. Swami Abhedananda saw the scrolls and made his own translation of the scrolls and published his book. He however omits the sections where Jesus criticized Buddhism and Hinduism.
Nicholas Roerich, wife, and son	1925	He published his testimony that the belief that Jesus had lived in India was widespread everywhere he went.
Madam Elizabeth Caspari and Mrs. Clarens Gasque	1939	Saw document: Shown by Lama Nawong Zangpo and took a photograph of the librarian displaying the scrolls.
William O. Douglas	1951	Visited Hemis. He testified that the people there believed that Jesus had visited Hemis and that the legends described his stay in Tibet in detail.
Edward F. Novak	1970s	A monk at Hemis, where he was a guest at, told him: "There are manuscripts that describe the journey and life of Jesus in India."
Dr. R. Ravetch	1975	Oral reference: informed by friend who was a local physician in Leh that there were scrolls at the monastery which stated that Jesus had been there.
U. Eichstadt	1974	Saw document

The real question to ask regarding the Notovich scrolls is, if Jesus was God or part of God, why did he need to study in Egypt, India, and Tibet? Is God not all knowing and infinitely wise? He would have been born with the knowledge and wisdom if he was truly the same or part of God. Jesus was not the Christ or Son of God; Jesus was a man that had a few main motives, one was that he planned to establish his own ministry and exert influence by using the teachings and knowledge he had acquired from the ancient masters and mystery schools of the East and Egypt. Jesus even planned his own death precisely when he intended it to be. Nobody who knew Jesus in a personal capacity ever wrote anything in any of the canonical Gospels of the New Testament.

As if this is not already enough proof that something is amiss concerning the wonderful Jesus story, millions of people align their lives strictly according to the instruction of the church, and they bring it forward as the will of God and state that everything can be recovered in the name of Jesus. All other religions are slandered and tainted with damnation. Again, I will mention the statement that appears in your Bible, "God is the God of all life." First, look within yourself, at your own faults, before you are tempted to judge others. Look at the plagiarism and fraud that comes from your own religion. Just because you were born into Christianity and became a Christian does not automatically mean that it is the truth.

The crucifix idealizes only suffering and death. It is disturbing that the central focus of Christianity is the image of a blood-soaked suffering savior. The religious organizations try and make you believe that suffering is desirable by God. No wonder mankind has little to no empathy for human beings that are suffering, be it from poverty, oppression, war, or disease; it does not matter how people suffer that should evoke empathy but instead just the fact that another human being is suffering should be cause enough.

The cross is more ancient than Christianity. The original meaning of a bare cross was that it symbolized the harmony between the vertical and the horizontal of the eternal with the limits of possible experience or knowledge of the realms beyond with the realms here and now on this plane where we reside. The crucifix is traditionally Christian, but it was only decreed by Emperor Justinian in AD 692 to replace the symbolical bare cross. Why do you want to praise an instrument of torture and death? This goes against what and who God is. It comes down to the true agendas of these religious institutions; they provide only distorted images and ideas of both God and Jesus to suit their own needs and motives.

The Christians preach of a God of love, but there is more hate, ostracism, and division among their own people, and there are more than ten thousand registered Christian churches and religions in the world. The rest of the global populations that do not proclaim that Jesus is the Christ are all labeled as either the Antichrist or as Gentiles; these people are completely shoved out of their life circle. The word "holy" has become ridiculous and absurd. On an almost daily basis, the church fathers come out with the most preposterous teachings in order to capture their members' or followers' attention.

The mystical drivel concerning unexplainable events that allegedly occurred with this or that individual is usually good enough reason to start a new movement. These days, there are innumerable so-called prophets who go around proclaiming that they are the kings of the kingdom of God, and therefore the priests are there to ensure that there is financial funding for them and their endeavors. These so-called prophets predict that there is a shifting process occurring within the community and congregation. This is usually a successful method to cause people to believe that God is busy calling the priests and kings together. These groups of people are actually living off the funds from the church. Only the church and religious fathers are enriched from the psychological manipulation that is imprinted in the minds of fearful mankind.

The Savior of Christendom has become a watered-down story over the years. The story of Jesus is infested with mythical fabrication and the statements, such as the wisdom of God is foolish by man, and that the wisdom of man is foolish by God. That is truly the most disgusting excuse that any reasonable person could conceive, but this statement tends to work time and again with those who are deeply religious.

These so-called church fathers who claim that they know their Savior and have a personal relationship with him cannot even tell you what happened to Jesus between the ages of twelve and thirty. They do not even know for certain when exactly this important person was born. These people who say that they were placed there to guide your life to heaven do not even know where exactly heaven is. They do not even know where Jesus is at the moment.

Ask these religious leaders what Jesus looked like. The most common answer is "that it is only through belief that they know Jesus." What is so personal about that? They claim to love Jesus. Is that not comical when you think that nobody even knows who he truly was or what he did for more than half his life, but they claim to know and love him?

It is so easy to suddenly turn around and say that it is only in spirit that they love Jesus. Let me show you what is written in your own Bible; it says, as it is in nature so too in spirit, but the Bible goes further and says that nature comes first and then the spirit. In other words, it means that I cannot love something in spirit if I do not know it in flesh.

God is a god of order. Does nature not show you this? Look at the order that God has in the universe; everything is in harmony that he placed there. Why would God, who is a logical god, be like nature, but when it concerns his children, he speaks to them in an illogical language full of riddles and symbolism? Which parent would speak to their child in foreign languages, riddles, and symbolism?

Awaken from your deep slumber and investigate these aspects; it even stands in your Bible, or is it just another case of pressing the snooze button and sleeping a little longer?

I listen to the other preachers who warn their members or followers against listening to anything that does not appear in their Bibles because it is perceived by them to be demonical. Who and what are now the misleaders? Show me the church fathers that go on their own to investigate these aspects without being biased. Or show me any that take the time to simply search through these aspects. I do not speak of theologians that scratch through their books and are instructed by their mediator to state what he wants them to say.

The Inquisition, which originated from Roman Catholicism, was a papal judicial institution; they used torture to obtain answers to their questions, and that is where the old expression "They put you to the question" comes from. People who were heretics or people suspected of being heretics were tortured, jailed, or burned alive at the stake. These barbarities in the name of religion only ceased a few hundred years ago. The strange part of this is that these brutalities were only performed in those parts of the world that were at the forefront of civilization, but even though these barbaric practices have ceased to exist, the inquisitorial mind remains to enforce their version of the so-called truth upon the minds of millions of people. This mind-set is part of a ruthless and cruel doctrine which coerces adherence, obedience, and subservience to its beliefs by using force, threats, and mental conditioning.

Unfortunately, there are other forms and tactics that are used to suppress the views of others that are different from conventional Christian beliefs. These religious structures will try and attack you in the lowest possible way, in a very crafty and sly manner in order to discredit you because then they need not bother about your condemning proof or arguments. By discrediting you, they need not evaluate or discuss any evidence you might have because the truth is these organizations are too petrified and reluctant to face any evidence that would go against what they have been telling you through the centuries. Why do they have this attitude? They behave in this fashion because they would be made out to be liars and betrayers among their members and followers of their faith.

Since when has the Son of God been claimed to be more than his Father? Why would God say that he is sending his Son if he himself was actually coming? Some claim that the appearance of God is too terrifying to look at. This stands in your Bible were the followers of Moses says this. Therefore, God had to send his Son, and then most obviously the Father and the Son cannot possibly be the same entity. Why do you worship the Son and not the Father? I thought that the Father and the Son were one of substance? As Jesus said in John 14:10: "Anyone who has seen me has seen the Father."

Let us stop here for a moment and have a look at the God or gods that you worship as a Christian. We are revisiting the Trinity God doctrine briefly. It is already evidently proven that this Trinity God is nothing more than the three gods that the Hebrews lived under during the time that they were roaming around.

God the Eternal Father is the strength and wisdom in our midst, the same as Isis the eternal mother who is the strength and wisdom in the people's midst. God states that he *Is*, just as Isis was known as *Is*.

The second God who is Jesus, the Son of God who is the Son of Righteousness. The second god that the Hebrews learned about was the sun god Amen-Ra, who was the son of God and the Son of Righteousness. Let me show you how close the conventional Christian religion is in comparison with the religion of Amen-Ra.

Ra, who is the sun god, his name is Amen. What you ask for in his name, he will provide for you. When you pray, how do you validate your prayer? Is it not with the word "Amen"? The Egyptians named a day after their Lord, and the day became the holy Sabbath, which means "the day of the Lord." Nobody was allowed to work on this day because it was only a day for worship. On which day do you go to church to worship? Who is using the word "Sabbath" now? I thought the Ra religion was a Gentile religion. Why does a Christian religion hold on to Gentile traditions? The entire world's Christians celebrate the birth of Jesus on December 25. That is actually the birth of the sun, the day the sun gives its life to the world in the northern section of Egypt.

The third god, the Holy Spirit—who is the comforter and known as the comforter, the one that will stay by mankind—is actually the god El, the comforter god who is associated with the planet Saturn. Saturday was named after the god El, which is also the reason why Saturday is still the Sabbath for the Jews. The Holy Spirit is synonymously associated with the white dove, as is Saturn associated with the white dove. The concept of the Holy Spirit originates from older mythical religions. The Buddha Gautama from the east was seen as the Holy Spirit in about 1200 BC. Today, Christians reject the eastern religions and conceive it as confusing.

It would seem as though the Christian religion originated from morsels of wisdom from all the so-called mythical and confusing traditions.

The old mythical religions used heavenly bodies as gods and later attached human characteristics to these gods. Here comes the Christian religion; they humanize the sun and make it their god. Now everyone is sitting back and waiting for a tall, blond, and blue-eyed man who will come one day on a cloud to fetch them and take them away to a better place than the earth.

What does your religious leader tell you is the actual meaning of sin? The usual answer is that it is a transgression against God. This is not at all what sin means. How could the Almighty God be utterly offended by something that his creatures have done by accident? Sin is more like missing the mark; in other words, if you try and you do not succeed with what you were trying to do, then you should try and get closer to the point or mark next time you try the same thing. You should constantly try to better yourself in understanding, actions, deeds, and wisdom.

Look at what your Bible is teaching you.

In your Bible, it says that the kingdom of God is by mankind. What is the difference between the kingdom of God and heaven? It is actually the same place. According to the Bible, God himself proclaims that who would search for him high in the heavens or over the vast oceans. God is only spirit, according to the Bible, and he resides by mankind. Therefore, if the kingdom of God and God himself is by mankind, his Son is by his Father in his kingdom, then where is the Son? But Jesus ascended, right? No, read your Bible correctly. It stands emphatically in the Bible that Jesus ascended to the height of a man. That is very high, is it not?

How ridiculous does your religion look now? That is what blind faith does to you.

I know that you will state that many great wonders have been done in the name of Jesus. Yes, you are correct. Just as many people have raised the dead in other names besides that of Jesus. Many sicknesses have been cured and not always done in the name of Jesus. Do not be like a sheep that walks among the masses of other sheep. Your own Bible says that you will find very few that chase after the truth, but that you will find many on the path to ruin. It is actually really funny that the Christians boast about their total right over the world. They are the most powerful organization ever. This Jesus of theirs has become a mighty giant.

You will only find God in truth. Is that not what your Bible teaches you?

The most important figure in the entire Christian religion and nobody even knows when he was born. There is also so much confusion about the crucifixion, funeral, and resurrection. Read the four canonical Gospels in the New Testament in your Bible, and you will see that there is not even any agreement or correspondence on these three points.

This brings us to the point where we move over to the next chapter concerning the four canonical Gospels of Mark, Luke, Matthew, and John.

Chapter 12

Matthew, Mark, Luke, and John

In order to provide the best understanding of what these four Gospels of inconsistent portraits of the same man are, a short introduction to the Gospels and their suspected history is important. These four canonical books of the Bible describe the life, wonders, crucifixion, funeral, and resurrection of Jesus. These Gospels are only four of many similar documents that were circulating in the first four centuries after the birth of Jesus.

As mentioned in earlier chapters, contrary to common belief, there was never a onetime truly universal decision as to which books should be included in the Bible. It took over a century of the spread, growth, and popularity of numerous writings before anyone even bothered to start picking and choosing, and then it was largely a cumulative, individual, and happenstance event, guided by chance, prejudice, and bias until priests and academics began pronouncing what was authoritative and holy, and even they were not unanimous. If it was inspired by God as many proclaim, would God make his children argue and differ on what his word is and was? Every church had its favored books, and since there was nothing like a clearly defined orthodoxy until the fourth century, there were in fact many simultaneous literary traditions. The illusion that it was otherwise is created by the fact that the church that came out on top simply preserved texts in its favor that suited its agenda and destroyed or let vanish opposing documents. Therefore, what we call "orthodoxy" simply means "the church that won." Can you still not see that everything you have been told by your church leaders has been a lie, that there were hidden agendas and human greed that formed the foundations of Christendom?

The Gospels cannot be accurately dated, and the real authors are not known. It is based on speculation that Mark was the first, written about AD 60, Matthew second, written between AD 70 to 80, Luke (and Acts) third, was written about AD 80, and John last, written between AD 90 to 100. Scholars have provided numerous other dates for each work, and the total range of possible dates runs from the 50s to the early 100s, but all these dates are hypothetical. It is strongly suggested that the Gospels did not exist before AD 58 simply because none of the Epistle writers or Paul mentions or quotes them. Mark is presumed earlier than the others because Mark is written in a simpler style, and it appears that Matthew and Luke borrowed material from Mark, material that was predominantly his own invention.

The Emperor Constantine began what was to become a century's long effort to eliminate any book in the original Bible that was considered unacceptable to the new doctrine of the church. At that time, it is believed there were up to six hundred books, which comprised the work we now know as the Bible. Through a series of decisions made by the early church leadership, all but eighty of those books, known as the King James Translation of 1611, were purged from the work, with a further reduction by the Protestant Reformation bringing the number to sixty-six in the "Authorized" King James Bible. The editing and formation of the Bible came from members of the early Christian Church. Since the fathers of the church possessed the scriptoria and determined what would appear in the Bible, there occurred plenty of opportunity and motive to change, modify, or create texts that might bolster the position of the church or the members of the church themselves. Constantine set a really bad president after the council of Nicaea in 325 when he yielded to the request of the victorious theological camp and banished those bishops into exile who would not think and vote correctly about the main item on their agenda, that is who and what Jesus really was. Unfortunately, the church has always retained this character flaw.

The traditional church has portrayed the authors of the canonical Gospels as the apostles Mark, Luke, Matthew, and John, but scholars know from critical textural research that there is no evidence that the Gospel authors could have served as the apostles described in the Gospel stories. Yet even today, we hear priests and ministers describing these authors as the actual disciples of Christ. Many Bibles still continue to label the stories as "the Gospel according to Saint Matthew," "Saint Mark," "Saint Luke," and "Saint John." No apostle would have announced his own sainthood before the church established sainthood.

The Gospel of Mark describes the first written Gospel of the New Testament, and although Mark strangely appears after the Matthew Gospel, the Gospel of Mark was written at least a generation before that of Matthew. Mark had not heard of Jesus nor served as his personal follower. Whoever wrote the Gospel simply accepted the mythology of Jesus without question and wrote a crude and simple account of the popular story at the time. Careful reading of the three Gospels of Matthew, Mark, and Luke will reveal that Mark served as the common element between Matthew and Luke and provided itself as the main source of information for both of them. Of Mark's verses, approximately six hundred appear in Matthew and three hundred in Luke. The author of Matthew had obviously gotten his information from Mark's Gospel and used them for his own needs. He fashioned his narrative to appeal to Jewish tradition and scripture. Matthew's Gospel improved the grammar of Mark's Gospel and placed more emphasis on the miracles and mysticism of Jesus. The author of Luke's Gospel admits that he is an interpreter of earlier material and not an eyewitness in Luke 1:1-4. The Gospel of John disagrees with events described in Mark, Matthew, and Luke.

You need to understand that the stories written and described in the canonical Gospels cannot serve as examples of eyewitness accounts since they are products from the minds of the unknown authors and not from the characters mentioned in the scriptures. The Gospels describe narrative stories, written predominantly in the third person. However, people who portray themselves as eyewitnesses will write in the first person and not in the third person. Moreover, many of the passages attributed to Jesus could only have come from the invention of its authors; for example, many of the statements of Jesus claim to have come from him while he was allegedly alone. If so, who heard him? It becomes even stranger when the evangelists report about what Jesus thought. To whom did Jesus confide his thoughts? Clearly, the Gospels use techniques that fictional writers use. In any case, the Gospels can only serve, at best, as hearsay; but they are most likely fictional, mythological, or falsified stories.

The most interesting point about the Gospels is not where they agree but where they differ or even conflict.

Numerous scholars have argued that the four Gospels of the New Testament were Gentile or Western documents in terms of their formulation, style, and orientation, with the exception of the Gospel of Mark; they were written after the fall of Jerusalem in the year AD 70. After this event, the Jews were no longer a strong united force. It has been suggested that the Gospels were formulated to subtly shift the blame of the death of Jesus away from the Romans and onto the Jews because they did not want to perturb the powers that were or the people that they were preaching to in Rome, Greece, and the western parts of the empire. Anti-Semitism was caused predominantly due to Christian hostility to Judaism because they blamed the Jews for the crucifixion of Jesus.

You must remember that every Christian states that each word in the Bible is inspired by God. That everything written in the Bible is true and that nobody may add or remove from that which is written in the Bible.

Look at nature; everything is exactly in place as it is meant to be. That is how God works, in perfection.

The original authors of these four books seem to be in a degree of disagreement because they tend to contradict one another. Not one of these books was written during the time that these events occurred.

Let us have a look at the crucifixion as Matthew, Mark, Luke, and John describes it.

Each of the authors describes the event as they perceived it to have happened. They did not personally witness the event. Let us use an example; if a person is called to the stand in a court as a witness and the individual states that they have heard about this or that, the court will dismiss the witness. How could someone be a reliable witness if they themselves did not personally witness the event? It is just as relevant when it concerns the crucifixion of Jesus.

Are you trying to tell me that none of the witnesses at the crucifixion of Jesus was literate? Nobody thought of writing it down and documenting the event? There is hardly any evidence that proves that Jesus was crucified, except for the Bible. The writers of these four Gospels have serious contradictions when compared to one another, so how could any reasonable person believe that it is the truth? Only those people who believe blindly would believe that all four different stories are true.

This is what Matthew describes about the crucifixion. Matthew speaks of a man from Cyrene by the name of Simon that was called to carry Jesus's cross to a place called Golgotha. In Hebrew, Golgotha means the place of a skull. They gave Jesus vinegar mixed with gall to drink, but he would not drink it.

After they had crucified Jesus, they parted his garments among the lot and sat to keep watch over Jesus. Set above his head, the accusation was written, "This is Jesus the King of the Jews." Two thieves were crucified with Jesus, one on the left and one on the right.

Matthew describes how the people that passed by mocked him, "If thou be the Son of God, come down from the cross." The chief priests, elders, and scribes also mocked Jesus. Matthew even describes how the two crucified thieves mocked Jesus as well. These sound like very accurate witnesses, just a pity that Matthew was not there in that time period. We go further and see how Matthew describes the rest of the crucifixion.

Did you notice how exact Matthew is with the time frames during these events? He writes that from the sixth hour there was darkness over all the land until the ninth hour. At the ninth hour, Jesus cried out with a loud voice saying: "Eli, Eli, lama sabachthani?" That is to say, "My God, my God, why hast thou forsaken me?" Some of the people that were there that heard this said, "This man calleth for Elijah." Jesus calls out with a loud voice, and yet nobody heard what he called out. This is almost an overdramatized story. That is unfortunately all that it is, a story.

As Matthew describes when Jesus blew out his last breath (gave up the ghost) and how everyone feared greatly saying, "Truly this was the Son of God." Matthew describes earthquakes and rocks that tore apart. Suddenly, the greatest proof emerges that the world ever witnessed, proof that it was truly the Son of God, but nobody attempted to record the event when it occurred.

This is how the testimony of Matthew looks like.

Let us look at how Mark describes the same events.

Mark also speaks of the man from Cyrene but places more emphasis on this man Simon. He describes that Simon came out of the country, and that he is the father of Alexander and Rufus. Mark asserts that Simon was somewhat forced to carry the cross of Jesus. They brought Jesus to Golgotha, the place of a skull. They gave him wine and myrrh to drink, but he did not drink it.

After Jesus was crucified, they distributed his clothes among the lot and gave to those as to who should have received it.

Mark is just as precise as Matthew with his time frames. Look at how precisely he knew that it was at the third hour when Jesus was crucified. Here is however a bit confused when it comes to the superscription of his accusation above his head. Mark does not see what Matthew saw. Mark only sees the words "The King of the Jews."

Mark also describes the two thieves and the exact words the passersby used when they mocked Jesus. However, Mark mentions that the scripture was fulfilled, that of the prophecy. He also writes about the time period between the sixth and ninth hour of where there was darkness over the whole land until the ninth hour. Mark also writes about the loud call of Jesus; however, his spelling of Eli is different.

Mark writes, "And at the ninth hour, Jesus cried with a loud voice, saying, "Eloi, Eloi, Lama Sabachthani." Mark noted that after the loud call from Jesus, one ran to fill a sponge with vinegar and placed it on a reed and gave it to Jesus. Mark also noted that Jesus gave another loud cry, blew out his last breath (gave up the ghost), and that the veil of the temple split in two. The centurion (head man) stated that "Truly, this man was the Son of God." Mark does not mention anything about earthquakes or rocks tearing apart.

Even though the description of Matthew and Mark are similar on merits, there are substantial differences.

The reason for the similarities in their stories originates from the prophecy that appeared in the scriptures; this was available to the public. It is a pity that the church fathers never placed this scripture about the prophecy in the Bible.

When we look at the descriptions from the book of Luke, we are given a completely different story. It is evident that these books were written as a theatrical piece, as if the writer actually attended and witnessed the events. The dramatization by Luke about them approaching Golgotha is more intense when compared to Matthew and Mark's descriptions. In the scriptures of Luke, Jesus has a talk with a woman. Luke mentions the destination as Calvary and not Golgotha. Here, Luke mentions how Jesus asks God to forgive the people because they do not know what they are doing. Should the people not have done this? If they did not, then the prophecy would not have been fulfilled.

Luke states that the superscription written above the head of Jesus was written in Greek, Latin, and Hebrew, "This is the King of the Jews." Luke writes that they crucified Jesus and the malefactors (felons) in Calvary, one on the right and the other on the left of Jesus. He does not mention that they were thieves. The one felon mocks Jesus, and the other answered and rebuked him, and said, "Dost thou not fear God?" This man asked Jesus to remember him when he goes to his kingdom. Jesus promises the man, "Verily I say unto thee, today shalt thou be with me in paradise." Even Luke describes the time frame between the sixth and ninth hour as there was darkness over the entire earth, and that the temple veil was torn. Luke never mentions earthquakes or rocks tearing apart. Luke also never mentions the loud call of Jesus as described by Matthew and Mark, "God, my God, why hast thou forsaken me?" Luke describes the event in more of a gracious fashion. The only loud call of Jesus as noted by Luke is, "Father, into thy hands I commend my spirit . . ." When Jesus had said this, he blew out his last breath (gave up the ghost). Luke states the events differently when compared to the first two Gospels, especially concerning the centurion (head man) that said, "Certainly this was a righteous man." The rest of the crowd beat their chests and left.

We already have three versions of the same events, and not one is identical to the other.

This brings us to John, the fourth witness, or should I rather say, we have four evangelistic canonical books with different descriptions. No wonder there are more than ten thousand registered Christian religions in the world.

Let us have a look at what John describes concerning the crucifixion.

In this story that John describes, Jesus carries his own cross to Golgotha, the place of a skull. Jesus is crucified along with two others on either side of him. In this story, Pilate wrote the title above Jesus's head himself which was written in Hebrew, Greek, and Latin; it said, "Jesus of Nazareth the King of the Jews." According to John, the chief priests of the Jews went to Pilate and requested that he changed the writing to what Jesus said, "I am King of the Jews" instead of the King of the Jews. Pilate answered, "What I have written I have written." Another contradiction with the other three Gospels is where the clothes of Jesus are divided into four parts, and that each soldier receives a part. There is also mention of Jesus's vest without seam that was not to be torn. We hear again about the prophecy that must be fulfilled.

In this story, Jesus has a conversation with his mother and a disciple. Also in this story, Jesus says that he is thirsty, and the guard filled a sponge with vinegar, placed it on a reed, and gave it to Jesus to drink. Now here is another difference; Jesus received the vinegar and said that the prophecy has been fulfilled ("It is now finished."), bowed his head, and blew out his last breath (gave up the ghost).

Here is mention the other two men that were crucified, that their legs were broken before the Sabbath but Jesus who represents the Lamb of God; his legs are not broken because he is already dead. One of the soldiers pierced the side of Jesus and only blood and water came out. John writes about the soldier, "And he that saw it bare, and his record is true; and he knoweth that he said true, that ye might believe." A pity that this soldier's name was never recorded so that research could be done.

We have four different versions of the crucifixion that only the Christians make out to be the truth. Unfortunately, it is purely based on their blind faith. Religion is one thing, but when facts are missing, it is difficult to believe, especially when there is so much proof of plagiarism and fabrication that has come forward over the years concerning the scriptures and the Bible. Religion that hosts so many myths, traditions, rituals, and symbolism cannot possibly hold any substance.

If you think the crucifixion was bewildering, then have a look at the different descriptions of the burial of Jesus, which is supposed to be the funeral of one person. It becomes more hilarious when you think of all the literate people who are becoming severely misled because they are clinging to their blind faith.

The burial as described by Matthew:

When it was evening, a rich man of Arimathea named Joseph, who was also a disciple of Jesus went to Pilate and begged for the body of Jesus. Pilate commanded that the body be delivered.

Is it not strange that even though Jesus only had twelve disciples, every second person who had something to do with Jesus was regarded as a disciple? Let us go further; Joseph took the body, wrapped it in clean linen, and laid the body of Jesus in a new tomb that he had made; he then rolled a large stone in front of the opening and left. Mary Magdalene and the other Mary sat over against the tomb.

The next day that followed, the day after the preparation, the chief priests and Pharisees went to Pilate and said that they remember what the deceiver had said when he was alive, that he would rise again after three days. They asked if the tomb could be made secure until the third day because his disciples might come to fetch his body and tell the people that he has risen from the dead. They said, "The last error shall be worse than the first." Therefore, Pilate said that they should place a guard to watch the tomb and seal the tomb as best they can. They went to seal the stone at the entrance of the tomb and set a guard to watch the tomb.

Let us have a look at how Mark describes the burial of Jesus.

When it was evening, it was the preparation, the day before the Sabbath. Joseph of Arimathea, an honorable counselor who also awaited the kingdom of God, came and went to Pilate to ask for the body of Jesus. Pilate was not sure if Jesus was dead already and asked the centurion if he was dead and when he found out that Jesus was dead, he gave the body to Joseph. Joseph bought fine linen, took

Jesus down from the cross, wrapped him in the linen, laid him down in a tomb that was hollowed out of the rock, and rolled a stone in front of the opening. Mary Magdalene and Mary the mother of Jesus observed where Jesus was laid.

So far it is obvious that the writers of the Gospels Matthew and Mark overheard these stories and described the events in their own version; these Gospels are not inspired by God. There are noticeable differences between how the Gospels describe the events.

The story that Luke describes is similar but also has differences such as the preparation of the herbs and the rest on the Sabbath as the commandment required.

Let us have a look at how John describes the burial of Jesus.

John confirms that Joseph of Arimathea was a disciple of Jesus but states that he was secretly a disciple of Jesus. Joseph asked Pilate for the body of Jesus and took the body away with him. Here is another change in the story; in the Bible, it says "And there came also Nicodemus, which at the first came to Jesus by night, and brought a mixture of myrrh and aloes, about a hundred pound weight." They, Joseph and Nicodemus, took the body and wound it in linen clothes with the spices in the same manner as the Jews bury. Some versions of the Bible say that the body of Jesus was laid in a garden where he was crucified inside a tomb while others say that his body was laid in a grave in a garden where he was crucified. There they laid Jesus because of the Jews preparation day was nearly at hand.

It does not amaze me that there has never been peace among the people of the Christian religion; there is not even any agreement or correspondence. Even the writers of the Bible have their own views with regard to the Christian religion. What do you expect, with fraud, corruption, and lies, there cannot be any peace and harmony. Just as the mythology of Zeus and Hercules are now portrayed as cartoons, so too is Christendom perceived by many that come to the realization that this religion has created a distorted image of God and how the church preys on the weak for money.

The Christian religion is scattered with myths, symbolisms, and rituals. This religion that represents itself as the true way to God is nothing more than a merging of myths from old traditions and ancient religions.

How can the Bible be considered holy when it is filled with lies and fraud? They talk about the will of God, but whose will is it actually? It comes from old decrepit men that used mankind's fear of hell and the eternal damnation. Christendom is yet just another religion that has created a perception of God from myths. This religion has an advantage for those that are in the driver's seat; this entails total control over people's feelings and the monetary power that is paired with it.

I do not come with stories of Jesus that was married, and I am not trying to start a new religion. If that was my motive, then I would have brought forward wonderful and alluring stories to attract people.

I know that what is written in this book will face immense resistance from many church fathers, along with persecution and scorn. You must keep in mind that I am scratching at a financially powerful organization that derives its main income from the churches.

Further, I will tell you that you are too slack-spined to do what God has commanded you to do. You call yourself an enlightened religion, but you are dangerously gambling with souls and that only for a favorable profit.

Pay attention to history and what is going on around you; more people have been hideously mutilated, brutally tortured, and gruesomely murdered in the name of religion than in the history of mankind when compared to natural disasters that have taken lives.

You speak of a god of love, but right through the entire Bible, I read of how God orders his people to go to war—to kill, overthrow, and conquer. Have a look at the Jews today; as far as history shows you, they have always been fighting one or another nation. They are shown to be the chosen people of God, but they do not even proclaim that Jesus was or is the Christ. With such a warped religion, there will never be peace on this earth. For two thousand years, the Christian religion has become a giant monster, like a dragon with numerous heads that causes devastation and destruction as far as it spreads and grows.

The following chapter discusses the Holy Spirit.

Chapter 13

The Holy Spirit

Be honest with yourself, you do not actually know who or what the Holy Spirit is. Mankind has created an image of the Holy Spirit which comes from ancient traditions and religions; a mystical wonder has replaced the true meaning of who and what the Holy Spirit is. The majority of Christians believe that the Holy Spirit is part of the Trinity, of which God is the Father, and includes the Son and the Holy Spirit. The concept of the Holy Spirit comes from the early periods of society when people believed that the elements and natural disasters were believed to be gods or a god, or the active manifestation of a god.

According to Christian religion, the Holy Spirit was left behind to act as the comforter. However, the Holy Spirit or Holy Ghost has undergone extreme metamorphoses throughout the Christian religion, as will be demonstrated by the texts from the Bible. The characteristics of this imaginary being are described within the Gospels; you are able to observe that the Holy Ghost has so many variations that it cannot maintain a definite character.

- Matthew 1:18, "She was found with child of the Holy Ghost." *King James Version 1611* The Holy Ghost becomes an agent in the procreation of another God; that is, this third member of the Trinity aids the first member (the Father) in the creation or generation of the second member of the Trinity—the Word, or Savior, or Son of God.

- Mark 1:8, "I indeed have baptized you with water: but he shall baptize you with the Holy Ghost." *King James Version 1611* The Holy Ghost is also considered to be a medium or element for baptism.

- Luke 2:26, "And it was revealed unto him by the Holy Ghost, that he should not see death, before he had seen the Lord's Christ." *King James Version 1611* The Holy Ghost is also the author of a revelation.

- Luke 4:1, "And Jesus being full of the Holy Ghost returned from Jordan . . ." *King James Version 1611* The Holy Ghost is a God within a God "Jesus being full of the Holy Ghost" and many other texts, we are taught people are filled with the Holy Ghost. How can Jesus be God or the essence of God if he is able to receive the God the Holy Spirit? If they are one in the same essence, it would not be necessary for the Holy Ghost to fill him because he would have all the qualities as that of the Holy Spirit.

- John 1:32, "John bare record, saying, I saw the Spirit descending from heaven like a dove, and it abode upon him." *King James Version 1611* The Holy Ghost is presented as an inanimate, senseless object only descending like a dove would descend. The Holy Ghost is of the neutral gender "it [the Holy Ghost] abode upon him."

- John 14:26, "the Comforter, which is the Holy Spirit, whom the Father will send in my name . . ." *King James Version 1611* The Holy Ghost is spoken of as a person or as a personal assistant to Jesus.

- John 20:22, "He breathed on them, and saith unto them, Receive ye the Holy Ghost." *King James Version 1611* The Holy Ghost has taken the form of breath, as I legitimately infer by it being breathed into the mouth of the recipient similar to various ancient Oriental customs.

- Acts 2:2, "And suddenly there came a sound from heaven as of a rushing wind . . . and began to speak with other tongues . . ." *King James Version 1611* The Holy Ghost is being described as "rushing wind that also enables them to speak in other tongues."

- Acts 2:3, "And there appeared unto them cloven tongues like as fire, and it sat upon each of them." *King James Version 1611* We learn the Holy Ghost sat upon each of them with reference to fire "cloven tongues of fire."

- Acts 8:17, "Then laid they their hands on them, and they received the Holy Ghost." *King James Version 1611* The Holy Ghost is imparted by the "laying on of hands." According to the Bible, the laying of hands can only be done by a living apostle.

- Acts 10:38, "How God anointed Jesus of Nazareth with the Holy Ghost and the power . . ." *King James Version 1611* The Holy Ghost, we infer, from its mode of application, is an ointment but yet also a power.

These are only a few examples of the ever-changing descriptions presented in the scriptures regarding the Holy Ghost. The Christian Holy Ghost undergoes a continual metamorphoses when it is presented on different occasions as a dove, a spirit, a rational entity or being, a god, the wind or a wind, an ointment, the breath or a breath, an inanimate object, cloven tongues of fire, one that reveals the will of God or is regarded as a divine messenger, a medium or element for baptism, an intelligent speaking being, a sexless being, a being possessing a body, an unconscious substance, a god dwelling within a god, and the author or agent of the incarnation of the second God in the Trinity, Jesus Christ. Many of these concepts of the Holy Spirit were derived from mythological sources.

<u>Baptism by or into the Holy Ghost Accompanied with Fire,</u> as in Matthew 3:11: "He shall baptize you with the Holy Ghost, and with fire . . ." *King James Version 1611* Paul mentions the necessity of being purified by fire, 1 Corinthians 3:15: "He himself will be saved, yet so as by fire." This is an ancient rite of purification which was practiced by some of the old mythological traditions, such as the pagans and Tuscans, or Etrurians, which were baptized with fire, wind, and water. Baptism into the first member of the Trinity (the Father) was with fire; baptism into the second member of the Trinity (the word) was with water; while baptism into the third member of the Trinity (the Holy Ghost or Holy Spirit) consisted of a spiritual or symbolical application of wind to represent the ghost or spirit. Some have stated that, in some of these ancient countries, a child was taken to the priest to be named; the priest named the child (christened) by the sacred fire; afterward, in another ceremony, the child was sprinkled with holy water from a vessel made from the sacred tree known as the Holme. There were several ways of using fire in the baptismal rite. In some cases, the candidate for immortality ran through blazing streams of fire, and some of the candidates who participated voluntarily in the baptism of fire sacrificed their lives in the operation because of the belief that it was necessary to purify the soul and would enable them to ascend to higher levels in the celestial or spiritual world.

<u>Baptism by the Holy Ghost:</u> This ceremony has ancient origins, such as the traditional American Indians; the priest or spiritual healer was to breathe into the mouth or upon the face of the person seeking purification, understanding, or divine experiences. The priests of the other traditions were believed to impart the Spirit of God through this process. The custom was anciently quite common in Oriental countries and was at a later date borrowed by Jesus and his apostles and integrated into the Christian ceremonies. We find that Jesus not only believed to have used it or sanctioned it but practiced it, as it is stated in the Bible when he met his disciples after his resurrection "he breathed on them, and saith unto them, Receive ye the Holy Ghost" (John 20:22 *King James Version 1611*). Keep in mind that breath, air, wind, spirit, and ghost have been used as synonymous terms throughout the Bible, and that the breathing was supposed to impart spiritual life and the Spirit of God. Baptism will be discussed in depth in chapter 22.

<u>The Holy Ghost Synonymous with the Dove:</u> In ancient Rome, a dove or pigeon was the emblem of the female procreative energy and frequently a legendary spirit. Shammuramat also known as Semiramis in Greek was the Assyrian queen of Shamshi-Adad V that ruled between 824 BC and 811 BC; she is represented with a golden dove on her head; the association of the fish and dove is found at Hierapolis Bambyce, the great Syrian temple. This bears similar resemblance to the dove on the head of Jesus at baptism.

In Saint Paul's Cathedral, at the feast of Whitsuntide also known as the Pentecost, is probably identified with one of the great summer pagan festivals that predated Christianity. The descent of the Holy Ghost was performed by a white dove or pigeon being let loose to fly out of a hole in the midst of the roof of the great isle. This also has ancient pagan and various Oriental religious origins. Whitsunday is a feast of Christianity which commemorates the descent of the Holy Spirit upon the apostles of Jesus, fifty days after his resurrection at Easter and ten days after the Ascension, as described in the New Testament in Acts 2.

In ancient India, a dove was the symbol of the Holy Spirit, or Spirit of God as the dove represents the third member of the Trinity, who is regarded as the regenerative power. This is similar to the Christian idea of "by the washing of regeneration, and renewing of the Holy Ghost . . ." (Titus 3:5 *King James Version 1611*).

<u>The Holy Ghost As Cloven Tongues of Fire:</u> The Buddha, an incarnate god of the Hindus of more than three thousand years ago, is often seen with a tongue of fire. The tradition of the visible expression of the Holy Ghost by fire was widespread among the ancient Buddhists, Celts, and Druids.

There are two variants of speaking in tongues: xenolalia, speaking in a foreign language; and glossolalia, speaking in gibberish, or at least in a tongue that no one understands.

As described in the scriptures, the Holy Ghost or Holy Spirit when visible was always in the form of a fire or a bird and is associated with wisdom, power, and truth. There is an ancient custom among the Hindus, Persians, and Chaldeans of making offerings to the solar fire, which was associated symbolically as the Holy Ghost or Holy Spirit.

So-called holy men of God, like some of the prophets, are considered by their followers to be inspired by the Holy Ghost; read 2 Peter 1:21 and Acts 28:25. The ancient Celts were also moved by the Holy Ghost, and they too claimed that their Salic laws were inspired by the Salo Ghost or Holy Ghost, also referred to as the Wisdom of the Spirit or the Voice of the Spirit. There are numerous similarities between pagan and Christian traditions.

Does the Holy Spirit truly exist, or is it also a myth?

In chapter 10, we saw that the Canaanite god El was their mediator and known as the Comforter. In the Christian religion, this god has become a watered-down story because the true meaning behind the advent of the so-called Holy Spirit as Christians understand it today has been lost. The old church fathers changed scriptures from ancient mythology, created images, and offered empty promises in the minds of mankind that are not true.

People symbolically relate the Holy Spirit to a dove. As we have briefly mentioned earlier, the dove or the descent like a dove is not a new or unique manifestation in tradition or religion. From the old mythological scriptures out of the Egyptian religion, it was a common representation that spirits of gods descended like doves upon people.

In the Greek and Inca traditions and religions, the dove was seen in a metaphorical sense to explain how gently the spirit of truth and wisdom reaches mankind.

In some of the Christian religions, when a member receives the Holy Spirit, they convulse, fall to the ground, and start foaming at the mouth. The preachers scream out the words "Now receive the Holy Spirit!" People become lame, and the services are held by incorporating this mystical ritual so as to make the audiences believe that they have been intoxicated with the so-called holiness. Since when does any form of truth force your body to convulse, fall to the ground, and foam at the mouth? This is absolute nonsense because it is an enacted dramatization and absolute madness. This is the absolute truth and not a perception.

In the Bible, it states that the Holy Spirit will come to you like a soft breeze. People who have the truth are calm and do not jump around like clowns. The truth would not make you scream and go ballistic because God is a god of order, as it is in nature so too in spirit. The concept of what the Holy Spirit is and how it is perceived is a myth. Distance yourself from worldly things that will distract you off of your path, become still within yourself.

When you search for the truth and live it, you will experience peace. That is why it is written in the Bible that you should search for the kingdom of God; when you have found the truth, everything that is in the kingdom and more will be granted to you. The kingdom is the truth that God wants you to live in today. However, unfortunately, many people believe that the easy way is to sit in the church benches; but actually, it is the most difficult path because you will not find the truth there, and therefore, you will not find God there either. You will only find God in the truth. Most people exert no effort to investigate; they predominantly follow the norms and accept that they are being told the truth.

How could it possibly be the truth if there are so many lies, myths, symbolisms, and mysticisms in the religion? Truth does not require any form of mysticism; the truth is straightforward and does not speak in riddles.

The churches exhibit the impression that they have done the research and investigation on your behalf. They go further and lie to your face when they tell you that they have found the truth and will show you how you must live your life, usually according to their ideals and views. What does God command of you?

You are commanded to search and investigate, not your churches. Search for the actual truth and behold it. Live it, and the truth will grow within you. This is what the spirit of truth means, not a bodily shape that descends onto you like a dove and neither something that places its hands on your shoulders to blow into your neck as some want to claim.

The churches create this perception with their members and followers that the Holy Spirit has human characteristics. Where the Bible clearly shows you that the Holy Spirit is nothing more than the spiritual truth that you and I need to find and live in. This spiritual truth is not the stories of ancient characters, but it is the strength in your midst today, the present.

One of the main problems already started many years ago when the church started humanizing energies and powers when gender titles were placed in front of the involved power or energy. You will never be free if you blindly believe and trust.

Look at how many Christians, Muslims, and many others sit in the churches or temples. Honestly, how many people do you know that make it their lifelong task to obtain and search for the naked truth, that do not only try to derive answers from the Bible or listen to what they are told by church leaders? That is why I do not expect you to believe me because I want you to search for the truth and answers for yourself, but open your eyes for the lies and fraud.

This does not mean that you must throw your moral values overboard and suddenly live a sinful and destructive life. In your searches, you will find a lot of wisdom, and the truth is locked within this wisdom because you need to understand before you become; it is a change of consciousness.

The truth is at times painful and difficult to accept, but it is necessary at times to hear these things to wake you from your slumber.

Believe in God and do not move out of the truth. When I talk about truth, I do not mean myths, traditions, habits, symbolism, and mysticism. God is true and orderly through all the years without needing to change every year as many churches try to change regularly. God has never changed; mankind has distorted, altered, and manipulated the perception of God.

Lies are able to wield immense strength, and arrogance has ravished the consciousness of millions of people.

If you doubt the word, as religion teaches you, you are threatened with hell and damnation or you have demons within you. Is this how the spirit of truth looks like? No, it definitely is not.

You will get many church leaders who will take what I have mentioned in this book and attempt to manipulate and distort what I have brought forward. These church leaders will say that the Holy Spirit was either created by God or that the Holy Spirit was inspired by God. Therefore, they will further say that it has only been Christianity that has brought the true meaning of the Holy Spirit to its followers. This is a complete and utter lie. The Holy Spirit does not exist as Christianity has portrayed it; the concept of the Holy Spirit is that it is spiritual truth and not what Christianity tries to make you believe it is.

This brings us to another so-called truth that is proclaimed, the Holy Nation of God; this is dealt with in the following chapter.

Chapter 14

The Israelites: God's Chosen People or Holy Nation

Let us begin this chapter with the truth, as I have done from the start of this book. The truth is not always easy on the ear and irrespective of how ugly the truth seems it is a true reflection of that which truly was.

It is astonishing how everything concerning this nation has suddenly become holy. I will not speak of this nation or refer to them as holy. I believe that by now you have realized that there are too many fabrications that appear throughout the Bible stories. That is why we need to be direct and straightforward.

Who and what is this nation that professes to be the only chosen nation of God? If God is the god of all life, then all life must belong to God. There are no boundaries when it comes to mankind because people are all part of one race, the human race, regardless of color, culture, and creed. For example, take a Jewish baby and allow the child to grow up in an English household and environment without any influence from the Jewish community. The child will not be able to speak Hebrew and will not be familiar with Jewish culture. That is why culture has nothing to do with the matter of holiness. Culture, religion, and tradition cannot make any human being holy or divine.

According to the Bible, it is stated that those people who do not declare that Jesus is the Christ are not born from God and do not belong to God. The Israelites do not believe in Jesus, and they do not acknowledge that Jesus is the Son of God. How can they be holy if according to the Bible, "they are not born from God" because they do not acknowledge Jesus to be the Son of God? Are they considered holy because the Bible says that the Israelites are holy?

Let us go to the beginning and see where this nation originated from.

On the southeast of Greece, there were a cluster of islands that was inhabited by a blend of cultures; this is also where the myth of the city Atlantis comes from, the population that lived on these islands were master builders and artisans in various fields. Egypt also had many dealings with these groups of people. When a volcano erupted on the main island, the island started to sink and disappeared under the ocean, and those who survived the disaster infiltrated into Egypt and went to see the Pharaoh. The reigning Egyptian Pharaoh allowed this nation of displaced people to enter the kingdom under exile and work as paid workers. These events occurred approximately in 3800 BC.

When these people advanced into Egypt, many married and merged with other nations. The Hebrews that arrived in Egypt under exile were a nation without land. They also did not originally have stringent traditional or religious services. The Egyptians were one of the first nations to have a structured religious or traditional service. Originally, the term "Hebrew" had nothing to do with race or ethnic origin. It derived from Habiru, a variant spelling of Ḫapiru (Apiru), a designation of a class of people who made their living by hiring themselves out for various services.

When we look at the history of Egypt, there is ample evidence of a long line of myths that existed in their religion for thousands of years. There were religions that went back more than ten thousand years prior to the arrival of the Hebrews. When we have a look at their religious structures, we see how they used numerous old myths to forge new habits and religious forms, which is similar to how new religions have originated and been formed.

During their time in Egypt, the Hebrews adopted many of the Egyptians habits and myths that they incorporated within their own belief structure. For example, when you think of Noah and the Ark and are able to decipher it, it is actually the "Arcka-Noa or Argha-Noa" from the old Egyptian era. We will discuss Noah's Ark and the Arcka-Noa more in depth in chapter 18. The same is applicable to the story of Moses that derived from the Egyptian mythological story of Mises also known as Missi; the two stories are identical to one another. Mises, placed in a reed basket, found by the daughter of the king and raised in the king's house. There is even the similarity of Mises on the mountain communicating with God as Moses did, and there are many other examples. Moses and Mises more in depth discussed in chapter 15. The Hebrew language itself did not appear until after the Hebrews left Egypt, and then only for religious ceremonial purposes by the priests during the first few years of their existence. In fact, many of the terms and names used in the Hebrew religion came from the Egyptian ceremonial rites.

The stories of Father Abraham and the story of Elijah and Moses appear in the Quran. The Muslim religion views these figures as their prophets. When they call "Azan" or "call to prayer" five times a day, the first prophet that they pray through in the morning is the prophet Abraham. The second prophet is the prophet Elijah; the third prophet is Moses. The fourth prophet is the prophet Jesus, and the last prophet they pray through is the prophet Mohammed. Four of these prophets are Christian and Jewish religious figures. Who is lying trying to lie to whom now? These religions originally sprout from the same sources.

For Muslims, Abraham is a prophet, the "messenger of God" who stands in the line from Noah to Muhammad, to whom Allah gave revelations (Quran 4:163), who "raised the foundations of the House" (Quran 2:127) with his first son, Ismail, a symbol of which is in every mosque. Ibrahim (Abraham) is the first in a genealogy for Muhammad. Islam considers Abraham to be the "first Muslim." To Muslims,

Jesus was merely another prophet in the long line of prophets that Allah has sent to mankind. In Islam, the Quran describes Elijah as a great and righteous prophet of God, and one who powerfully preached against the worship of Baal. According to Islam, all Muslims must have faith in every mentioned prophet and messengers in the Quran, which includes Moses and his brother Aaron.

The main reason why the Jewish nation is referred to or known as the holy or chosen people of God is because Jesus was a Nazarene; he called the Jewish people his nation.

With the sufficient evidence given so far, the Bible and Christianity portray a distorted and mythical version of Jesus. Jesus was not the divine entity that the Bible or Christianity depicts.

If the Jews are the chosen nation of the eternal and living God, then what chance do you and I have to inherit the kingdom of God? According to the Bible, we must be more like Gentile nations.

In chapter 11, when we discussed the saviors and predecessors of Jesus that had the same life patterns and striking similarities, we discussed the two large gaps in the life of Jesus in which the Bible remains silent. It is highly unlikely that Jesus was the chosen one or son of God. The point is that some Jews followed Jesus and crowned him as their Christ. Christ means savior, redeemer, and messiah.

The Hebrews gave the elements human characteristics and used old myths to develop a comprehensive religion over the years. The Bible as we know it is only five hundred years old. Why do the scriptures of the Dead Sea Scrolls not appear in the Bible? There are mysteries and secrets kept from the followers of the faith. Why are the secrets not made known to the people who serve that religion? Even the Vatican has original documents and scriptures that they do not make available to the public. These teachings, scriptures, and ancient books is knowledge that everyone should be entitled to, but it is the religious powers that control what information is allowed to be public knowledge.

Have a look at how the Christian religion has changed the last five hundred years. I thought that God was an unchangeable god, as he was, he still is and so shall he be until the end of time. Humankind changes the way the church services, and teachings are conducted in the churches on a regular basis to suit the times. In order to suit the needs of people, these changes are incorporated. You serve a very willing god, a god that changes according to your requests.

The most probable date for the Exodus is about 1290 BC. If this is true, then the oppressive Pharaoh noted in Exodus (1:2-2:23) was Seti I who reigned in 1318-04, and the Pharaoh during the Exodus was Ramses II who reigned c. 1304-c. 1237. The Hebrews' Exodus from Egypt did not happen as the Bible states; they did not leave at once in a large group. The history books tell the story differently. The Hebrews left Egypt at night in small groups over a period of forty years; they went through the Reed Sea, not the Red Sea, and the Reed Sea was only knee deep.

When the Hebrews were living and traveling through the desert, they raided travelers of all their valuables, i.e., food, water, fabric, jewels, etc. in order to survive. After forty years, when the last groups of Hebrews fled from Egypt, they traveled to Canaan, and that is where they continue to live today.

The stories regarding idol worship during their time in the desert is possible because there was little to no amusement for the people, and the young boys did not have woman available for their desires. These limitations lead to sodomy and prostitution to take place. People tried to develop their own religious beliefs in order to justify their actions and allow such deeds. As in any society, you have extremes; you will always get your stubborn and unmanageable individuals, and then you get those that remain on the same old path and uphold old traditions.

The story that all the Hebrews fled from Egypt is also false. Many stayed behind and adopted the Egyptian culture. Bloodlines prove this as well. The idea that all the Hebrews were not welcome into Egypt after they had fled is a myth. The Jews still maintained trade relations with the Egyptians after these Hebrew groups had left. Jesus and his parents went to reside in Egypt for approximately twelve years. Thereafter, they returned to Bethlehem for a short while, and Jesus went to India and Tibet to study at the mystery schools of the ancient masters until the age of twenty-nine. These are provable facts. Why do your church leaders not tell you these things? If they told you the truth, the church would lose money and struggle to survive. The truth does not suit their agendas.

Israel, the nation that rides on their renown as the chosen people of God, receives protection from each Christian country because they are perceived as the holy nation of God. The nation infected with corruption and hate. They are always involved with some or other war, usually with people that do not agree with them. A nation that shows no love from God and that does not acknowledge Jesus as the Son of God. How could you still refer to them as holy?

This nation states that Moses led them to the Holy Land; there is no evidence that there even was a Moses; the figure of Moses is a myth. Let me show you the wonderful Moses story, and then you can decide for yourself.

Chapter 15

The Moses Story

Moses has had such an immense impact on the religious structure of the world that even the Muslim religion sees this so-called prophet as a man of God.

The story of salvation that comes from the oppression of those whom opposed them.

However, what troubles me is that the Christian and Muslim religions stand opposite one another, like day and night. The Christians proclaim that Abraham, Elijah, and Moses are actually associated with their religion. The Muslims proclaim that these prophets were not Christians but rather the prophets of God or Allah, the name they use when they refer to God.

Let us look at the story and history of Moses and explain a few myths and fabrications with the lies and fraud that is contained within it.

Where does the story of the mythical Moses come from?

First, keep in mind that numerous ancient religions have identical stories as those that appear in the Christian Bible. Many are found in the Bhagavad Gita, Tan-gyur, Kan-gyur, and many more.

The first trace of the Moses story has its origin in Babylon. The story is about a king and prophet of God by the name of Nebu, who was a man with golden hair. Nebo went into the mountain of God, which was the pyramid, and received the Great Law which is known as the Great Law of Hammurabi. Nebu emerges from the mountain of God, the pyramid, with tablets of stone and gives the Great Law to the Babylonian people.

The Egyptians later picked up this story and made it their own. The Egyptian great lawgiver was known as Mises (pronounced as Me-seas), who was a man with golden hair. Like Moses, he had a rod that he worked miracles with, and the rod could turn into a serpent. Mises uses his rod to divide the rivers Orontes and Hydastus, and he even strikes a rock with it to provide water for his thirsty army. Mises went up into the holy mountain, the pyramid, and received the law. He brought the law down on two stone tablets, but when Mises saw that the Egyptians did not respect the divine law, he broke the stones with the great law.

The Hebrews later took the same story during the period when they went to Palestine, when they were worshiping the god El; they came out with the story of Moses. Moses is Mises, and Mises is Nebo. It is all the same story, throughout the thousands of years.

According to the Bible, the father of Moses took a wife in his young years, a daughter of Levi. Moses's father's name was Amram, and his mother's name was Jochebed (whose other children were Aaron and Miriam). One of the measures taken by the Egyptians to restrict the growth of the Hebrews was to order the death of all newborn Hebrew males. According to the Bible, Moses's parents, hid him for three months and then set him afloat on the Nile in a reed basket. The child, found by the Pharaoh's daughter while bathing, was reared in the Egyptian court. It is well known that the pharaoh during the Exodus was Ramses II (c. 1304-c. 1237). Here is the first problem; Ramses II only had a daughter very late in his life. According to the Bible, the Pharaoh's daughter named the child. It surprises me that the name of the Pharaoh's daughter is never mentioned.

The name Moses has many meanings: master, is born, superior, rival, etc. The name Moses is originally derived from the names Moesoek and Moesoep.

From research, there is no evidence or trace that a Pharaoh's daughter lived in the house or court of the Pharaoh with a boy by the name of Moses, not even a single sign of a guard that was murdered by such a boy as Moses.

The Bible of today refers constantly to the Israelites, but they were not known by this name, and the name Israel only emerged much later in history, even after the time of Jesus.

I read in the story of Moses about his plight and the wonderful things that happened to him. Even about the circumcision of the ear to the mouth. There is mention of his wife whose name was Zipporah and his father-in-law's name who was Jethro.

Moses goes back to Egypt and speaks with the Pharaoh. There is no evidence of this encounter in any Egyptian book or manuscript. Not even the ten plagues are mentioned in any Egyptian history or literature. There is no record of the Pharaoh's firstborn son dying, as stated in the tenth plague in the Bible. The firstborn son of Ramses II was known as Atum; he never died in a plague. Atum died on the battlefield at the age of thirty-six.

This brings us to the great Exodus of the Hebrews from Egypt. According to the Egyptian history records of that time period, the rebellious Hebrews left in small groups under the cover of night and went through the Reed Sea that was actually marshland. They joined up with other Hebrew groups in the desert and hunted other groups for survival. This departure from Egypt took place over a period of forty years and not as the Bible states that the Exodus happened at once with a large group of Hebrews.

The manna mentioned in the Bible is actually mushrooms; they are called psilocybin magic mushrooms. Mushrooms sprout in the early hours of the morning when there is dew. The manna or mushrooms, when digested, causes the individual to hallucinate which creates the impression that they are experiencing the divine or God.

If there was ever a Moses that was at the forefront of the Exodus, he definitely did not negotiate their departure with the Pharaoh. The Pharaoh Ramses II did not drown in the Red Sea as described in the Bible. With thorough research, it has been found that not one Pharaoh, king, or high ruler has ever drowned in the history of Egypt. We researched before the time of Ramses II to as far back as Amenhotep I who reigned c.1525-1504. There is no shred of evidence that any Pharaoh drowned, except for the alleged story in the Bible.

We went and looked at the house of Levi to determine who the mother of Moses was. There is no trace or evidence of any son-in-law by the name of Amram marrying one of the daughters of Levi. The story of the Ten Commandments is a story that originates from ancient Egyptian mythology that was performed by Mises, the conqueror and the rescuer. It is remarkable how similar the stories of Moses and Mises are. Mises comes from a time period of about c.1228 before the time of Moses and the Exodus.

Even the story of Mises is suspicious because a very similar story appeared eight hundred years ago in the Orient before the time period of Mises; this mythical individual was known as Nebu, the savior from the Orient.

This is yet another tantalizing and classic story that has been around for ages in mythology. These are tales that are developed and told to reflect the will of the gods, which shows how mercy and redemption are intertwined with each other.

The story of Moses closes off on a more dramatized tone. Moses goes up the mountain of God and never returned; there is not even any sign of a grave found on the mountain. Strangely enough, Moses and Elijah appear separately with Jesus on a mountain at a much later stage.

Elijah ascended as Jesus had with his body to heaven and would return again as it is stated in the Bible; it is believed that Elijah did return. Read Matthew 17. This point will be discussed further in chapter 16.

Therefore, Moses also went to heaven because there was no sign that he had died. To be honest, there is no trace or evidence that there ever was a man known as Moses; he never existed.

There are five books that are believed to be written by Moses; however, there is no proof that it was the same person that led the Hebrews out of Egypt that is believed to have written them. It is unbelievable that all these leaders or men of God appear in secret and that only other leaders see these leaders or men of God. It appears to come forward in an extremely secretive way because only much later these leaders are revealed and proclaimed to the people. This is all about mystical secrecy. People are left with no answers, only unexplained mysteries; however, God states that nothing will be kept a mystery or a secret from his children.

If this is true, that nothing will be withheld from the children of God and that everything will be revealed to them, then it is obvious that the church and those who are in their advice are not children of God. The reason I say this is because everything in the Christian religion is unexplainable and mysterious. Even those things they tell you are illogical and marvelous. I thought that God was a god of logic and order. Does nature not teach you this?

Without breaking down the lovely story of a nation that is saved, we need to acknowledge that the lies, myths, and fraud in the entire Moses story makes it difficult to state that any section of the story is holy.

To proclaim that certain events took place through the will of God, and we know that the story is in actual fact a fable, which would mean that the name of God was used in vain, and that it is blasphemous. It might sound harsh, but it is the truth.

How can you build your religion on myths, lies, fables, symbols, and rituals? Do you also drum to the same drummer with the norms of your religion in the hope that what you are doing will become holy because everyone is doing it. Do you honestly believe that pretty stories based on lies and myths will save you or make you holy? If you just believe and trust, you will be saved! People continue to cling to ancient unproven old myths as the truth. What is religion without actions or deeds, or without trying to be a better person?

The Old Testament of the Bible was originally used by the Orthodox Jews and is known as the Torah. Torah means law. These are the scriptures of their religion, and here come the Christians and state that it is actually their religion; they wrote and added a few books together that formed the New Testament and claimed that it is the will of God. The Muslims accept the Old Testament scriptures but reject the New Testament, even though they accept Jesus as a prophet and believe that he will return one day. When Jesus returns to defeat the devil, the Muslim community will place the body of Jesus in his designated grave next to Mohammed in Mecca.

The Muslims pray through the following prophets: Abraham, Elijah, Moses, Jesus, and Mohammed. Despite this, they hate the Christians, and the Christians in turn hate the Muslims and label them as Gentiles. The Muslims pray to and accept the Christian figures but are judged because they have another prophet who came to them after the time of Jesus.

Christians are quick to assign the differences in their church to differences in culture, but because the culture of the Muslims is different from theirs, they are judged harshly. Are they not also as lost as you who follow the Christian religion? They also pray to Moses who never existed. The story of Moses is a mythical fable designed to give people a sense of strength.

Build your existence on religion, hope, and love. I ask you earnestly, which religion? Why do we still persist with ancient ignorance and myths in the form of religion? What do you hope for? What type of love comes from lies, myths, symbols, and mysticism? These are aspects put in place to keep you and your feelings at bay. These aspects make people more governable and aids in maintaining your subservience to the powers that be so that you do not investigate. They do these things because they know that once people start investigating, their powerful organizations will fall when the truth is revealed because the truth will shake the foundations of Christianity. This is the absolute truth.

Perhaps you know these things or suspect that something is not right; you doubt but are too scared and lazy to stand up for your own soul, and by doing nothing, you go against what God commanded you to do; he commanded you to investigate everything and behold only the good.

How could it be a sin to investigate if it is a command from God? It is your religious leaders who have conditioned your mind to such an extent that you have become too ignorant to see.

Again, I say to you that you look but do not see; you hear but do not listen. Perhaps you would want to sleep a bit longer and keep putting it off until it is far too late.

Do you honestly want to be like Moses? Do you also want to be just a myth?

Let us move on to the next chapter to see more revelations. Let us see who is lying to whom. Then you can read from your own Bible, the book that you may not add to or remove from what stands in it.

Chapter 16

John the Baptist

Let us look at another mythical story that originated from the Egyptian myth of Anup the Baptist, who baptized the son of Osiris with water.

It is remarkable how similar this story is; it has been adapted and modified slightly from the original Egyptian story by the Hebrews that resided in Egypt. Only the names and places have been changed to suit the Jewish religion, and it was later adapted to suit the agendas of Christianity, as they had already placed Jesus as the central figure of their religion who was based on the Egyptian figure Horus; therefore, they also had to add John the Baptist who is actually Anup. This was an attempt at confirming their religion as the so-called only truth.

From the story in the Gospel of Luke, when Mary (the mother of Jesus) went to Elizabeth, who was six months pregnant with John, Mary told Elizabeth that she was bearing the Son of God; John leaped up in Elizabeth's womb (Luke 1:41).

From Egyptian mythology, when Isis (the mother of Horus) went to Bethesiba, who was pregnant with Anup, Isis told Bethesiba that she was bearing the son of God, the son of Osiris, and Anup then leaped up in Bethesiba's womb.

- Mary and Elizabeth were cousins. = Isis and Bethesiba were cousins.

- John baptized people with water; they were reborn through this process and dedicated their lives to God. = Anup baptized people with water; they were reborn through this process and dedicated their lives to God (Osiris).

- John baptized Jesus with water in the Jordan River; the Spirit descended like a dove unto Jesus, and there came a voice from heaven proclaiming that Jesus is the Son of God. = Anup baptized Horus with water in a river; there a voice came from the heavens that proclaimed that Horus is the son of Osiris.

- John the Baptist from the Jordan is Anup the Baptist from Tat-Ann.

- After Jesus was baptized, John the Baptist sent his disciples to Jesus and asked him if he is the Messiah or if they must wait for another to come. = After Anup baptized Horus, Anup sent his sister to Horus to make sure that he was the son of Osiris.

John and Jesus were cousins and most probably played together as children. Even Elizabeth would surely have told John that his cousin Jesus was the Son of God. Yet John sent two of his disciples to Jesus to ask if he was the Messiah, in Matthew 11:2 "Now when John had heard in the prison the works of Christ, he sent two of his disciples, and said unto them, 'Art thou he that should come, or do we look for another?'"

According to the Bible, John states that he himself is not the light but only testifies of the light. John states further that the one who is after him will be the Savior, and that this savior will be baptized with the Holy Spirit.

What is John the Baptist's main task; is it to prepare the path for Jesus? Who and what was this character, known as John the Baptist? In the Gospel of John, John the Baptist says: "I am the voice of one crying in the wilderness, Make straight the way of the Lord, as said the prophet Isaiah" (John 1:23 *King James Version 1611*); this would imply that John knew more about Jesus than he was prepared to admit or was John in doubt? John did not know at that point that he was Elijah, John 1:21 "And they asked him, what then? Art thou Elijah? In addition, he saith, I am not. Art thou the Prophet? And he answered, No." *King James Version 1611*

Let us have a further look into this uncertainty.

I do not want to stray too far from the point, but I need to show you something that your church does not want to see.

Let us read a few verses in the Holy Bible, Matthew 17:10-13.

Verse 10: "And his disciples asked him, saying, why then say the scribes that Elijah must first come?" *King James Version 1611*

Verse 11: "And Jesus answered and said unto them, Elijah truly shall first come, and restore all things." *King James Version 1611*

Verse 12: "But I say unto you, That Elijah is come already, and they knew him not, but have done unto him whatsoever they listed. Likewise shall also the Son of man suffer of them." *King James Version 1611*

Verse 13: "Then the disciples understood that he spake of John the Baptist." *King James Version 1611*

That means that John the Baptist and Elijah are actually the same person. What the Bible is promoting here is reincarnation.

Read verse 12 again; here, Jesus predicts that the same will happen to him when he returns again. In other words, it means that Jesus will be reincarnated.

What surprises me the most with the story of Elijah is when he says that he will arrive with the second coming of Jesus just before the world comes to an end. However, Jesus would certainly never lie; he says that Elijah has already returned in the form of John the Baptist. Here we see that Elijah had to go through the entire birth process again and had to occupy a new body and grow up with new parents. Jesus states that the same process will occur with him. Therefore, Jesus will be born again, occupy a new body, grow up with new parents, and go through the same growing process.

When we look at the Bible, Elijah, Moses, and Jesus ascended to heaven with their physical bodies. Elijah has already returned and Jesus is still coming, but is the mythical Moses coming again?

Look carefully at the role of Moses; he saves the nation of God from oppression and leads them to the Promised Land.

Jesus saves the children of God from sin and promises them the Holy City, the new city Jerusalem with streets of gold.

Elijah will come to restore everything.

Now that we know that Elijah is John the Baptist, what did John restore? Or is he also coming back?

All these aspects that come from the Bible that are so clear to see are rejected by Christians as evil or devil's works. What am I talking about? Let us have a look.

In Matthew 17, the Son of God states that Elijah has been born in the form of John the Baptist. We are talking about reincarnation here. For those of you that do not know what reincarnation is, let me briefly explain.

Reincarnation is the rebirth of a soul in a new body. Let me explain further; reincarnation means that a person with an immortal soul comes into life through the normal conception and birth processes as a certain person (e.g., Josh) and lives a fulfilling life, were he (e.g., Josh) dies. Then this person's (Josh) immortal soul will enter life again to go through another birth and live another life as someone else (e.g., Benjamin) with a new family. Therefore, the same immortal soul has lived two lives and has lived as two different people, but it is actually only one entity.

Christians are strongly against reincarnation; they completely reject the idea even though it appears as clear as daylight in their own Bibles, Jesus states in the Bible that reincarnation is real. However, Christians continue to believe that reincarnation is evil or demonic.

The story and life of Elijah is very different from the story and life of John the Baptist. Yet according to Jesus, they are the same entity.

This brings me to an important question. According to the Bible, Elijah will arrive with the second coming of Jesus before the end of the world. Jesus states that Elijah has already returned as John the Baptist, but that was not the second coming and neither was it the end of the world. Therefore, this could mean one of two things.

Either Jesus lied and John the Baptist was not Elijah, or Jesus was telling the truth that Elijah and John will return at the end when the Son of God returns to man on a cloud.

The latter statement is the most accepted among Christians. That statement actually means that reincarnation exists, and that it is not something the devil concocted.

Reincarnation is a doctrine generally held to be true of many of the world's major religions. Over millennia, various groups of ancient Greeks, Egyptians, Muslims, Hindus, Native Americans, and Africans have believed in some form of reincarnation. However, the religion most associated and founded on reincarnation is Tibetan Buddhism. Similar to other religions, they believe that a soul keeps being reincarnated, until that soul finally becomes enlightened and achieves nirvana. Do your recall that Jesus studied in India and Tibet? That would explain where this concept of reincarnation came from and how it managed to be part of the Bible and automatically form part of Christianity.

Wisdom is strongly associated with God, and our next chapter deals with another so-called holy and wise character that is almost too perfect when compared to the average person; we will discuss Solomon next.

Chapter 17

King Solomon

When we look at the story of King Solomon, we see that we have to do with a person that lives the wonderful wisdom of God.

He was given a choice between riches and wisdom.

The main reason why this story was included in the Bible was to show people that it is better to attain wisdom than riches. Therefore, it is better to live your life according to the church instead of chasing after wealth.

Is it not true that the knowledge that the church provides is disclosed to you as wisdom?

Let us go back to the story of Solomon. According to the Bible, this was a person that in all aspects revealed wisdom. Strength was born from this wisdom and the self-explanatory wealth that was brought about from it.

The name Solomon is the son which is personified three times.

- Sol: means sun in Latin
- Om: means sun in the Orient
- Mon: means sun in Hebrew/Greek

The personification of the sun is transformed into a human being. This figure, Solomon, represents the strength and wisdom that is brought forward in mankind. This mythical figure demonstrates how the strength and wisdom of God can work through a person.

Through this story of Solomon, we can see that we are not supposed to chase after wealth but instead that we should desire the wisdom and strength of God. The entrenched promise exists that if you hang on to and desire the wisdom and strength of God, you will automatically receive wealth.

When you actually look at the religious pattern, you will notice the manipulation that manifested when certain values, divergent stories, and aspects were incorporated into religion only to suit its agenda and needs.

The entire story has to do with the wonderful wisdom and strength that came in the form of mankind to mankind.

The issue of who King Solomon was and whether he actually existed has plagued biblical scholars for decades. While this personage is attested to in the Old Testament, there is no mention of such a person in any contemporary sources, even though many of Israel's and Judah's later kings are attested to in contemporary sources. The name Solomon does not appear anywhere else in the preexilic ancient world. Equally problematic is that there is no archaeological evidence of a large Israelite state as described by the Bible at the time King "Solomon" was supposed to have lived around tenth century BC and thought to have ruled from 971 BC to 931 BC. Nor are there any documentary records of a king Solomon or any archaeological sites that can be attributed to a King Solomon, though some once were. There is no unequivocal archaeological evidence of King Solomon at all. There are a number of archaeologists who specialize in ancient Israel that have expressed doubts that there ever was a King Solomon. No discovery has been made in Jerusalem which can be dated to the time of David and Solomon.

It is true that biblical, Judaic, and Arabic traditions have always ascribed great wisdom to "Solomon." However, in this regard, bear in mind also that the authors of the Bible were highly influenced by the surrounding Babylonian culture, particularly its literature and myths.

In 2001, a stone stela from allegedly 1000 BC was offered to the Israel Museum for $10 million. The stela was valuable because it referred to repairs of the temple of Solomon, the very first time that any contemporary text had ever been found that mentioned the temple of Solomon at all. That is why the Solomon stone would have been so important and that is why the finding was so sensational. The artifact was traced to a Jerusalem antiquity collector called Oded Golan, the man who "coincidentally" owned the James Ossuary. A police raid found both of these amazing relics in Golan's luxury apartment in Jerusalem, along with many other lesser but still remarkable relics and a workshop.

Dr. Yuval Goren, a geo-archaeologist and head of the Archaeological Institute at Tel Aviv University, declared it a sophisticated forgery, as was the James Ossuary also declared a fake. The stone had been taken from a Crusader castle and used for the inscription, and then this had been aged and faked so well that scholars must have been among those that had done it. An error the forgers made was that the tablet was not of basalt, the stone often used for ancient monumental inscriptions but of stone that is not native to Israel, and that could not have been found in Judah in the reign of King Jehoash, its supposed author. Another error was in using chalk to fake the patina, thus leaving minute fossils on the stone that could not have been there had it been a genuine relic from the region.

Oded Golan was arrested. His workshop was full of tools, materials, and relics that were still in the process of being made, showing that for years, a relic forging scam was being run from there. The whole archaeological record has been contaminated by the forgers. Dr. Goren has shown that many of the world's Jewish artifacts, particularly bullae and clay seals that were easy to forge were held in prestigious museums and bought over the last two decades are actually fakes. Museums and collectors around the world have paid hundreds of thousands of dollars for relics forged in Oded Golan's scam. The more honest biblical archaeologists think everything that came to the Palestinian antiquities market in the last twenty years is likely to be forged, and so cannot be assumed to be genuine. The clever forgers have played on the desire of believers to have their beliefs confirmed. They have proved their gullibility and cast doubt on all supposed evidence of the Bible.

What evidence is there for the Temple of Solomon? Those indoctrinated into biblical mythologies that believe it to be true factual history might be surprised to know that the only evidence of King Solomon is found in the Bible.

However, even if there was a historical "Solomon" who ruled an Israel in the tenth century BC, as the biblical conventional accounts say, his realm would have been rather small. The mighty empire of "David" and "Solomon" as described in the Bible did not occur until the reign of King Omri in the ninth century BC. Had such a huge empire existed, it would certainly have been mentioned in Babylonian, Assyrian, or Egyptian sources of the same time period. Unlike King Omri, there are nonbiblical accounts of his existence; the kingdom of David and Solomon was not mentioned by any of the surrounding cultures.

The absence of any historical confirmation of a Solomon simply does not deter some people because God has told them there was a Solomon, so who can contradict it? The fact is that the ancient religious and church fathers added, modified, removed, and changed numerous old writings, history, and myths.

Many of the stories of David and Solomon were added by the scribes of the Maccabees in an effort to justify their setting up of a Jewish-free state. They depicted their own battles with the Greeks, and these were interpreted symbolically as having taking place with the Philistines and Canaanites.

Another interesting fact concerning Solomon is that there are many parallels with King Nabu Na'id also known as Nabonidus; he was king of Babylonia who ruled from 556 until 539 BC. The biblical stories about "Solomon" were probably written a century or three after the time of Nabonidus; it becomes easy to see how the biblical writers could have adopted many of the stories about Nabonidus, his legendary wisdom and power, his relations with Hiram, king of Tyre, their joint naval presence at Etzion Gaber and long-distance trading ventures by sea, as well as Nabonidus's contacts with the Queen of Sheba, the glass floor of his throne room, and his possession of gold mines in western Arabia, and then adapted them and ascribed them to their own legendary and entirely mythical ruler whom they called King Solomon, "Shlomo" (in Hebrew) or "Sulayman" (in modern Arabic). The conclusion to all this is that the name Solomon is the personification of the sun in three languages, and the character Solomon in the Bible is based on the life of King Nabonidus.

During Neo-Babylonian times, the "Hay Zida" temple, which was dedicated to the god Nabu in Borsippa, had a pure glass surface. The outer bricks were made of pure glass that covered the regular mud and clay bricks that formed the core of the temple. In other words, where Nabonidus built his temple, palace, or throne room in Tayma, with the floor which was made of glass bricks; he would only be following a custom already established in Mesopotamia. Whereas for a king of Israel in the tenth century BC to build a palace floor out of glass, as the Quran story indicates, it would be highly out of place as it was not customary. The science of manufacturing glass was certainly advanced enough by the sixth century BC but not at the time of the tenth century.

In terms of the Queen of Sheba visiting, it is more relevant concerning King Nabonidus than it is to the mythical King Solomon. The book of Job mentions that Job and his people were being harassed by both the Babylonians and the Sabaeans. The passages in the book of Job indicate that the empires of Babylon and Sheba were rubbing up against each other in the mid-sixth century BC. Such a situation would have warranted a visit by the ruler of Sheba to go to the Babylonian ruler in order to sort out the border issues and work out their international relations, especially if that Babylonian ruler had headquarters in Tayma, Arabia, as Nabonidus had during the mid-sixth century BC. It is well-known that Nabonidus, as king of Babylon, moved his capital to Tayma for a ten-year period in 552-543 BC. This is attested to not only in the Babylonian Chronicles but by writings of Nabonidus himself and by the archaeological evidence on the ground in Tayma.

The gold mines of "mahad azh-zhahab" (the so-called mines of Solomon) are situated precisely in the area, near Yathrib in modern Medina, that would have been in dispute between a Babylonian Empire centered in Tayma and the kingdom of Sheba that was centered in Yemen. Additionally, a Babylonian Empire holding vast areas of western Arabia as far south as Yathrib, according to Babylonian accounts, would have had great need for maritime contact with the Levant. A port at Etzion Gaber would have been most logical and probably necessary. The Babylonians, being a great land power, had no naval expertise themselves so they would have had to turn to the Phoenicians, who at that time were in a subservient position to King Nabonidus. It so happens that the king of Tyre during Nabonidus's time was named Hiram, who provided the ships for the port at Etzion Gaber.

Let us look at the values of Solomon, which are considered to be holy, that we now consider being unholy today.

This man that had all the wisdom of God also had three hundred wives. It is portrayed as a blessing bestowed upon Solomon from God. We are told that a man should only have one wife. Even Adam was only given one wife.

Let us have a look at Ephesians 5.

- "Husbands, love your wives just as Christ loved the church." It does not say, "Husband, love your wives."

- Then the Bible says to the woman, "Wives, submit yourselves unto your own husbands." It does not say, "Wives, submit yourselves to your husband."

There is a lot of talk about culture in the churches. Then I need to ask, for which culture was the Bible written for?

I read in the Bible that Abraham impregnated his wife's slave and received a son from her. This after God told him that his wife Sarah would bear him a son. Throughout the Bible, there is mention of holy men who desire a woman but receive another, and later he takes the other woman as well. This is polygamy. There are even laws against multiple spouses.

This sort of behavior is not in line with what the Bible stands for, yet God finds these people favorable.

Culture is not supposed to influence God's plan. They talk about one religion, one baptism, one Lord, in everyone and through everyone. I thought the Christian God is an unchangeable god, as he was, he is, and he always will be.

Everything in the Bible is blindly recognized and believed to be true and holy because God gave it. People accept the wisdom of Solomon as holy, even though he goes against what the Bible stands for, or do you believe that the scriptures were not relevant to him?

People's brains become foggy and hazy when it concerns religion, and when you look at the actuality of reality, you will see that everything that is upheld as godly wisdom is actually a bunch of myths and fables that is brightened up by mysticism.

The unrealistic aspects are entrenched with statements such as:

- By God, nothing is impossible.
- God is almighty.
- The wisdom of God is foolish by man.
- It was the will of God that is why it had to happen.

The list goes on; you can continue listening to excuses because the churches do not have explanations for these things.

God is a god of order; God does not change, and God is reliable and fair.

God is the perfect, positive strength and wisdom by humankind. These are not linked to culture and do not change from time to time. God does not desire transient things and will not bless you with transient things. God warns us against striving for riches that the moths and rust will destroy.

God did not bless a man with three hundred wives, and neither will God give you worldly riches. God has delight in the souls of people, that which is everlasting and eternal. God does not care for the desires of humanity. God said that he gave you your own will, and that he left his will by you.

God has never promised earthly rewards such as wealth to his children. You will receive your reward at the end of your days, the crown of your victory. You will not receive new houses, cars, or lump sums of money. You can pray until you are blue in the face, but if you do get it, just remember that God did not give it to you, at least not from the eternal God.

An eternal god will offer you eternal things. A transient god will offer you transient things.

These two gods stand opposite each other, as day is to night. Through the manner in which you live your life and through your actions, you will know who your God is.

Wisdom has never been rewarded with transient things.

Do not confuse knowledge with wisdom. You can pick up knowledge on every street corner. Wisdom is what you have in your heart and mind; it is how you live your life in connection with your attitude, behavior, and actions. You cannot buy or learn wisdom from books; wisdom is a gift that you receive.

Wisdom does not come from myths, lies, symbolism, or rituals. It does not even come from culture or traditions.

Dismiss those that try to enchant you with tricks that they bring forward as wisdom; they are able to capture you because they are devious and cunning. Wisdom does not want honor or compensation. Therefore, the wisdom of Solomon or the story about it is a fable and farce to charm and captivate you.

Let us go to the next chapter that deals with Noah and the Ark, the lies behind the story, the ignorant mistakes made, and the blind oversight of the impractical.

Chapter 18

Noah and the Ark

This is one of the first Bible stories that I had to hear when I was a child. The story tells of how Noah, his wife, three sons Shem, Ham, and Japheth with their wives, and all the animals in pairs of two that were on the earth had to sail in a large boat that Noah had built. This story captivates children and lets their imaginations run wild. There is not one Christian child that does not have an image of the ark in their minds, of how the rains came that caused the floods and that caused the death of the people who were on earth.

Show me any Christian child that does not know that Noah first sent out a crow and later a dove that returned with an olive twig. How Noah came from the ark and planted a vineyard, drank the wine, and became drunk. This story is long winded and told with detail; they even describe the type of wood used to build the ark.

Here are again myths, fables, and lies in this story.

The biblical flood story of the "Flood or Deluge" was a late remake of the ancient flood myths known throughout the ancient world. Thousands of years before the Bible was written, an ark was built by the Sumerian Ziusudra. In Akkad, the flood hero's name was Atrakhasis. In Babylon, he was Utnapishtim, the only mortal to become immortal. In Greece, he was Deucalion, who repopulated the earth after the waters subsided, whose ark landed on Mount Parnassus. In Armenia, the hero was Xisuthros, who was a corruption of Sumerian Ziusudra, whose ark landed on Mount Ararat.

Also consider the names of Noah's sons, Shem, Ham, and Japheth. It is related in Padmapooraun that Satyavrata, whose miraculous preservation from a general flood is told at large in the Matsya, had three sons, the eldest of whom was named Jyapeti or Lord of the Earth; the others were Charma and Sharma; the last names are in the vulgar dialects which are usually pronounced Cham and Sham. Can you see the similarity?

Let us begin by looking at the type of wood that Noah used—gopher wood.

Gopher wood comes from the gopher bush, also known as Diospyros genus. You cannot even use this wood to make matches; it is similar to cork.

Then we look at the measurements of the ark. According to the Bible, the length was three hundred cubits, the breadth, fifty cubits, and the height, thirty cubits. The hatch was only one cubit by one cubit. The cubit, generally taken as equal to 18 inches or 457 mm, was based on the length of the arm from the elbow to the tip of the middle finger and was considered the equivalent of 6 palms or 2 spans. In some ancient cultures, it was as long as 21 inches or 531 mm. The cubit unit of measurement has been used by many ancient peoples. It originated in Egypt about 3000 BC.

All the animals of the earth, a pair of each living creature, a male and female, had to enter the ark. How did Noah manage to get the animals through the door of the ark? It was far too small for most large animals. Where were the herbivores and carnivores placed? What did these animals eat during their time on the ark? Then we get the usual answer from the church, that God made provision for everything because everything is possible for God.

God is not a magician; God is a god of order. According to the Bible, God created everything, so why would God use a man and a boat to save the animals and mankind? God can create more animals and human beings, as he did in the beginning.

Again we hear of the number 40, also mentioned in the Moses story.

Why does God do all these things in a human way? It seems that God is starting to think more and more like a human being. Look at the entire story; there is no wisdom in this tale. This is not the way that God is. Compare Genesis 1 with this story; it does not sound like the same God. In Genesis, we hear "And God said and it was so." In the story of Noah, God is tired of mankind and wants to destroy them. He uses the most stupid method to start over. It is blatantly obvious that there is only so-called human wisdom that fills the pages of this story.

Naturally, this story originates from ancient mythologies, as all the other stories from the Bible do. There is an ancient myth from Egypt and Central Africa known as the Archa-Noa/Argha-Noa.

In ancient times, the Nile Delta became flooded due to the monsoon rains that gather and run down the Nile River; it was considered a great tragedy at first; this happened each year, which came and washed away the Egyptian world. The Egyptians called these waters the Waters of Chaos; they were terrible and destructive, but they also brought new life because without the Waters of Chaos, the desert would claim back the agricultural lands on the riverbanks of the Nile and nothing would grow. When the floods came, it looked as if the whole world was flooded because there was water everywhere they looked.

The Egyptians however discovered that the Waters of Chaos was truly a blessing that brought new life. Seeds and fertile soil was carried down the river with the floods; it was then deposited on the banks of the Nile. As soon as the floodwaters subsided, the warm desert sun accelerated the growth of these seeds. It literally became green overnight. They celebrated every year the coming of the Waters of Chaos for bringing new life. This celebration was called the Argha-Noa.

The Argha Noa was the coming of the great flood that washed away the old world and brought new life, and therefore Egypt was born again. The moon was always in the lower quarter; this quarter of the moon became known as the Argha-Noa, also known as the Wet Moon; this resembled an arch in the sky. Noah is in fact a solar myth, and the ark represents the sun entering into the "moon ark," the Egyptian "Argha," which is the crescent or arc-shaped lower quarter of the moon. The ark often signifies the female generative power, carrying the life essence of nature and mankind.

When the water breaks, there comes new life. This is symbolical to a pregnant woman's water breaking because from that comes new life. Baptism also originated from this ancient mythological story, where the sins and old life are washed away with water, the rebirth and new life through water.

Regarding Noah's Ark, the word "ark" originates from Egypt. It means a chest or box for preserving something sacred. Another idea that is by no means original; the Hindus had their Argha, the Greeks their Cista, and the Argonauts their Argo.

When Noah was seeking land, he sent a raven and later a dove. The Babylonian Noah, Utnapishtim, sent a dove, then a swallow, and finally a raven. The Babylonian ark rested on Mount Nisir, the Hindu ark on Mount Himalaya, and the Greek ark on Mount Parnassus. The word "Ararat" or "Arath" is the Aramaic source of the word "earth."

God made a covenant with Noah to never again destroy the earth by a flood. To ensure that he did not forget his promise, God made a rainbow in the sky as a reminder. So there were no rainbows that ever appeared before the time of Noah?

Let me show you a few similarities found between religions regarding the "Noah" story.

Zeus, known as Jupiter to the Romans, also became offended with his own creation. He also decided to drown them all, sparing only Deucalion and Pyrrha, who had "found grace" in his eyes. He allowed them to escape in a boat which finally landed on Mount Parnassus. The Babylonian account can be found on the tablets of Assurbanipal.

Here, the god Enlil, who was also offended by mankind's wickedness, decides to destroy them with water, but Ea, the god of wisdom, learns of Enlil's plan and tells a man by the name of Utnapishtim about it. Like Noah, Utnapishtim is tenth in line from the first man and walks with Ea. Ea tells him to build an enormous boat, one that will hold him and his family and also, all the beasts, birds, and creatures. As soon as it was finished, a storm started, and it began to rain, a storm so great that even the lesser gods "trembled in fear." It rained for six days and nights, and on the seventh, it stopped. The boat floated around until it finally came to rest on Mount Nisir. It should be noted that Mount Nisir sits between Medea and Armenia, making it practically identical with Ararat. Utnapishtim also sent out a dove, but others were swallow and raven when seeking land. He built an altar upon making land and offered incense upon it. The gods smelled the "sweet savor" and gathered around; and Ishtar, who was "the lady of the rainbow," hung out her multicolored necklace.

With the Persian and Hindu myths, it is not physical birds and beasts that are brought into the ark, but their seeds: "Take the seeds of sheep, oxen, men and women, dogs, and birds and every kind of tree and fruit, two of every kind, into the ark seal it up with a golden ring and make in it a door and window." An avatar of Vishnu warns the Hindu Noah, Vaivasvata, about the flood and tells him to build a vessel for his family and bring on board plant seeds and a pair of animals. After the flood, the boat comes to rest on Mount Himalaya, and the number of days the storm lasted is forty days; this coincides exactly with the number in the Hebrew account.

The Tepanecs or Tepanecas of Mexico also reported a great flood that lasted exactly forty days and nights. The Society Islanders say the god Tangaloa was angered by the wickedness of man that he created such a mighty flood to punish them and that only the mountaintops remained. According to Inca mythology, the god Viracocha promised to never drown humankind again, and to confirm his promise, he placed a rainbow for them to see. Bochica, a god of the Chibchas of Bogota, perched on a rainbow and quelled the flood.

Many Bible believers would try and argue that these other accounts were copied from the Hebrew account; however, it should be noted that the Chaldean, Hindu, Babylonian, and Egyptian accounts predate the Hebrew versions by many centuries.

Even though the story of Noah is a myth, people are still trying to find the biblical ark on Mount Ararat. Knowing that yet another story from the Bible is nothing but a fairy tale, how can anyone continue to believe in the legitimacy of the Bible?

It is wrong that people base their lives on these biblical, mythical stories. God gave you a life to live and allowed you to make your own mistakes so that you can learn from them. How can you ever expect to grow spiritually when you believe that life is like a mythical story? If you do live your life this way, you are false because you are acting instead of living your life to be the best, positive, and unique individual that you can be. Religion is slavery, and only truth can make you free. Freedom through truth is the comfort that God talks about.

Stop trying to satisfy your church, the norms, and people. Instead try and satisfy God.

I do not say that it is wrong to use symbolism, but inform people that it is only symbolism and do not make it holy. You know just as well as I do that invented fables mislead people easily, and I believe that neither you or I would want to be responsible for misleading anyone or cost someone their salvation.

Let us move on. I will show you where the shedding of the blood, the offering of blood, and the cleansing by blood came from that are present in religion. All these myths have ill-defined the true religion of the living God in the minds of people. The churches have taken over in order to pursue money in the name of God.

The churches are as false as the fable of Noah, and you want to make it holy. Can the churches use the Bible as a yardstick in order to establish how you must live your life? Religious authorities have an immense arrogance to believe that they can force you into a direction by using the fear of hell and the fear of being cast away by God. They also bank on the backing of various governments for protection. They ensure that you always feel weak and powerless to the extent that you believe that you need the blessing of the church to enable you to do anything. God has given you the wisdom and strength to be able to be strong. Investigate everything and keep the good, which is exactly what truth is. Pray to God and loosen yourself from distorted images and unrealistic promises.

I am not moving away from the chapter, but I am using the contents to bring you to your senses and show you that I am not trying to estrange you from God. Your soul will show you that what you see is the truth, and this will bring fear unto you.

Fear not, for now is the time to stop the monster that has misled you and to tell him: "You have been misleading me for long enough. I am now going to investigate and find the truth with the strength and wisdom that God has given me in order to live my life accordingly." Do not judge the individual. Judge the lies and fraud in their midst that has come over for generations. Move away from it and hold on to the hand of your creator.

All that I am yet to show you will not be easy on the ear. It will not pacify your conscience at first. Trust me, it is the purest naked truth, and it is not my purpose to destroy any person; I will only destroy the house of lies and fraud that has over the centuries held you and your loved ones as prisoners.

What I offer you is only the naked truth, and through truth you will achieve the actual path to salvation. I am not a preacher or minister. I am the one that brings you the truth, and you will either accept it or reject it. Do not love the lie and push away the truth.

I speak very frankly because I am not trying to bring forward any fabrications. The God that I am showing you is the actual God, and he is not far from you. He does not hide in the places that you are unfamiliar with. God wants you to see him and strive toward him. Do not strive toward earthly possessions. I do not promise you a wonderful life after this one that God has given you. I bring you peace of mind and enlightenment that you will experience after you have accepted what has been revealed.

Alone you entered this world and alone you will leave. Come onto the path where you will no longer be alone and lost but where you walk in unity with your creator. Fulfill your task that God has given you.

Let us move over to the next chapter for you to see the lies, so that you will know it for what it is.

Chapter 19

The Shedding of Blood, the Purification, and the Sacrifice

The shedding of a man's blood has become symbolic in religion. Blood also symbolizes the sacrifices that are made. Concepts such as the goblet filled with blood, how blood gives your soul salvation, and how blood purifies have become prominent in many religions.

Have you ever heard the phrase "That man is sweating blood," but we have never seen anyone sweat blood.

In old mythology and traditions, offerings of animals or people were commonplace. Blood has universal connotations in the religious imagination of humanity; it symbolizes life, fertility, and the violence of sacrifice, whether as an offering, a punishment, or for atonement. Like any highly symbolic and potentially "holy" substance, blood has numerous meanings and functions; it contaminates and purifies, convicts, and redeems. The variety of sacrificial offerings are (1) blood offerings (animal and human); (2) bloodless offerings (food and vegetation); and (3) divine offerings.

Ritual sacrifice worldwide has been predominantly blood sacrifice; it is with blood that gods are bribed, appeased, or enlisted in human enterprises, as hunting or war. For the Incas of Peru and the Aztecs of Mexico, human blood sacrifice ensured cosmic regularity; for the Israelites, blood sacrifice established and maintained the covenant of God with his people. In each case, ritually spilled blood reinstates or ensures the continuation of order and proper human relations with the gods or God.

The practice of sacrifice is in the oldest records of humankind. The archaeological records contain human and animal corpses with sacrificial marks long before any written records of the practice were documented. Sacrifices are a common theme in most religions, though the frequencies of animal and human sacrifices are rarely performed today. Animal sacrifice has turned up in almost all cultures, from the Hebrews to the Greeks and Romans and from the Aztecs to the Yoruba.

Some occasions that required human sacrifice in multiple cultures include the following:

- Human sacrifice performed to the dedication of a new temple.
- Sacrifice of people upon the death of a king, high priest, or great leader; those sacrificed were supposed to serve or accompany the deceased leader in the next life.

- Human sacrifice in times of natural disasters, such as droughts, earthquakes, volcanic eruptions, etc. were seen as a sign of anger or displeasure by the gods, and sacrifices were supposed to lessen the wrath of these gods or God.

Blood sacrifice from an animal or human is archaic, ancient, and barbaric. Blood has no power; it cannot purify or enable soul salvation in any way. How could anyone that is educated or someone of average intelligence possibly believe in these myths? They believe in these myths because it is tradition or custom that has been passed down from generation to generation.

Blood sacrifice was considered to be a powerful method of talking with the gods and remains an act of extreme piety that challenges our modern idea of morality. Jesus's death on the cross is a blood sacrifice to God the Father that atones for the sins of humanity, thus reestablishing the harmony between humanity and God that had been destroyed by sin. This act is considered to be the greatest act of love. God's justice required atonement for sin from humanity if human beings were to be restored to their place in creation and saved from damnation. The central Christian ritual, the Eucharist, establishes participation in this redemptive sacrifice through the drinking of the holy blood and the eating of his body.

In the Roman Catholic Church, the Eastern Orthodox churches, as well as among some High Church Anglicans, the Eucharist or Mass is seen as a sacrifice. It is, however, not a separate or additional sacrifice to Jesus on the cross; it is rather exactly the same sacrifice, which transcends time and space; it is renewed and made present, the only distinction being that it is offered in a nonbloody manner. The Orthodox Church sees the celebration of the Eucharist as a continuation rather than a reenactment of the Last Supper. Some Protestants reject the idea of the Eucharist as a sacrifice, inclining to see it as merely a holy meal.

The concept of self-sacrifice and martyrs are central to Christianity. Often found in Catholic and Orthodox Christianity is the idea of joining one's own suffering to the sacrifice of Christ on the cross. Therefore, one can offer up involuntary suffering, such as illness or purposefully embrace suffering in acts of Penance.

How many times have you heard that parents are willing to give their lives to their children? Have you heard someone say that they would be prepared to die for the one that they love? All of these are symbolic statements.

The crucifixion catches hold of each Christian's imagination. The bloodshed by the savior and that he had to die for their sins. Each Christian claims that Jesus died for them, that he suffered, died, and rose again to go to his Father to prepare a place for them. This demonstrates the intense arrogance of this lie-filled religion that proclaims that if you do not attest that their Messiah is the Savior, then you are not from God.

Only God can give life, and each human being on this earth has life within them. I know and see how the lies and fraud in the Christian religion rape and murder souls through sly, twisted lies and myths used in the name of God. Now they will label me as the Antichrist and the misleader just because I can see the damage and devastation that they cause. What blood exists that can wash your soul as white as snow? What salvation can blood offer your soul? This is all symbolism. The songs written and sung in church of the strength in the blood make use of symbolism.

Again, they use hidden mysticism, symbolism, and rituals in their stories. Does God need to use mysticism, symbolism, and rituals to get through to humankind? The Christians keep talking about the love that they have for God and the love that God has for them, but I have never seen so much mysticism, symbolism, rituals, and traditions that are needed to keep reminding them of the love from and for God. When you love someone, you know that they love you, you feel it, and you live in it. You certainly do not need constant reminders, such as rituals and symbolism that you love that person.

Have a look; the church controls all these rituals and activities or they take place at the church and sometimes money is collected. Does God then need money to exist, or do the church fathers want a better life? Large buildings are erected with soft benches and the latest technology incorporated to attract volumes of people to their church.

If I truly love my wife and children there is nothing that I do for them that will be a sacrifice. Whereas, the churches keep announcing the sacrifices that God has to do for us; so if love is sacrifice, then I do not want it. The church makes it sound as if we are in a huge indebtedness to God because he loves us.

Then they tell you that you should be God fearing. Why? I do not fear the one that I love. Why do I say this? In the Bible, every time when there is a phenomenon or a manifestation, people feel fear and throw themselves to the ground. They shake and experience utter fear. Why would you fear your father? Religion that is supposed to bring you joy makes you fearful. Only children who have something to hide from their father have reason to be scared of him. Children who have a healthy relationship with their father enjoy peace and happiness.

The Holy Spirit is the comforter and spirit of peace; this is the spirit of truth. When you have the truth, then you have no need to fear.

You pray and yearn to go to God, but you forget that God is with you and that his kingdom is by humankind. God is the spirit, strength, and wisdom in you. What do you yearn for? Where do you want to go? Does your soul, which is only spirit, actually need a place to go to? You are offering up your life, the life that God gave you by chasing after the will of the church. You investigate nothing, you only go through the Bible that everyone reads or knows about. You announce viewpoints from the Bible as your church has given it to you, so that the number of members in the church can go up, and you think that you are doing God a favor. Matthew 7:13-14 says "Enter ye in at the strait gate: for wide is the gate, and broad is the way, that leadeth to destruction, and many there be which go thereat: because strait is the gate, and narrow is the way, which leadeth unto life, and few there be that find it."

Christianity stands as one of the most powerful religions, and you are part of it either directly or indirectly. You are part of their norms that cling on to myths, traditions, symbolism, and mysticism. Christians state that they proclaim the light, but they do not know where the light comes from; they cannot proclaim with conviction that they know the light or can see the light because God is the light. You claim that you can see the reflection of the light, as the sunlight reflects off the moon. That would mean that you walk in the darkness, and that is why you feel fear.

You move in ignorance, and you fear the unknown. God states that nothing will be hidden from his children, and that his children will not be left in ignorance. The churches fill you with explanations, but when you ask where God is, nobody knows. They make you believe that you will meet a man one day that will be either Jesus or God. Again, they plant distorted images in your mind and raise your expectations.

God does not have the form of man, so why would you meet a man? They plant a twisted image of heaven in your mind as well, a heaven that has golden streets and houses made of gemstones, things that only humans think of. Read the following that comes from the Bible, Romans 8:5-6: "For they that are after the flesh do mind the things of the flesh; but they that are after the Spirit, the things of the Spirit. For to be carnally minded is death; but to be spiritually minded is life and peace." This passage speaks of peace and not fear. Let us also have a look at Jude verse 10, "But these speak evil of those things which they know not: but what they know naturally, as brute beasts, in those things they corrupt themselves." C It cannot be stated clearer than that. I do not intend on misleading anyone; your own Bible confirms what I have told you about your church fathers who talk about things that they know not.

The church instills fear with you by the understanding that it is actually a type of godly happiness. They tell you that you should not see it as fear but rather as respect toward God, and the fear that they say you should have is the fear of not getting to heaven.

If you know the truth and it forms part of who you are, it is logical that you will live according to the truth. Why people are unable to stay faithful to their religion is because people cannot cling on to rituals, symbolical nonsense, and traditions while living the life that God gave them. Show me one individual who does not wonder about certain aspects in their religion. They remain silent and subservient, as they do not want to be branded as nonbelievers.

People are scared to ask because the church prohibits them from questioning. They expect you to believe blindly and tell you that your blind faith will save you. It is expected from you to be like a child because children do not ask questions and accept everything that they are told. When I was a child, I reasoned like a child, but now that I am fully grown and have the wisdom of God within me, I know that I must investigate everything as God has commanded me to do. Therefore, I will not allow anyone to stop me from seeing what God gave me to investigate.

Beware of those who will come to you as an angel from God that know the languages of mankind and of angels, they that state that you must be obedient to the laws of Moses and those that leave you in suspense with regard to the coming of your savior. There are people that proclaim the Savior must still come, but those of you that proclaim that God is with you and that his kingdom is with you have the truth and the peace within you. You need to live a spiritual life.

What is salvation? What is soul salvation? What is the eternal life?

Salvation is liberation from ignorance or illusion and deliverance from danger or difficulty.

To experience salvation would entail happiness, joy, pleasure, glory, and prosperity.

To experience soul salvation would entail soul happiness, soul joy, soul pleasure, soul glory, and soul prosperity.

When you manage to feel these emotions and these states of being, your soul, heart, and mind are in a state of absolute bliss and contentment. These are not things that God only wants you to experience after the grave. God wants you to live and experience these things now with the life that he has given you. Do not believe that it will be different when you are dead; God is an unchangeable god, as God was, so he is and so he shall forever be. When you are in God and live in him, you will also be unchangeable.

Your soul also has no end; therefore, you will live forever in spirit and not in the flesh as you know it, which means that you have nothing to sacrifice. During your lifetime, give humanity that which belongs to humanity, but give to God that which belongs to God.

The myth that blood will purify you is a fable; and human beings, not God, instated these rituals. Blood has no power to purify you or make you holy. The blood that circulates though your body is the life essence of your body. The blood of someone else that you are supposed to wash with cannot purify your soul. The purification of heart, mind, and soul comes from the truth. The truth will set you free and loosen the ties made by lies.

The Holy Spirit is the spirit of truth that will comfort you. It is the truth that God wants you to find within yourself. That is what you need to search for and investigate. When you find the truth, you will be filled with peace and happiness, which is the salvation that you already have within you.

God only walks in the truth; when you have the truth, you also have God within you. You will receive strength from the truth and acquire wisdom from it. There are no empty promises or unrealistic dreams of one day when you are dead that you will rule as kings and priests, with streets of gold and houses made of gemstones because these are carnal things that humanity cling on to; God has no care for carnal or human things.

Let us go to the next chapter, "Holy Communion."

Chapter 20

Holy Communion

Holy Communion, also called the Eucharist, the Sacrament of the Altar, the Blessed Sacrament, the Lord's Supper, and other names, is a Christian sacrament or ordinance. It is celebrated in accordance with Jesus's instruction at the Last Supper as recorded in several books of the New Testament, that his followers do in remembrance of him as when he gave his disciples bread, saying, "This is my body" and gave them wine, saying, "This is my blood." The bread has become the symbol of Jesus's body, and the wine became the symbol for the blood of Jesus. Blood is also symbolically seen as sacrifice.

Besides baptism, Holy Communion is one of the most popular rituals and symbols practiced in the Christian religion structure. There are disagreements between the numerous Christian faiths when it comes to Holy Communion. Some have divergent views as to what the ritual means, if a communal cup or multiple smaller cups need to be used, should alcohol or grape juice be served, and the list goes on.

Varying views and theories concerning Holy Communion:

- The Catholic Church teaches that the signs of bread and wine become, in a way surpassing understanding, the body and blood of Christ.
- Many Christian denominations classify the Eucharist as a sacrament. Some Protestants prefer to call it an ordinance, viewing it not as a specific channel of divine grace but as an expression of faith and of obedience to Christ.
- Lutherans believe that the body and blood of Jesus are present "in, with, and under" the forms of bread and wine, a concept known as the sacramental union.
- The Reformed churches, following the teachings of John Calvin, believe in an immaterial, spiritual presence of Christ by the power of the Holy Spirit and received by faith.
- Anglicans adhere to a range of views, although the teaching on the matter in the Articles of Religion holds that the presence is real only in a heavenly and spiritual sense.
- Some Christians reject the concept of the real presence, believing that the Eucharist is only a memorial of the death of Christ.

A divided church cannot stand . . . because a divided church is not a church at all.

The Catholic Church teaches that when the bread and wine are consecrated in the Eucharist, they cease to be bread and wine and become, respectively, the body and blood of Christ, each of which is accompanied by the other and by Christ's soul and divinity. The empirical appearance and physical properties are not changed, but for Catholics, the reality is. The consecration of the bread and wine represents the separation of Jesus's body from his blood at Calvary. However, since he has risen, the church teaches that his body and blood can no longer be truly separated. Where one is, the other must be. Therefore, although the priest or minister says "The body of Christ" when administering the bread (host) and "The blood of Christ" when presenting the chalice, the communicant who receives either one receives Christ, wholly and entirely.

The baptism, Eucharist, and ministry document of the World Council of Churches are attempting to present the common understanding of the Eucharist to Christians and describes it as "essentially the sacrament of the gift which God makes to us in Christ through the power of the Holy Spirit," "Thanksgiving to the Father," "Anamnesis or Memorial of Christ," "the sacrament of the unique sacrifice of Christ, whoever lives to make intercession for us," "the sacrament of the body and blood of Christ, the sacrament of his real presence," "Invocation of the Spirit," "Communion of the Faithful," and "Meal of the Kingdom."

What do the Gospels say? The synoptic Gospels, first Mark, and then Matthew and Luke, depict Jesus as presiding over the Last Supper. References to Jesus's body and blood foreshadow his crucifixion, and he identifies them as a new covenant. In the Gospel of John, the account of the Last Supper has no mention of Jesus taking bread and wine and speaking of them as his body and blood; instead, it recounts his humble act of washing the disciples' feet, the prophecy of the betrayal, which set in motion the events that would lead to the cross, and his long discourse in response to some questions posed by his followers, in which he went on to speak of the importance of the unity of the disciples with him and each other.

Oldest practicing group: Holy Qurbana or Qurbana Qadisha, the Holy Offering or Holy Sacrifice, refers to the Eucharist as celebrated according to the East Syrian and West Syrian traditions of Syriac Christianity. The main anaphora of the East Syrian tradition is the Holy Qurbana of Addai and Mari, while that of the West Syrian tradition is the Liturgy of Saint James. Both are extremely old, going back at least to the third century, and are the oldest extant liturgies continually in use.

Let us talk more about what is believed, viewed, and thought of during this ancient ritual in the minds of those who practice it.

Some Christian religious sects believe that the bread symbolizes the word of God and that the word of God comes to the congregation of the church from within the church. Unleavened bread also known as matzah is used during Holy Communion because they believe that this bread is nourishing to one's soul.

The unleavened bread represents the spiritual message that has not been prepared beforehand (as the bread used was not allowed to the ferment). This is symbolical as well because it reflects this Christian sect's method of preaching as they do not prepare their message to their congregation before any services take place. They claim that they allow the message of the spirit of God the opportunity to speak through a person to the people of the congregation. This sect judges harshly over the others that prepare their sermons before the Sunday service; there are many religious leaders that prepare their sermons beforehand. They see the preparation of sermons as bread that has been allowed to ferment.

This same Christian sect believes that the bread represents the "herder" method and style of speaking which is used to speak about spiritual life to the congregation. This method and style of spiritual speaking is believed not to be fit for the unborn souls; what they believe to be unborn souls are people who have not found their spiritual path in their church. The method of preaching used for unborn souls is different; they speak straight from the Bible to these people, and this style and method is referred to as the "evangelic stream" of speaking. Whereas the "herder stream" of speaking is believed to clarify evangelic talk used for the church members according to how they explain and understand it. This method and style of delivering religious and spiritual messages has been developed to cater only for their congregations that form part of their religious sect.

This religious sect believes symbolically that their members are the bread, and therefore their members form the body of Christ. When they receive Holy Communion, they commemorate the body of Christ. They also believe symbolically that the goblet used during Holy Communion represents their body because they form the body of Christ and therefore represents that they have made their body available during the month for the service of the church. The wine or grape juice used during this ritual is symbolic for the sacrifices that each member makes during the month in service of the church. As a member of the body of Christ, they have suffered and sacrificed by following the path of their religion through their dedication, service, activities, and duties. This is what they commemorate when they drink from the goblet.

During this ceremonial ritual, the tithes (to give a tenth of one's income) are blessed. The blessing is made by using the following phrase: "Father, it is not the cabinet or its contents that we ask your blessing for, but for the faithful that long for your blessing Father." The congregation is blessed with outstretched arms for their faithfulness concerning the offerings or tithes.

Many other Christian religions view and commemorate the symbolic ritual of the Eucharist or Holy Communion as follows:

- The death of Jesus and his resurrection,
- The Last Supper that Jesus had with his disciples,

- The bread is the body of Jesus and the wine his blood that flowed for the sins of humanity.

When you look at the previous chapters and see where the Christian religion originated from, it is understandable that there is hardly any agreement between them regarding rituals and their symbolic value. Now that you have read through this chapter, I ask you, can this ritual possibly make you holy? Will you not attain heaven if you do not take part in this ritual? Do you think God requires you to perform this ritual in order for you to inherit his kingdom?

This ritual was implemented as a monthly event through the good intentions of the church fathers; it is not a holy day. It would seem as though everything that has been brought in by the church fathers are believed to be the will of God. People are then actually proclaiming that the church fathers are their god.

Concerning the prophet: It is claimed that the prophet has fulfilled his task because the prophet's purpose is to edify (build or establish) the congregation; thereafter, the church is then established and registered. Is this the establishment that the Bible speaks of? Actually, what the Bible means is that the prophet is meant to spiritually improve the congregation. Look at how unedifying some churches are. The clapping of hands and stamping of feet, the Bible warns you against those who clap their hands and stamp their feet in the name of the Lord. Their defense is that they dance and rejoice with joy in the name of their God.

Let us have a look at the next chapter concerning baptism with water and the symbolic rituals and myths connected to baptism.

Chapter 21

Baptism with Water

Baptism is certainly the most popular sacrament or mythical ritual in the Christian religion. There is also no other aspect in the various religious structures that is as varied in application and view. The variants of baptism are as follows: christening for babies by sprinkling water on the forehead, baptism for adults in the form of full body submersion, and baptism for adults by sprinkling water on the forehead.

Baptism through water began in Babylonia as part of the Babylonian Mystery School religion. The Egyptians are the descendants of the Babylonians. "Bab" means gate or gateway in ancient Babylonian. Babylonia itself means "the land of the gateway" to the mysteries of death. Babylonia in ancient times was famous for the immensely large Gates of Isis and the mystery school that was functioning within the great walled city. Baptism originally was a method of drowning and resuscitation. It was a method of opening the "gate" to death that gave a person what is now termed a "near death" experience. As a person symbolically died and was reborn, it was used originally as an initiation ritual and as a method of conversion from the old life and ways of living to a new life and way of living. This ancient ritual was experienced and witnessed by the Hebrews who were living in Egypt; they adopted this ritual and slightly modified it into their own religion. Baptism was performed through water and through fire. Many Hebrews rejected fire baptism and therefore never included it into their religion.

Mithraism, which existed about four thousand years ago, performed ceremonies where spiritual purification was believed to come from sprinkling or fully submerging a person being baptized with bull's blood or ram's blood; this ritual purification meant that the person was born again as part of their spiritual transformation journey.

The followers of Mithra were called Mithras; they referred to Mithra as the Light of the World and as a symbol of truth and justice. Mithra was a mediator between heaven and earth and was a member of a Holy Trinity in the ancient Persian culture. People who underwent baptism were born again followers of him when they were baptized. Does this not sound strangely familiar to conventional religions such as Christianity?

Baptism by Water: Baptism by water is an ancient rite that has been practiced by the pagans, Zoroasters, Romans, Egyptians, Persians, and numerous other nations. It was also popular among the Hindus during ancient times. The method used to baptize was to submerge the person three times in the water element;

176

some of the Christian sects now practice much in the same manner as other older religions practiced the baptism rite. During the ceremonial rite, the following prayer was spoken over the individual being baptized: "O Lord, this man is impure, like the mud of this stream but do thou cleanse and deliver his soul from sin as the water cleanses his body." They believed that water possessed the mystical power of being able to purify both soul and body; the soul was purified from sin, and the body was literally and symbolically purified from dirt. The ancient Mexicans, Persians, Hindus, and Jews used to baptize their newly born infants almost immediately after they were born, and the water used during the rite was called "the water of regeneration." Those people who touched the nonbaptized infants were deemed as having been contaminated and made impure; these people had to be baptized again. It was obviously unavoidable for the mothers of these infants; they therefore had to purify themselves on the eighth day by the priest in the temple. The Romans baptized girls on the eighth day and boys on the ninth day after their birth, and the child was named during baptism.

Baptism by Sprinkling Water on the Forehead: This method of performing the baptism rite was partially done due to the scarcity or lack of water in some countries and the infant fatalities that sometimes resulted from the practice of full submersion baptizing of infants. Therefore, a new mode of baptism was introduced, today known as "sprinkling," in which times water or blood was used, dependent on culture and religion. It has been stated by some scholars that the practice of blood baptism was prevalent among the ancient Romans and Latin. Blood was considered "the life essence" of humankind, and therefore it was deemed to be more powerful than water, and therefore they often used blood instead of water. The Greeks kept a "holy vessel" for this purpose known as the *facina*. The Romans made use of a brush to apply the blood and later water on the foreheads of the individuals partaking in the baptism rite. The Hindus and Persians used a branch made from laurel and other shrubs for sprinkling the repentant candidate.

In some countries, the rite was used as a magical charm to ward off evil spirits. The followers of the Mexican religions had to sprinkle themselves with blood, usually their own, before they were allowed access to their sacred altar. They had to perform this ritual to pay their respects to the powers that be and to cleanse themselves from all evil. This ancient ritual is very similar to that of the Jews that sprinkled the walls and doorposts of their temples with blood under the requisition of the Levitical code. This mode of purification by sprinkling with either water or blood is mentioned and recognized in the scriptures of the Christian Bible in the Old and New Testaments.

Baptism by Fire was a method used and introduced from the ancient belief that fire held a higher power for the purification process. There were numerous ways of using fire in the baptismal rite. In some cases, the candidate who underwent spiritual purification to attain immortality ran through blazing streams of fire, a custom called "the baptism of fire." Some scholars suggest that baptism by fire was prevalent in India, Chaldea, Syria, and throughout most of eastern Asia and would seem to have evolved from deity worship, which resembled the sun. Unfortunately, a small group of radicals voluntarily sacrificed their lives during a form of fire baptism; they believed it was necessary to purify the soul in that manner and that the ritual would enable them to ascend to a higher plane in the spiritual world. Some other religious sects believed that some sins committed could not be purified by fire, and that they would be punished by fire in the life to come.

Baptism by the Holy Ghost: This ancient ritual ceremony exists in many religions, including the Christian religion. The ritual was performed by breathing or blowing into or upon the candidate in exchange for divine favors from the gods or from God, i.e., blessings, fertility, to cure sickness, etc. A holy or spiritual leader, such as a medicine man or priest, was allegedly able to impart the spirit of the gods or of God to the candidate by performing this process; only they were authorized to conduct this ritual. There are various places in the Bible that speaks of Jesus and the apostles imparting the Holy Spirit onto people.

Baptism of the Dead: It was customary among ancient traditions to postpone baptism until near the supposed time of death in order to purify the soul and wash away all their sins, so that they could cross over without being judged for what sins they had committed during their lives. Obviously, the time of anyone's death cannot be precisely guessed, and many people died unexpectedly before the ritual was performed. Here, a new devised baptism practice emerged to baptize the deceased person's body or to baptize someone in that person's place instead because their souls could not be deprived from the soul salvation ritual. The most common method used to baptize a person's corpse was to use a living person, the living person laid under the bed, and the corpse placed lying on top of the bed. When the deceased's corpse was asked if he or she would be baptized, the living individual would respond and answer the question on behalf of the deceased, and the corpse was then submerged into a prepared liquid to finalize the baptism ritual. This is truly a senseless, mythical, and superstitious practice.

Christians believe that only those who have been baptized can inherit the kingdom of God. Immense value has been associated with this ritual, but many have forgotten the actual meaning and purpose of baptism.

Let us have a look at baptism as it is written in the Bible and then see if baptism is authentically Christian, as the Christians tend to make it out to be.

Baptism has its origins in the ancient Egyptian religions. Anup the Baptist baptized Horus with water, and a voice emanated from the clouds and said, "This is the beloved son of Osiris." This so-called mythical baptism of Jesus is actually a retelling from the old Egyptian religion. This is as close to actual plagiarism as you can get, and you make baptism out to be holy.

Let me show you a few aspects from the Bible that concerns baptism.

Many religious leaders say, "Stay in the bathwater of the word."

What type of water is referred to in the following Bible verse: Proverbs 18:4 "The words of a man's mouth are as deep waters, and the wellspring of wisdom as a flowing brook."

In conventional Christianity, water symbolically represents the word. Even the "evangelic words" are referred to as "evangelic waters." Are you not supposed to be baptized in the baptism of spiritual water? Do you think that God has any desire or pleasure in your rituals and symbolic elements? Certainly not.

I think you are making yourself out to be a joke in the eyes of God, especially if you think that the symbolic ritual of baptizing with normal water will cleanse and free you from your sins and save you as a "reborn" Christian.

The entire baptism ceremony as you know it today has been incorporated by human influence and has no holy powers or holy value in its symbolical form. This ceremony only pacifies your own conscience, and you perform the ritual to show the world that you are saved. Have you actually been saved?

The Bible speaks of baptism by fire, so why do the Christians not have a ritual for this form of baptism?

In the Bible, it mentions five baptisms that each person must go through. Do you believe that baptism with water is enough now that you know that baptism was not incorporated into the religion by God but that it was actually copied from the ancient Egyptian religion?

People are obsessed with the fact that Jesus was baptized by full body submersion in the Jordan River. However, nowhere in any scripture has it been recorded that Jesus was completely submerged in water. In the Bible, it says that Jesus went up out of the water, but the Jordan River is only ankle deep. If the baptism took place, then John could only have thrown some water over Jesus's head. Who will actually ever know, especially that there never was and there is any existing evidence that it actually occurred. This is another example of blind faith and the trust people have in others that claim it to be true.

How can baptism be considered holy if it is solely based on these points?

Let me assure you that baptism with water is nothing more than a fable and a symbolic myth. There is no power present from this ritual or action. God does not have any desire or concern with any human rituals. This ritual is a transient deed that forms part of religion only for the individual to be accepted and acknowledged by their congregation and religious members.

Do you need certain rituals to remind you of what you are supposed to know concerning your religion?

Will the physical baptism ritual free you from the hustle and bustle of the world? Certainly not. Why would you then perform the ritual? Do you feel compelled to take part because the church and your religion expect it from you? Just do not attempt to say that it is the will of God and that God has commanded you to perform the mythical ritual of baptism. You will know within yourself that you are simply just saying it, but in fact, you do not truly believe yourself especially now that you know the truth.

There are various texts in the Bible that state that you must be baptized. However, not one of these texts state that you must be fully immerged under water during baptism, as there also is no text that states that anyone must be sprinkled during baptism. In fact, there is no text that states that you need to be baptized with natural water in order to be saved.

The baptism ritual has been developed and instated by humanity and not by God as many say it is. Christians are quick to say that Jesus was baptized with water, and therefore they too must be baptized in the same fashion.

I have listened to the preachers when they baptize people, and I wonder; they say the following during the ritual, "I baptize you in the name of God the Father, I baptize you in the name of God the Son, and I baptize you in the name of God the Holy Spirit, Amen." Every time the priest says, "I baptize you . . ." the individual is submerged in water. Let us assume for a moment that the priest said nothing during this ritual and simply went ahead to submerge you in water three consecutive times. Would you have been baptized or not? Which part of the ritual confirms the baptism? Is it the water or the words that are spoken that baptizes you?

In Ephesians 4:5, "One Lord, one faith, one baptism," which one of the more than ten thousand Christian religions would be the right religion? The Bible does not mention what type of god or what type of baptism. The Bible is however very specific when it says that there is one Lord, one faith, and one baptism.

Let us have a look at christening or the small baptism.

In Mark 10:13-16, "Suffer the little children to come to me, and forbid them not; for of such is the kingdom of God. Verily I say unto you, Whosoever shall not receive the kingdom of God as a little child, he shall not enter therein." In other words, you need to become like a child in order to inherit the kingdom of God. Unfortunately, the churches and adults become childish instead of becoming childlike. Is there perhaps any truth behind the christening ritual that the churches perform?

I looked at a text that states that you must stay in the baptism. Why have they not made a ritual for this religious aspect yet?

It is astounding at how many myths and rituals are strewn throughout the religion. In order for the church to cover all its bases, they sprinkle water on the child's forehead when they are christened and the adults are fully emerged under water, just in case the one method is actually correct instead of the other. Do you honestly believe that God is concerned or pleased by any of the rituals that the churches perform with vigor? The answer to this question is in Jude verse 10, "But these speak evil of those things which they know not: but what they know naturally, as brute beasts, in those things they corrupt themselves."

It is ironic that people are quick to say that you are not allowed to add or remove anything that is written in the Bible. People are always ready to attack each other over aspects that they believe they understand, and they show how clear the Bible is concerning the aspect; they do this only when it suits them and their agendas.

The Bible is idolized because it is written that God gave everything described in the Bible. Now that there are texts from their own Bible that show that the religion that they follow and worship is a farce and a lie, they become angry and think that I am trying to slander their religion. The truth cuts close to the bone at times, and I will not distort the truth to find favor with you.

Look deep within yourself and see the rotting diseased stories that you make out to be holy; all the lies, myths, rituals, symbolism, and habits. All these things were brought in by the church to attract crowds of members and followers, all the mystical music and red-hot sermons that keep the people sitting on the edges of their seats. Many have famous singers and events to attract the young generations to the church. Thousands are spent to make the experience of church as comfortable and enjoyable as possible. There are even Bible study groups to further indoctrinate the masses. There is not one religion that tells its followers to look a bit broader and wider to find the truth. They make you believe that what they bring to you is the only existing truth that there is. This is just another technique used to keep you in their group.

God commands you to search and investigate for the truth, but the moment you hear or read something that challenges your religion, you dismiss it off the bat and make it out to be the devil's work without taking the time to look into it.

As I have mentioned throughout the book, I am not here to mislead you because I will not benefit from it and do not want to be responsible for your downfall. I do not intend on starting a new religion or sect. All that I am offering you is the truth, so that you can follow the path to your spiritual awakening and your own spiritual journey that you need to be traveling on in order to live a fulfilled life and fulfill your task for this life.

Some of the church leaders will defend these myths by proclaiming that some of these aspects are meant purely on a spiritual basis whereas their own church approved and practiced rituals will be claimed as the will of God. Many religious leaders will even tell you that what I have showed you is a complete lie, but this they do out of fear of you finding out the truth. You see, these religious leaders tell you which aspects are natural and which are spiritual, but the Bible states that all things should first be considered on a natural basis and then only on a spiritual basis. These church fathers will do anything to convince you that they represent the truth that God has given Christianity.

Let me show you how strangely some people view their religion in a natural way and mislead you with false hope in order to keep you in their group while they also take your money. Let us move onto the next chapter that deals with the return of the savior, as the churches bring it to you and the truth to it all as God actually meant it.

Chapter 22

The Return of the Savior

In chapter 11, we discussed the mythical figure of Jesus, the myth that the churches had distorted and created. We already know that there was a man named Jesus, but he was not the Son of God. There is no doubt however that Jesus the Nazarene lived, that he performed great feats and was the founder of Christianity. The return of the mythical Jesus is yet another fabrication. Why you might ask. Because the church fathers needed to incorporate this made-up story to maintain power and control over their followers. At the end of the day, what does the story of the "return of the savior" entail concerning the church fathers and their members? That is simple; you are made to believe that Jesus was real as the Bible portrays him and therefore automatically the return should be real; now that you believe this nonsense, you must listen to the church and live your life their way so that Jesus can fetch his chosen people. They forget that in the Bible, Jesus will only fetch the 144,000 sealed souls. So what chance do you and I or the billions that lived before us have of inheriting the kingdom of God?

Your church fathers will make you believe that as long as you believe and give your life to Jesus and the church, you will inherit the kingdom of God. This promise was made to millions and billions of people before you. They have the audacity to continue promising every church member that as long as they do the will of God according to their church, they will inherit eternal life in heaven. How many millions of kings and priests are currently residing in heaven? Can you not see how many contradictions, false promises, and lies fill the pages of the Bible?

According to some sources, it is thought that the story of the savior's return originated from the Romans because whenever the Roman Empire faced times of crises, the aristocracy would refer their matters to the Sibylline Oracles, who were kept housed in the Temple of Jupiter in Rome, to aid them in their time of crisis. They believed that oracles possessed mystical powers and could foretell future events. The Roman aristocracy primarily worshipped the Greek gods like Apollo, Zeus, etc., and they anticipated the return of Apollo to earth to usher in a New Age. Since the Sibylline Oracles were familiar with the popular myths such as Apollo and the mythology of Horus, the Cumaean Sibyl prophesied the return of Horus who would usher in the New Age.

Many popular traditions myths were adapted and distorted by the Roman aristocracy in conjunction with the early Christian forgers in the early history of the church. These myths were used as the basis to invent the myth surrounding the coming of Jesus and the end of the world as written in the book of Revelation.

Sibylline Oracles prophesied numerous prophecies in which Jewish or Christian doctrines were allegedly confirmed by a sibyl. The prophecies were originally the work of a few early Jewish and Christian writers from about 150 BC to about AD 180. In the Oracles, the sibyl proved her so-called reliability by first "predicting" events that had actually recently occurred; she then predicted future events and set forth doctrines that were considered to be eccentric to Hellenistic Judaism and Christianity. The Jewish apologist Josephus and a few Christian apologists thought the works were the genuine prophecy of the sibyls and were immensely impressed by the manner in which their doctrines were apparently confirmed by external testimony. You must understand that these early church fathers tried to link any sources to strengthen their religious strategy, irrespective of how unreliable these sources were. Both Theophilus of Antioch and Clement of Alexandria, second-century Christian theologians, referred to the sibyl as a "prophetess" who was considered just as inspirational as the Old Testament prophets.

All that can be said about the origin of the myth of "the return of the savior" is that its origins, like so many other stories in the Bible, have their origins from numerous ancient religions myths.

In the Bible, it is written in Luke 17:20 that the kingdom of God does not come with visible signs. Many Christians perceive this in a natural sense. However, it says in Jude verse 10, "But these speak evil of those things which they know not: but what they know naturally, as brute beasts, in those things they corrupt themselves." In other words, anyone who understands the aspects of the Bible in a natural way will corrupt himself or herself.

In the Bible, God asks who will go to the highest places to search for him and who will go over the waters to search for him there. Did you not know that God came so close to you that on your tongue and in your heart he wants to live? The churches state that this text means that the spirit of God wants to reside by humanity, but God says that he does not have the form of man, that he is only spirit. God states that he is the strength and wisdom in our midst. Further proof that the early church fathers were writing their own religion, as they believed it to be, by using Christianity to their advantage in the process, i.e., they had their own motives, such as control and power. These writers as a whole remained faithful to the primal myths but filled many religious writings with their own insights into the nature of God, man, and the universe.

Let us stop here for a moment and sum up the points mentioned.

- The kingdom of God that does not come with visible signs is by humanity.
- God that is only spirit resides by humanity.
- The Son went to his Father. Where is the Son?

The Son proclaims that he is the way, the truth, and the life. Think about this; the way that humanity must take to get to God, the truth that everyone must walk in to get to God, and the life you need to lead in order to keep God in your life.

- The way: it is nothing more than the manner in which you live your life.
- The truth is not strewn with rituals, myths, and symbolism; it is the actual truth that you need to possess.
- The life: that you as a human being need to live, as God has given it to you.

In your search for the truth, in the cloud of true witness, you will experience the true God and discover facts instead of sifting through man's wisdom. The truth will surround and comfort you like a cloud; this does not come to you with visible signs. A cloud is broken-up water; water is words from a person's mouth. In Proverbs 18:4, "The words of a man's mouth are as deep waters, and the wellspring of wisdom as a flowing brook." Is this not perhaps what they meant concerning the return of Jesus, that the "waters" the truth would return to humanity and not the physical mythological Jesus.

In the Bible when it says, "Every eye will see him," which eye are they speaking of, if you are not supposed to see things in a natural way? Let us have a look.

If I should explain something to you and you do not understand what I mean, then you would say that you do not see what I mean. It is not your natural eye that does not "see" but your mind that does not comprehend or understand what challenges you. When you use this expression, you are actually saying that you do not understand. If I then explain that which you do not understand and you then understand it, that is when you say, "Now I see." What you are actually telling me is that you understand. These things are not "opened" to you by flesh and blood, and you do not see with your physical eye because flesh and blood cannot see the kingdom of God.

In the Bible, it is written that every eye that sees God will surely die. Paul says that he dies a thousand deaths each day. What death does he talk about or mean? You must die in order to live; therefore, if you see God, you will surely die because it means that your own will shall die, just as Paul said to God that he does not live anymore, that God lives in and through him.

You are not meant to "see" in a natural sense; you are supposed to understand the truth and not declare things in a natural way.

Let us look at the return of the savior in a natural way and see if it still makes sense to you.

The Son of God comes on a natural cloud to fetch his chosen people and take them to God. Those that are left behind will suffer terribly, and they will want to end their lives, but death will not come. Those that stay behind are lost and doomed to eternal hell.

Already this does not make sense because it does not agree with what the Bible says. Jesus says that he will come and imprison the devil for a thousand years. Then Jesus will come again to free the devil for a short while, and then Jesus will come again to slay the devil, and that will be the end. The end of what?

Look at the whole story.

The promise that Jesus will come on a cloud to fetch his children and those that stay behind will be lost and doomed. Jesus will also imprison the devil. No devil means that there will be no sin or heartache. Therefore, those that stay behind will have no sin or temptation. This sounds more like a heavenly state of existence.

Why would Jesus return if he has already taken his chosen people? Those people that stay behind belong to the devil.

So people will not be snatched from their bodies; what happens to this idea now?

Many near Eastern religions include a story about a battle between a divine being and a dragon or another monster representing chaos, a theme found, for example, in the Enuma Elish. A number of scholars call this story the "combat myth." A number of scholars have argued that the ancient Israelites incorporated the combat myth into their religious imagery, such as the figures of Leviathan and Rahab, the Song of the Sea, Isaiah 51:9-10's description of God's deliverance of his people from Babylon, and the portrayals of enemies, such as Pharaoh and Nebuchadnezzar. The idea of Satan as the opponent of both Jesus and God may have developed under the influence of the combat myth. Scholars have also suggested that the book of Revelation uses combat myth imagery in its descriptions of cosmic conflict.

The apocalypse described in the book of Daniel, which he sees as a record of historical events, is presented as a prophecy of future events and was originally based on previous existing ancient mythic structures, such as the Hellenistic kingdom that is represented as a terrifying monster. This concept comes from the Eastern pagan myth of "the dragon of chaos."

This entire story as it is in Christianity has so many holes in it that it falls apart. The promise that the Bible makes was written by church fathers, and it is not a promise from God. You have been misled.

If God is by humanity, his kingdom is by humanity, the Son is by his Father, and then the Son must be by humankind. Why do you then wait for the Son to come on Mount Zion that is in Muslim territory, to come and fetch you to take you to God, who is already by humanity?

I read in the Bible, where Jesus was resurrected, in Matthew 27:52: "And the graves were opened; and many bodies of the saints which slept arose." What happened to them? Was King David and Solomon not recognized, and what happened to them? Were they supposed to stay behind in the earthly life?

Do you not think that this would have been the best proof that Jesus was the Son of God? Why do you not ever hear again about the dead believers that stood up out of their death? There is no proof that anything like that ever happened in those times, except for the one place in the Bible. If this event took place that many witnessed, they would have made many records about it.

Jesus supposedly said there are some of you that stand here that will not see death before the Son of God has returned to humankind. In Mark 9:1, it is stated differently, "And he said verily I say unto you, that there are some of them that stand here, which shall not taste of death, till they have seen the kingdom of God come with power."

Did Jesus lie?

Where are the people that are older than two thousand years? Did Jesus already return, as Elijah returned in the form of John the Baptist? As it says in Matthew 17:12-14, "But I say unto you, that Elijah is come already, and they knew him not . . . Then the disciples understood that he spake unto them of John the Baptist." Was this story of Elijah and John also a distortion and myth? That is possible because we already know that many things have been changed, removed, and added in the Bible to suit the agenda of the church. However, what we have learned about the actual return of Elijah suggests another possibility: that Jesus's return may take place through the birth of a child, just as Jesus came into the world the first time through reincarnation.

There are consistent patterns that appear throughout the Hebrew and Christian Bible such as the primordial struggle between good and evil. There exists a distinctive characteristic of the Hebrew and Christian Bible; there are numerous reinterpretations of various myths based on history, even though some are further from the truth than they would ever admit.

The most dangerous disease for the soul is ignorance.

With the return of Jesus and the Last Judgment comes the end of the world. Let us have a look at that in the next chapter.

Chapter 23

The End of the World: The End of Time

The Last Judgment is a general and sometimes an individual, judging of the thoughts, words, and deeds of people by God, the gods, or by the laws of cause and effect. In some religions like that of Christianity, the judgment concerns both the living and the dead. In the Asian religions of Hinduism, Jainism, and Buddhism, they believe in reincarnation; the concept of a Last Judgment is rare but not uncommon.

Let us see what some religions and traditions believe concerning the myth of the Last Judgment or the end of days.

Mayan

The Maya calendar does not end in 2012, as some have said, and the ancients never viewed that year as the time of the end of the world. December 21, 2012, is the time when the largest grand cycle in the Mayan calendar overturns and a new cycle begins. The Mayan calendar is a system of calendars used in pre-Columbian Mesoamerica and in many modern communities in highland Guatemala and in Veracruz, Oaxaca, and Chiapas, Mexico.

Both the Hopis and Mayans recognized that we would be approaching the end of a World Age in 2012, even though they were off only by a few years. In both cases, however, the Hopi and Mayan elders do not prophesy that the world would end. Rather, this is a time of transition from one zodiac age into another, which they called the "world age." The message they give us concerns our making a choice of how we enter the future ahead. Our moving through the age with either resistance or acceptance will determine whether the transition will happen with cataclysmic and disastrous change or gradual peace and tranquility. The same mythological story can be found reflected in the prophecies of many other Native American, Eastern, and ancient visionaries from numerous traditions and religions.

The Mayans did pass down a graphic yet undated end-of-the-world scenario, described on the final page of a circa-1100 text known as the Dresden Codex. The document describes a world destroyed by flood, a scenario imagined in many cultures and probably experienced on a much less apocalyptic scale by ancient peoples.

Hinduism

The End Time, as we understand from other religions, does not exist as such in Hinduism. Hindu traditional prophecies, as described in the Paranas and several other texts, say that the world shall fall into chaos and degradation. There will then be a rapid increase of perversity, greed, and conflict. The wrongdoings or such things committed by humans shall have no effect on the end of time.

In Hinduism, there is no eternal damnation of souls or actual end times. After this evil cycle of Kali Yuga ends, the next cycle would be Satya Yuga where everyone will be righteous, and this cycle will continually move onto others because their cycles keep repeating infinitely. Each cycle does however have its own start and end; these cycles can last for up to 8.6 billion years.

Buddhism

Buddhists generally believe in cycles of destruction, and creation continues and infinite cycles with their own beginning and end. The closest description to the end of time as Christians understand it is that the teaching of the Buddha would disappear after about five thousand years, when no one would any longer practice the actual teachings anymore.

According to the Sutta Pitaka, the "ten wholesome courses of conduct" will disappear and people will follow the ten unwholesome concepts of theft, violence, murder, lying, false speech, sexual misconduct, abusive and idle talk, covetousness and ill will, wanton greed, and uncontrolled lust that will result in poverty and the total breakdown of law and the regard for the dharma. During the final stage, the memory of the Buddha himself would have been forgotten. Sometime following this period or cycle, a new Buddha named Maitreya will arise to rediscover and reveal the timeless teachings of dharma and rediscover the path to nirvana. Maitreya is currently residing in the Tushita world before his final rebirth in the human world. This cycle would usher in a new age, one of rebirth.

Norse Mythology

In Norse mythology, Ragnarok, meaning "final destiny of the gods" in Old Norse, refers to a series of events that include a great battle foretold to take place that would result in the death of a number of major gods, such as Odin, Thor, Loki, and others. The events that were supposed to take place consisted of various natural disasters including the world being submerged in water. Afterward, the world would resurface being renewed and fertile. The surviving gods would get together after this event, and two human survivors would repopulate the world.

Zoroastrianism

Zoroastrian tradition is one of the oldest found in recorded history. By the year 500 BC, a fully developed ideology was developed of the end of the world in Zoroastrianism. According to Zoroastrian philosophy, as written in the Zand-i Vohuman Yasht, "at the end of thy tenth hundredth winter . . . the sun is more unseen and more spotted; the year, month, and day are shorter; and the earth is more barren; and the crop will not yield the seed; and men . . . become more deceitful and more given to vile practices. They have no gratitude." "Honourable wealth will all proceed to those of perverted faith . . . and a dark cloud makes the whole sky night . . . and it will rain more noxious creatures than winter."

At the end of this spiritual battle between the righteous and wicked, a final judgment of all souls will take place. Sinners who have more bad deeds than good deeds will be punished for three days, but their sins will eventually be forgiven. They believe that the world will reach a state perfection because all evil, such as old age, disease, thirst, hunger, poverty, and death will disappear from the face of the earth. Zoroastrian concepts are parallel with the religions and beliefs of Judaism, Christianity, and Islam.

Judaism

In Judaism, the End Times is usually referred to as the End of Days. This phrase appears several times in the Tanakh. The idea of a peaceful age has a definite place in Jewish thought. This event has a predetermined date (that is relatively unknown) but can come earlier if they are obedient toward their religion and only practice good deeds. According to Jewish tradition, this era (The End of Days) will be one of global peace and harmony, an era free of struggle and suffering and one that would promote further knowledge of the Creator.

There is another tradition within Judaism that states that each of the seven days of the week, which are based upon the seven days of creation, correspond to the seven millennia of creation. They believe that the seventh millennium begins with the year 6000, and that this is the latest that the Messiah can return.

Islam

Islam, like the other Abrahamic religions, teaches about the bodily resurrection of the dead, the fulfillment of a divine plan for creation and the immortality of the human soul. The righteous are rewarded with the pleasures of heaven, while the unrighteous are punished in hell. A significant fraction of the Quran deals with these beliefs.

End of Time beliefs in Shia Islamic thought are based on references from the Quran and instruction from the Prophet Muhammad and from Ahl al-Bayt. Their scriptures go on to speak of earthquakes that will erupt from the various corners of the globe. Smoke will spread and cause nonbelievers to fall ill, whereas the believers will only catch a mere cold. Later, Allah will send a cool wind, taking life gently from all the believers, leaving only the nonbelievers to see the last Day of Judgment.

The Latter-day Saints:

The Latter-day Saints, also known as the Mormons, states that humanity is living in the last days.

They do not speculate as to the time, day, or year of the second coming but watch for biblical indications or Signs of the Times that the event is approaching. A number of Mormon leaders have taught that the human family has been allotted seven thousand years, and that the earth is nearing the end of the sixth such millennium. Jesus's second coming and the ushering in of the millennial kingdom, which will be Earth's Sabbath and day of rest, will mark the seventh thousandth year. They believe that the seven seals and seven trumpets of the book of Revelation relate to the seven millennia that was allotted to Earth.

After the coming of Jesus to the Mount of Olives and the destruction of the wicked, the righteous will live on the earth in relative peace and prosperity under the leadership of Jesus during the seventh millennium. While the exact time of Jesus's return is not known by the Latter-Day Saints, they too believe in the myth that there will be certain signs that will point to his return.

Jehovah's Witnesses

Witnesses believe that the last days already began in 1914 with the events surrounding the outbreak of World War I. They believe that in the future, God will cleanse the earth of all wickedness, and that Satan will be bound for a thousand years. During this time, they state that people will be resurrected to live on earth, and that those that stay behind will be given a chance to learn about God (Jehovah) without the influence of Satan. They state further that Jesus will rule over the earth from heaven with his 144,000 corulers to restore earth to its original paradise state, as that of Genesis. They teach that biblical prophecy shows there will be no more death or sickness, and that people will live in peace and harmony as God originally planned for it to be for humankind. They do not believe that the planet will be destroyed but that only the wicked will be destroyed.

With only perfect humanity remaining, Jesus will give the kingdom back to the Almighty God, Jehovah. Those righteous people, who survive the final test at the end of the thousand-year rule, will live forever in paradise on earth. They do not generally use the expression "end of the world" with its associated perceptions of the destruction of humanity or the planet but prefer to use the expression "conclusion of a system of things."

While most religious traditions await the end of time, some believe that the events have already been fulfilled. Several established religions believe that their founder represents the coming of the Promised One of previous scriptures, and that the spread of their teachings will ultimately bring a desired society of unity, justice, and peace.

Bahá'í Faith

Concerning the concept of the end times, it has been claimed that the Battle of Armageddon had already passed within the historical context of the Bahá'í Faith. Bahá'ís expect their faith to be eventually embraced by the masses of the world, thus ushering in a golden age for society.

The cornerstone of Bahá'í belief is the belief that Bahá'u'lláh and his forerunner, who was known as the Bab, were manifestations of God. Bahá'ís believe that all the founders of the world's great religions have been manifestations of God and have been agents of a divine plan to educate the human race.

The founder of the Bahá'í Faith, Bahá'u'lláh, claimed that he was Jesus who had returned; there were also prophecies made by other religions of the expected return of Jesus; Bahá'u'lláh happened to fit the description of some of these prophecies. One of these prophecies was the Millerite prophecy that claimed the year 1844 to be the return of Jesus; the inception of the Bahá'í Faith coincided with this prophecy.

In connection with the previous chapter, most Christians know that when the Last Judgment approaches, Jesus would take his 144,000 sealed souls to heaven and then that would be the end of the world. Some proclaim it the end of the world while others proclaim that it will be the end of time. The Western prophetic religions, such as Zoroastrianism, Judaism, Christianity, and Islam developed concepts from ancient mythical sources that enabled them to create their impression of the Last Judgment; their imagery is rather detailed and dramatic.

Then I read the Bible where people asked Jesus about the end of days, the end of time, and he spoke about the time that will come. He meant the end of time and the time that would come.

Read Mark 14:13-14: "And he sendeth forth two disciples, and saith unto them, Go ye into the city, and there shall meet you a man bearing a pitcher of water: follow him.—say ye to the goodman of the house . . ." King James Version 1611

Let us have a look at a few strange phenomena that appear in the Bible that are not authentically Christian.

It is well know that Christendom is associated with two fish; Jesus that fed the crowd with two fish and five loaves of bread; the fisherman, etc. These fish stickers are pasted onto the back of motorcars so that everyone can see that they are Christians. The symbol of the fish also refers to nature. For the last two thousand years, the solar system has moved through the age of Pisces (the two fish).

Let me explain. It takes the earth approximately two thousand years to move through each zodiac house, and it takes approximately twenty years for the transition of the one house to the next to take place, as explained in the last section of chapter 4. The earth's axis is on a 23.5 degree angle; however, it adjusts to three degrees and back. This change is due to the procession of the equinoxes and influences by celestial bodies including the planets. The earth shifts in a systematic way. This motion is called precession and consists of a cyclic wobbling in the orientation of the earth's axis of rotation, which has a period of approximately twenty-six thousand years. Precession is caused by the gravitational influence of the sun, moon, and planets acting on the earth's equatorial bulge.

In 1998, the solar system began to move away from the Pisces house and is now moving into Aquarius. In 2018, our solar system will be predominantly in the house of Aquarius. The house of Pisces will no longer have an effect on the earth, and the natural balance will return to some normalcy once it has moved over completely.

Can you see that the end that is spoken of is not the end of the earth or existence as we know it, but instead that it is the end of a period, the period of Pisces? We are truly at the end of time, the time of Pisces.

These aspects have nothing to do with myth or symbolism; these are the hard, cold facts. The universe works like clockwork and will continue to do so for thousands of years. Read John 14:2, "In my Father's house are many mansions: if it were not so, I would have told you." King James Version 1611. We know of twelve houses, the twelve houses of the zodiac.

The return of the savior, the Last Judgment, and the end of the world is not what your church leaders have always told you it is. We know now that all that it means is that the end of an age and the dawning of another will occur. The end of time does not mean the end of the world. Even the Bible speaks of the time that will come.

There are, however, certain Christian religious sects that view the end of the world or the end of time very differently from mainstream Christian religion.

To them, the earth represents a person's mind and conscience. The Bible also defines it this way. In Luke, there is something written of a sower and good earth. In the Bible, Luke 8:11 says, "The seed is the word of God," and your mind is the earth.

According to this sect and the Bible, the end of the world is referred to as the end of world thought that each person carries within them. Therefore, the end of the world is when each person no longer chases after worldly things and instead lives their lives close to God. The end of the world is the day that they no longer follow their own selfish will, but instead they will do the will of God, and that God will live in and through them. To a large degree, this makes sense, but is this the true meaning of the scriptures, bearing in mind that so many parts of the scriptures are false and mythological?

This end of the time or the end of the world was not what the people were expecting it to be. The churches have made it out to be an overexaggerated and dramatized day that according to them would have occurred. They purposefully instilled fear in their followers because the end can come at any time; therefore, they have more influence over you.

The book of Revelation and many others incorporate imagery from ancient mythology. The end time, end of days, or end of the world is a time period described in the many ancient writings in the three Abrahamic religions of Judaism, Christianity, and Islam. There are various non-Abrahamic religions that have similar doomsday scenarios. In Islam, Yawm al-Qiyamah (the Day of Resurrection) or Yawm ad-Din (the Day of Judgment), Allah's final assessment of humanity, is preceded by the end of the world. In Judaism, the term "End of Days" is a reference to the Messianic era and the Jewish belief in the coming of Meshach and the Olam Haba. Various other religions also have very similar beliefs associated with a hero or savior returning and redemption.

The return of a physical savior on a white horse on a white cloud is another fabrication from ancient mythology. The story of the return of the savior that the Christian churches teach you is so flimsy that is also falling apart. The end of the world in the book of Revelation is just as distorted as the book of Genesis concerning the creation. The churches state that these aspects should be seen spiritually and that people are not meant to understand. Yet in the Bible, it says that nothing will be hidden from God's children. Why would God want his children to live in ignorance?

There is another thing; in the Bible, it also says that as things are in nature, they are in spirit. The church says you must understand it in a spiritual sense and not naturally, even though the Bible states it differently, and they instead continue to say that you are not meant to know these things. This makes no sense at all. There are so many contradictions that there is no wonder that there is no agreement among the Christian religions. They are all fables.

The only end that will take place will be the end of age-old myths and lies that have deceived and messed with the souls of God. Churches and so-called holy figures have stolen your life, and they had the backing of many governments and political institutions, even some laws prohibit you to think otherwise. The means to end these lies rests in your hands because your soul is your responsibility and nobody is going to do it for you.

You will always find those people that will continue clinging for dear life on to the dreams and myths that they believed to be true. Do not judge them. Those that do not know cannot sin, but those who have heard the truth and continue doing nothing, they have no excuse. It is the end for them because they no longer have anything to live for. Those are the people that pray their lives away; their life that God gave them in the belief that there awaits them a better life after this, which nobody can prove exists.

Live your life now, in the present. Seek and you shall find, ask and you shall receive. Search and investigate but keep only the good. What might be good for you is not necessarily good for the next person; therefore, do not judge.

There are so many that look but do not see, and there are so many that hear but do not listen. These people are blinded by an empty promise, and they pretend to be deaf because they are afraid to hear the truth; they do not want to be wrong.

The end of a time has broken for you now. Change and chase after the truth. Let go of all the old myths, traditions, rituals, and symbolism with their mystical wonders. Investigate everything and place your trust in the true God, he who has given you strength and wisdom.

Get away from the idols created to represent God; you know now that God is not who the churches tell you he is. See God in spirit and in truth.

Let us go to the next chapter that sums up the entire book, so that you can clearly see the big picture.

Chapter 24

Summary

- <u>Religion: Origin and History</u>

    o   Religion evolved with human culture, civilizations' law and moral codes, social structure, and society at large.
    o   The earliest evidence of religious ideas dates back several hundred thousand years.
    o   Religion is how human beings relate to that which they regard as holy, sacred, spiritual, or divine.
    o   Conviction plays a prominent role; without conviction, there cannot be any belief.
    o   Humanity witnessed the magnitude of power that the various natural elements held and therefore attributed each element or a combination of elements to various gods, goddesses, and deities.
    o   The portrayal of the elements as gods with human qualities made humankind capable of relating to them in a divine and spiritual way.
    o   Since the earliest of times, there were individuals that exploited the emotions of people through their religious beliefs. They work on people's fears and overpower them with threats, fear, force, and guilt. The early church leaders had learned how to have complete authority over the religious followers. This is the most successful recipe for psychological manipulation that continues to persist today.

Why do we follow a severally distorted version out of fear; are we afraid to question or inquire? Believing in something is beneficial to spiritual growth as our spiritual well-being is connected to all facets of our lives. However, our faith should be based on proven facts and the admission of ultimate truth. God does undeniably and undoubtedly exist, just not the way your religion teaches you.

Religion in general has made human beings stupid and totally illogical.

- <u>God: The Concepts by Man</u>

    o   In Christian theology, two tendencies stand in constant tension with each other. On the one hand, there is the tendency to arrange and organize the idea of God as far as possible. On the other, there is the tendency to eliminate the accumulated collection of current conceptions of God and to return to the understanding of the utter transcendence of God as they perceive this to be the only way to understand God.

○ The word or the name God is generally familiar to every person, irrespective of culture or creed. This concept is considered holy with everyone whether you are a Christian, Hindu, Muslim, or a shaman. It does not matter if you do not belong to a religion; there is still however a higher power that is in essence a God to you.

○ In the Christian understanding of "Christ" as being one with the Father, there is a constant possibility that the figure of the Son in the life of faith will overshadow the figure of the Father and therefore cause it to disappear and that the figure of the Creator, Sustainer, and Judge of the world will recede behind the figure of the Redeemer, Jesus.

○ People are truly arrogant. Why do I say so? Because people have always believed that they are the center of everything or at least at the center of something in some form or another.

○ Why did God give us the capability of inquiring and being curious if we were not meant to be that way? The God that is portrayed from the Old Testament is psychotic, vengeful, insecure, neurotic, and an unstable entity. Nobody can deny these traits; have a look for yourself in your Bible. This is the God that the Jews managed to foster in Christianity. This is not who God is.

Did God also simply become a myth or a symbol in your mind, just as the religion that you are chasing after? Blind faith without the right to question or ask? At the end of the day, how people perceive God to be is not the real God.

- <u>The Church and Its Religious Structure</u>

  ○ Early church figures such as Tertullian went to great lengths to break mythical associations between Christianity and other religions, even claiming that the devil caused the similarities to occur.

  ○ The concept of the church is a human-formulated concept which is not an authentically Christian invention. Churches and places of worship existed before Christianity existed. The so-called holiness that is associated with the church was incorporated by humanity and not by God.

- Churches are filled with myths, symbols, traditions, rituals, and habits.
- The most effective weapon used by the churches is natural psychological manipulation.
- All the Christian entities state that their beliefs of the Christian religion and of God are the only true religion, and they judge the other churches as sects. There are more than ten thousand registered Christian churches in the world. Each has their own form of worship and rituals.
- Most of the more than ten thousand known Christian churches are registered as a company or a nonprofit organization. The general law of companies states that companies must have a bookkeeping system, and they must show a profit or money flow. You cannot serve God and Mammon at the same time.
- What is the will of God, and what is the will of humankind?
- If God was truly in control of the church, as the church leaders claim, there would not have been discrimination between the Christian churches.

The truth is not always pleasant to hear, and sometimes it is even painful. It is at times easier to live in a lie than it is to live in the truth.

- Astrotheology and the Origin of the Bible

  - Contrary to common belief, there was never a onetime truly universal decision as to which books should be included in the Bible. It took over a century of the proliferation of numerous writings before anyone even bothered to start picking and choosing, and then it was largely a cumulative, individual, and happenstance event, guided by chance and prejudice, until priests and academics began pronouncing what was authoritative and holy, and even they were not unanimous. If it was inspired by God as many proclaim, would God make his children argue and differ on what his word is and was?
  - The Lost Books of the Bible: Human history has allowed few precious ancient religious writings to survive the onslaught of the more aggressive and powerful religious forces, which seek only to gain territory and wealth.
  - Christianity has been the victim of the Roman Empire, under the Emperor Constantine, who blended the Christian Church with the institutionalized "pagan" practices of Rome and eliminated any resemblance of either the Jewish religious influence or the first church Jesus established during his ministry.

THE HOLIEST LIE EVER

- ○ Through a series of decisions made by the early church leadership, all but eighty of those books, known as the King James Translation of 1611, were purged from the work, with a further reduction by the Protestant Reformation bringing the number to sixty-six in the Authorized King James Bible.
- ○ Besides the Apocryphal books eliminated from the Bible used by the Protestant Church, there are at least twenty-eight other books mentioned in scripture which do not appear in the Bible.
- ○ The Bible speaks of astrology.

When the words "God" or "holy" are used in a sentence, it evokes fear by people and because they are under the disguise of the holy cloak and they walk the "righteous way"; people trust and accept without question everything that they are told by these church fathers. This comes forward as if people that are part of a church or congregation fear their church fathers warnings more than the orders that God has given.

- • <u>Old Scriptures: The Naked Truth</u>

    - ○ As Christians, you are told repeatedly to blindly believe in the Bible and what is written in it.

Your god is a true and existing God of today. He is not a dream god of after the grave. Become blessed and content, even within your soul. Allow the pressure to be lifted off you so that you are able to enjoy a joyous and fortunate life in peace. It is your life, and God gives you the strength to transform the desert in you into a paradise.

Do not hinder your life any further by praying it away or by waiting for a better life after this one. Know happiness so that you are accustomed to happiness before you move on from this life. Do not allow your life to revolve around fear. Do not blindly believe but instead investigate these aspects of truth for yourselves.

- • <u>Satan, the Devil, Lucifer, or the Prince of Darkness</u>

    - ○ As God is the strength and wisdom in our midst, so the devil or Satan is the weakness and ignorance in our midst.
    - ○ These are energies and powers, not people. The best description would be that they are positive strengths and negative powers.
    - ○ For the last two thousand years, the church leaders ensured that deep-rooted fears are instilled about the devil. These fears are

so immense that people are petrified to read material that goes against their religious beliefs or their religious institutions.

- Do not call on the name of the devil or Satan in your life. Live without him and the grief he brings. Equip yourself with love, patience, tolerance, and all the other fruits of the soul.
- God allows that certain things happen to us so that we are equipped and experienced to deal with a future task.
- When you have the truth within you, then you do not need to fear the devil.
- If your refuge is by God, the darkness cannot attack you.

People and especially the church are obsessed with what is right and wrong. They play word games, but they justify the fact that they humanize God. Live in God and remove the thoughts of wickedness from your life. The struggle that I have and many other people should have is with lies and misrepresentation that the churches portray and sell as holy truths. Our endeavor is to strive against the evil powers of the light, those that are perceived as angels that display great wonders.

- The Concept of Heaven and Hell

  - Concept of Heaven is thought of by most as the dwelling place of God, gods, or other spiritual entities which is also the home or state of being of the "saved" when they pass over to the afterlife or when the time comes after the last judgment.
  - The concept of heaven is interpreted in various ways in the different religions of the world.
  - Christianity, which has its origins from Judaism, views heaven as the destination of the true believers and followers of "Christ."
  - Concept of Hell: the place or state of being of evil spirits or souls that is damned to punishment after death.
  - The concept of a state of being or of a place that separates the good from the evil or the living from the dead are found in most religions of the world.
  - If heaven cannot be a physical place, then hell can also not be a physical place.
  - You are either in a heavenly state or in a hellish state, an internal fight.

A person is so accustomed to accept without question and not to actually listen to what you are being told. As long as the wonder of the mysticism is present, then it is all in order. When you are told of this wonderful place that you will go to when you pass on, then people forget to live their life that God gave them. God warns us that we must not live in the past and neither in the future of dreams, but instead that we live now in the present, the present that God gave us.

- Eternal God: The Mortal Virgin and the Holy Child

  - This story is ancient and has been used in various religions before Christendom existed.
  - Mary, the mortal human being, has been raised above all other humans because she has been upheld to a godlike status.
  - Over and over throughout time, the same story has been claimed as the holy truth, and man has been clinging on to it.

How is it possible that the same story comes up through the ages, over and over again? Is man then so ignorant that he does not realize that he is being fed the same regurgitated story over and over again? There is just a touch of mysticism here and there that gives the story another flavor, but the core remains the same.

- Myths, Traditions, Rituals, Habits, and Symbolism

  - Since the existence of mankind when it evolved as a species that could rationalize and conceive ideas, myths, traditions, rituals, habits, and symbolism became part of the pattern of thought and behavior.
  - Mysticism became part of religion; whereas myths, rituals, symbolism, and the like originated from mankind's curious nature in their attempt to find answers and tolerate their fear to a degree of the unknown.
  - Mysticism conforms to fantasy because it deals predominantly with beautiful ideas that instill calmness over the mind and heart while being perceived as holy, automatically, and wrongly in turn being associated with God.

It is through myths, traditions, rituals, habits, symbolism, and mysticism being used over the years in the pursuit of the good that religion evolved into a church service pattern today and became one of the most powerful forms of manipulation. Show me a church that does not subtly manipulate the scriptures in order to secure your tenth in the form of money. How can you hold up your religion as true when it is scattered with numerous myths, traditions, rituals, habits, and symbols?

- The Trinity God

  - The Trinity has been an essential feature in the religion of many Oriental nations.
  - The Trinity doctrine forms part of antiquity.
  - The Christian doctrine of the Trinity defines God as three divine entities meaning that God the Son and God the Holy

Spirit have exactly the same nature or entity as God the Father in every way. These three manifestations of one God are conveyed differently by each church structure.

○ Christianity, which in itself has its origins from pagan Egyptian and Stoic sources, also having emerged from Judaism, is a monotheistic religion. Never in the New Testament does the Trinitarian concept become a "tritheism" (three gods) nor even two.

○ In 325, the First Council of Nicaea established the doctrine and crucial formula of the Trinity as orthodoxy.

There is only one God. There is no father or mother. God will not come forth in the form of a man or a dove. God is the strength and the wisdom from which everything was created. If God is the creator of all life, then all life belongs to God. Then how can people state that those who do not follow their religion are then not from God?

- The Jesus Story and His Predecessors

  ○ Jesus founded a religion, and mankind crowned him with the name Christ.

  ○ Jesus promised his 144,000 anointed members of his ministry a place in the kingdom of God and promised that they would rule as kings and priests.

  ○ However, there are more than sixteen identical stories with the same life sequence lived as Jesus. Be honest with yourself. How is it possible that there were so many people that lived the same or similar lives and you proclaim the latest Savior as the true Son of God?

  ○ There is no doubt, however, that Jesus the Nazarene lived, that he performed great feats and was the founder of a church which through human intervention became the mythically based Christianity.

  ○ The ancient story of a messiah, mediator, or savior has remained unchanged throughout the ages.

  ○ In light of all the similarities between the religions and their teachings, it is absolutely tragic that the religions that grew up around those teachings became the heart of the division and conflict that exists among them.

  ○ Jesus is portrayed as a magnificent being that performed many miracles, but yet there were numerous historians that lived in and around the Mediterranean during or shortly after the life of Jesus that made no mention of him at all.

The empty promises from religious leaders are only used to manipulate people psychologically. It happens to work so effectively that most people accept it blindly while only very few have noticed the many contradictions and discrepancies. The salvation that the Bible speaks of is not something that awaits you in another life, as the churches want to make you believe. It is something that you must experience in this life. Salvation is liberation from ignorance or illusion. With the sufficient evidence given so far, the Bible and Christianity portray a distorted and mythical version of Jesus. Jesus was not the divine entity that the Bible or Christianity depicts that he was.

- Matthew, Mark, Luke, and John

    - The Gospels cannot be accurately dated, and the real authors are not known.
    - The traditional church has portrayed the authors of the canonical Gospels as the apostles Mark, Luke, Matthew, and John, but scholars know from critical textural research that there is no evidence that the Gospel authors could have served as the apostles described in the Gospel stories.
    - The Gospels describe narrative stories, written predominantly in the third person.
    - The most interesting point about the Gospels is not where they agree but where they differ or even conflict.
    - Not one of these books was written during the time that these events occurred. Each of the authors describes the events as they perceived it to have happened.

How can the Bible be considered holy when it is filled with lies and fraud? They talk about the will of God, but whose will is it actually? It comes from old decrepit men that used mankind's fear of hell and the eternal damnation. Christendom is yet just another religion that has created a perception of God from myths. This religion has an advantage for those that are in the driver's seat; this entails total control over people's feelings and the monetary power that is paired with it.

- The Holy Spirit

    - According to Christian religion, the Holy Spirit was left behind to act as the comforter. However, the Holy Spirit or Holy Ghost has undergone extreme metamorphoses throughout the Christian religion.
    - Many of the concepts associated with the Holy Spirit were derived from mythological sources.

- o In the Christian religion, this "God" has become a watered-down story because the true meaning behind the advent of the so-called Holy Spirit as Christians understands it today has been lost.

The churches create this perception with their members and followers that the Holy Spirit has human characteristics, where the Bible clearly shows you that the Holy Spirit is nothing more than the spiritual truth that you and I need to find and live in. This spiritual truth is not the stories of ancient characters, but it is the strength in your midst today, the present. This does not mean that you must throw your moral values overboard and suddenly live a sinful and destructive life. In your searches, you will find a lot of wisdom, and the truth is locked within this wisdom because you need to understand before you become; it is a change of consciousness.

- • The Israelites: God's Chosen People or Holy Nation

    - o The Israelites do not believe in Jesus, and they do not acknowledge that Jesus is the Son of God.
    - o The main reason why the Jewish nation is referred to or known as the holy or chosen people of God is because Jesus was a Nazarene; he called the Jewish people his nation.
    - o The story that all the Hebrews fled from Egypt is also untrue.
    - o The Bible of today refers constantly to the Israelites, but they were not known by this name, and the name Israel only emerged much later in history, even after the time of Jesus.

There are no boundaries when it comes to mankind because people are all part of one race—the human race—regardless of color, culture, and creed. Israel, the nation that rides on their renown as the chosen people of God, they receive protection from each Christian country because they are perceived as the holy nation of God, the nation infected with corruption and hate. They are always involved with some or other war, usually with people that do not agree with them. A nation that shows no love but who worship the God of unconditional love, and they do not acknowledge Jesus as the Son of God.

- • The Moses Story

    - o Moses has had such an immense impact on the religious structure of the world that even the Muslim religion sees this so-called prophet as a man of God.
    - o The first trace of the Moses story has its origin in Babylon. The story is about a king and prophet of God by the name of Nebu.

- ○ The Pharaoh Ramses II did not drown in the Red Sea as described in the Bible.
- ○ There are five books that are believed to be written by Moses; however, there is no proof that it was the same person that led the Hebrews out of Egypt.
- ○ The story of Moses is a mythical fable designed to give people a sense of strength.

How can you build your religion on myths, lies, fables, symbols, and rituals? Do you also drum to the same drummer with the norms of your religion in the hope that what you are doing will become holy because everyone is doing it? Christians are quick to assign the differences in their church to differences in culture, but because the culture of the Muslims is different from theirs, they are judged harshly. Are they not also as lost as you who follow the Christian religion? They also pray to Moses, who never existed.

- • John the Baptist

  - ○ John the Baptist and Elijah are actually the same person. What the Bible is promoting here is reincarnation.
  - ○ The story and life of Elijah is very different from the story and life of John the Baptist. Yet according to Jesus, they are the same entity.
  - ○ The story of John the Baptist is based on ancient mythology.

Christians are strongly against reincarnation; they completely reject the idea even though it appears as clear as daylight in their own Bibles. Jesus states in the Bible that reincarnation is real. However, Christians continue to believe that reincarnation is evil or demonic. Reincarnation is a doctrine generally held to be true of many of the world's major religions. Over millennia, various groups of ancient Greeks, Egyptians, Muslims, Hindus, Native Americans, and Africans have believed in some form of reincarnation.

- • King Solomon

  - ○ This mythical figure, Solomon, is supposed to represent the strength and wisdom that is brought forward in mankind. This mythical figure demonstrates how the strength and wisdom of God can work through a person.

  - ○ Many of the stories of David and Solomon were added by the scribes of the Maccabees in an effort to justify their setting up of a Jewish-free state.

- o   An interesting fact concerning Solomon is that there are many parallels with King Nabu Na'id also known as Nabonidus.

- o   The name Solomon does not appear anywhere else in the pre-exilic ancient world.

- o   Those indoctrinated into biblical mythologies that believe it to be true factual history might be surprised to know that the only evidence of King Solomon is found in the Bible.

It is true that biblical, Judaic, and Arabic traditions have always ascribed great wisdom to "Solomon." However, in this regard, bear in mind also that the authors of the Bible were highly influenced by the surrounding Babylonian culture, particularly its literature and myths. Everything in the Bible is blindly recognized and believed to be true and holy because, allegedly, God gave it. People accept the wisdom of Solomon as holy, even though he goes against what the Bible stands for.

- •   Noah and the Ark

  - o   Naturally, this story originates from ancient mythologies, as all the other stories from the Bible do. There is an ancient myth from Egypt and Central Africa known as the Archa-Noa/Argha-Noa.
  - o   There are a few striking similarities found between various religions regarding the "Noah" story.
  - o   The story of Noah is yet another myth that is glorified in the Bible.

God is not a magician; God is a god of order. According to the Bible, God created everything, so why would God use a man and a boat to save the animals and mankind? God can create more animals and human beings, as he did in the beginning. Many Bible believers would try and argue that these other accounts were copied from the Hebrew account; however, it should be noted that the Chaldean, Hindu, Babylonian, and Egyptian accounts predate the Hebrew versions by many centuries. The churches are as false as the fable of Noah, and you make their institution out to be holy.

- •   The Shedding of Blood; the Purification and the Sacrifice

  - o   The shedding of a man's blood has become symbolic in religion.
  - o   Blood has universal connotations in the religious imagination of humanity: it symbolizes life, fertility, and the violence

THE HOLIEST LIE EVER

of sacrifice, whether as an offering, a punishment, or for atonement.

- ○ In the Roman Catholic Church, the Eastern Orthodox churches, as well as among some High Church Anglicans, the Eucharist or Mass is seen as a sacrifice.
- ○ The concept of self-sacrifice and martyrs are central to Christianity.
- ○ To experience soul salvation would entail soul happiness, soul joy, soul pleasure, soul glory, and soul prosperity.
- ○ The myth that blood will purify you is a fable and human beings, not God, instated these rituals. Blood has no power to purify you or make you holy.

Only God can give life, and each human being on this earth has life within them. I know and see how the lies and fraud in the Christian religion rape and murder souls through sly, twisted lies, and myths used in the name of God. I am quite sure that many others have seen these aspects too.

The Christians keep talking about the love that they have for God and the love that God has for them, but I have never seen so much mysticism, symbolism, rituals, and traditions that are needed to keep reminding them of the love from and for God.

- • Holy Communion

    - ○ Besides baptism, Holy Communion is one of the most popular rituals and symbols practiced in the Christian religion structure.

When you look at the previous chapters and see where the Christian religion originated from, it is understandable that there is hardly any agreement between them regarding rituals and their symbolic value.

- • Baptism with Water

    - ○ Baptism is certainly the most popular sacrament or mythical ritual in the Christian religion.
    - ○ Baptism through water began in Babylonia as part of the Babylonian Mystery School religion.
    - ○ Baptism by water is an ancient rite that has been practiced by the pagans, Zoroasters, Romans, Egyptians, Persians, and numerous other nations.

207

- o Baptism by fire was a method used and introduced from the ancient belief that fire held a higher power for the purification process.
- o Baptism by the Holy Ghost: This ancient ritual ceremony exists in many religions, including the Christian religion.

Christians believe that only those who have been baptized can inherit the kingdom of God. Immense value has been associated with this ritual, but many have forgotten the actual meaning and purpose of baptism. The entire baptism ceremony as you know it today has been incorporated by human influence and has no holy powers or holy value in its symbolical form. This ceremony only pacifies your own conscience. Let me assure you that baptism with water is nothing more than a fable and a symbolic myth. There is no power present from this ritual or action.

- • The Return of the Savior

  - o Jesus as he is portrayed in the Bible is a myth; therefore, the return of Jesus is also a myth.
  - o Many near Eastern religions include a story about a battle between a divine being and a dragon or another monster representing chaos.
  - o The apocalypse described in the book of Daniel, which he sees as a record of historical events, is presented as a prophecy of future events and was originally based on previous existing ancient mythic structures.
  - o There are numerous reinterpretations of various myths based on history, even though some are further from the truth than they would ever admit.

Your church fathers will make you believe that as long as you believe and give your life to Jesus and the church, you will inherit the kingdom of God. This promise was made to millions and billions of people before you. They have the audacity to continue promising every church member that as long as they do the will of God according to their church, they will inherit eternal life in heaven. How many millions of kings and priests are currently residing in heaven? Can you not see how many contradictions, false promises, and lies fill the pages of the Bible?

The return of the mythical Jesus is yet another fabrication. Why you might ask. Because the church fathers needed to incorporate this made-up story to maintain power and control over their followers. At the end of the day, what does the story of the "return of the savior" entail concerning the church fathers and their members? That is simple; you are made to believe that Jesus was real as the Bible portrays him and therefore automatically the return should be real; now that you believe this nonsense, you must listen to the church and live your life their way so that Jesus can fetch his chosen people. They forget that in the Bible, Jesus will only fetch the 144,000 sealed souls. So what chance do you and I or the billions that lived before us have of inheriting the kingdom of God?

- The End of the World: The End of Time

    o The Western prophetic religions, such as Zoroastrianism, Judaism, Christianity, and Islam developed concepts from ancient mythical sources that enabled them to create their impression of the Last Judgment.
    o The end of the world as Christians know it is a lie. It is the end of an age.
    o The book of Revelation and many others incorporates imagery from ancient mythology.

The end of the world in the book of Revelation is just as distorted as the book of Genesis concerning the creation. The churches state that these aspects should be seen spiritually, and that people are not meant to understand. Yet in the Bible, it says that nothing will be hidden from God's children. Why would God want his children to live in ignorance? The only end that will take place will be the end of age-old myths and lies that have deceived and messed with the souls of God.

End Note

Do not lose your faith in God just because you have seen the myths and lies for what they are. To break away from the lies is not simple and effortless because these lies and myths have been all you have ever known and have become your comfort zone. You will experience conflict within yourself, and thoughts such as "What will people say?" or "What if?" will emerge.

Many will hear this and not accept a word of it; these are the people that follow norms and allow darkness to dwell in their consciousness in the name of their fictitious gods.

All I can offer you is advice and show you the facts; I have tried throughout this book to be as helpful as I can. I worship God entirely and live my life to the fullest, as God gives it to me because I am not bound to any particular institution of religion.

The Christian religion has certain measures in place to help ensure that they are protected and that the religion will not be dismantled. That is why when anyone reveals the fraud and corruption of the Christian religion, they are immediately labeled as a blasphemer and seen as a demonic power.

When I say that you must put all of these ideologies and doctrines away and look within yourselves for the enlightenment, for the contentment, for the happiness, and for the incorruptibility of the self, not one of you is willing to do it or at least very few. Religious organizations cannot make you free because they were built and formed on myths, lies, and deceit with the monetary and governmental structures strongly behind them.

The fact is that the ancient religious and church fathers added, modified, removed, and changed numerous old writings, history, and myths to suit their agendas.

It is wrong that people base their lives on these biblical, mythical stories. God gave you a life to live and allowed you to make you own mistakes so that you can learn from them. How can you ever expect to grow spiritually when you believe that life is like a mythical story? If you do live your life this way, you are false because you are acting instead of living your life to be the best, positive, and unique individual that you can be. Religion is slavery, and only truth can make you free. Freedom through truth is the comfort that God talks about.

Fear not, for now is the time to stop the monster that has misled you and to tell him "You have been misleading me for long enough. I am now going to investigate and find the truth with the strength and wisdom that God has given me in order to live my life accordingly." Do not judge the individual. Judge the lies and fraud in their midst that has come over for generations. Move away from it and hold on to the hand of your creator. They, like you, also need to find the truth; they are not holy. There is no point in following them any further. Instead free yourself from the bondages you are entangled in because your church or religious leaders cannot offer you freedom and do not want you to have total freedom; that includes the monetary system and governmental institutions.

Those people or religious leaders that knew the truth and still chose to mislead people must live with their own conscience because that is their punishment. At the end of the day, your conscience will be your judge.

If you know the truth and it forms part of who you are, it is logical that you will live according to the truth.

The Bible is idolized because it is written that God gave everything described in the Bible. Now that there are texts from their own Bible that show that their religion and worship are farces and lies, they become angry and think that I am trying to slander their religion. You will not find God where there are lies; therefore, those who follow these religions are with the godless. The truth cuts close to the bone at times, and I will not distort the truth to find favor with you.

Knowledge and truth is power, but knowledge is not necessarily truth.

There are some truths and wisdom within the Bible that you can use. Unfortunately, religious structures have been built on lies and deception. The Bible has been based on lies.

The contents within this book are already enough to prove to the world and its people that the Christian institutions in total, with their so-called good intentions, are based on fraud, deceit, and lies.

In the future, more books concerning religion and related subjects will be provided after we have compiled them. The aspects covered within this book were merely to introduce you to disturbing aspects that everyone has a right to know about. This was but only the tip of the iceberg. We will break this open into the core to show you how deeply entrenched the corruption and lies are. The corruption and lies have rooted themselves into your everyday life, your society, and even into your government.

I understand that you are upset and a little confused, but do not kill the messenger. Rather, stop the deceivers.

We have reached the end of our walk together for now. We have discussed many aspects, and I believe you have received some answers that you were searching for. It is time for you to make a choice and reflect on your spiritual growth.

Until we meet again for our next walk together in the truth.

I wish you love, happiness, and strength for your spiritual journey ahead . . . May you become truly enlightened and content within yourself and within creation.

Go forth with love and live your life to the fullest.